Teresa Hiergeist, Alex Lachkar, Stefanie Mayer (eds.)
Queer and Feminist Relationships in Contemporary Fiction

Queer Studies | Volume 42

Teresa Hiergeist is a professor of French and Spanish literature and cultural studies at the Department of Romance Studies at Universität Wien. Her research focuses on alternative concepts of society and education, imaginations of social and communal cohesion, negotiations of the sacred and spiritual, human-animal relations in literature and culture.

Alex Lachkar is currently working on his PhD between Vienna and the Université Paris-8 on the theorization of the »Despentes Generation«, a group of young authors of lesbian literature in contemporary France. His research focuses on contemporary lesbian and trans literature and the links between generations of writers in France.

Stefanie Mayer works at the Department of Romance Studies at Universität Wien. She is currently working on her doctoral project on authorship in the 21st century with a focus on the Mexican writer Cristina Rivera Garza. Her research interests lie in contemporary Latin American literature and cinema, with a focus on gender issues.

Teresa Hiergeist, Alex Lachkar, Stefanie Mayer (eds.)
Queer and Feminist Relationships in Contemporary Fiction

Concepts, Practices, and Aesthetics in Romance Cultures

Assisted by Flori Haack

Bibliographic information published by the Deutsche Nationalbibliothek
The Deutsche Nationalbibliothek lists this publication in the Deutsche Nationalbibliografie; detailed bibliographic data are available in the Internet at https://dnb.dnb.de/

© 2025 transcript Verlag, Bielefeld

All rights reserved. No part of this book may be reprinted or reproduced or utilized in any form or by any electronic, mechanical, or other means, now known or hereafter invented, including photocopying and recording, or in any information storage or retrieval system, without permission in writing from the publisher.

Cover layout: Maria Arndt, Bielefeld, based on a design by Stefanie Mayer
Cover illustration: Stefanie Mayer
Printed by: Elanders Waiblingen GmbH, Waiblingen
https://doi.org/10.14361/9783839473429
Print-ISBN: 978-3-8376-7342-5
PDF-ISBN: 978-3-8394-7342-9
ISSN of series: 2703-1365
eISSN of series: 2703-1373

Printed on permanent acid-free text paper.

Contents

Queer and Feminist Relationships in Contemporary Fiction of Romance Cultures
Introduction
Teresa Hiergeist, Alex Lachkar, Stefanie Mayer 9

Make Kin, Not Babies
Human-Animal Proximity, Queering Kinship and Embodied Choice in Guadalupe Nettel's »Felina«
Vera Lucía Wurst 15

Nomadic Motherhood
Constance Debré and Eva Baltasar Resignifying Queer-Feminist Kinship Through Impediment
Gabrielle Jourde 31

Virginie Despentes
Vernon's Failing as a Way of Literary Queering
Michaela Rumpikova 47

Negative Affects, Futurity and Queer Relationality in and around *De la terreur, mes sœurs!* (Alexis Langlois, 2019)
Pierre Niedergang 61

Dissolving into Love as Crisis
Queer Feminist Relationality in the Films *A felicidade delas* (2019), *Trenque Lauquen* (2022) and *Três tigres tristes* (2022)
Alkisti Efthymiou 75

»You Cannot Confine Imagination«
Contemporary Corona Fictions Embracing Lesbian Relationships
Julia Obermayr 95

The Poet's Choice
Céline Sciamma's Lesbian Utopias
Anna Langewiesche, Arthur Ségard 121

The *Making-With* of Queer Dystopia
Entangled Relationships in Wendy Delorme's *Viendra le temps du feu*
Audrey da Rocha 139

Let's Kill the Author
Cristina Rivera Garza and Collective Authorship
Stefanie Mayer 157

Citation as/and Relation
Chronic Pain, Autotheory, and Horizontal Writing in Jennifer Bélanger
and Martine Delvaux's *Les allongées*
Hannah Volland 171

Exploring the *Intersectional I* in Transgender Autobiography
A Study of Camila Sosa's Early Works
Juan Zapata 189

Fighting to Exist in a World Where You Don't Belong
Forms of Relationships and Struggles in Lauren Delphe's
Faite de cyprine et de punaises (2022)
Alex Lachkar 203

»D'autres femmes continueront, elles réussiront«
Reception of Violette Leduc's Work in *Colza* d'Al Baylac, *Fiévreuse plébéienne*
d'Élodie Petit et *Au temps du sublime* de Louise-Amada D.
Alexandre Antolin, Luciano Verzeletti 219

Literary Performance Festivals as a Space for Feminist and Queer Sociability
Anna Levy 233

Contributors 247

Queer and Feminist Relationships in Contemporary Fiction of Romance Cultures
Introduction

Teresa Hiergeist, Alex Lachkar, Stefanie Mayer

Since the 2000s, diverse collective queer and feminist initiatives came to life, which perpetuate traditions of solidarity and togetherness, and give way to the development and circulation of different forms of relations and relationships (Zaytun/Ezekiel 2016: 209; Duncan 2023: viii). Also, following the uprising of digital movements and campaigns such as the hashtag campaigns *#MeToo, #Balancetonporc, #Niunamenos, #MeuAmigoSecreto, #RopaSucia, #SinMujeresNoHayLibertad, #YaEsHora* and the renewal of a protest culture multiplying demonstrations, marches and flashmobs in the public space (*Un violador en tu camino* by LASTESIS; *Canción sin miedo* by Vivir Quintana), a new level of connectedness, communitarization and solidarity has been achieved (Armstrong/Mahone 2023: 185; Renn 2019: 454). This transformation is also perceptible within the artistic field. Numerous queer and feminist publishing houses, film companies and distribution systems have emerged in the last years; crowdfunding of art projects contributes to make evading institutional discrimination possible; and numerous new blogs, podcasts and databases (*HablemosEscritoras, Ingrávida*), dedicated to queer and/or feminist creators, make them visible to the public eye and bring them into contact with each other. Production processes are also in constant evolution: Co-authoring projects such as *Les Allongées* (2022) by Delvaux and Jennifer Bélanger, *Morgana* by Michela Murgia and Chiara Tagliaferri or *L'Évaporée* by Fanny Chiarello and Wendy Delorme, writing in collectives (for example *Auch+, Mujeres Audiovisuales, MujeresAlBorde, Mujeres Creando, RER Q*; creational workshops like *Disoluta*) and concepts like queer kinship (Bradway/Freeman 2022), the concept of disappropriation by Rivera Garza (2019) or the concept of creative constellations (Turbiau et al. 2022) break with the idea of the author as an individualistic genius who, by tradition, works especially for male, heterosexual, bourgeois, abled structures. Over and beyond, queer and/or feminist creators refer to each other in their texts and films, knitting a close network of intertextual and intermedial references in which they express solidarity for one another and create new ways of reading and watching their work. These connections go beyond simple references as ideas such as feminist/queer genealogies or counter-canons and terms as ›autotheory‹ show (cf. Cavitch 2022). By focusing on collectiveness and connectedness, these ways of creating are seen by many as a counter-model to to the genialistic-individualistic concepts of authorship itself (cf. Falconí Trávez 2019).

The mentioned feminist and queer particularities are also perceptible in the sphere of reception. Relationships between public, artists and their works have been challenged and transformed, for example in the context of literary performance festivals such as the *MAD* in Brussels, the *Littérature etc.* festival in Lille and the *Sturmfreifestival* in Paris, or are completely different to begin with as the spectatorship often can be part of the same community as the artists (such as the actors in the movies by Alexis Langlois). It is noticeable that queer and feminist authors and directors tend to transcend the boundaries of the works, interact with their readers and viewers and establish a relationship with them. This brings literature to the fore as a performance that can be actively shaped and has a decidedly material dimension.

In addition, the importance of negotiating relationships within texts and films is particularly striking: currently, there are many works of fiction that specifically focus on social togetherness within queer and/or feminist communities (*Portrait de la jeune fille en feu* by Céline Sciamma, *Três Tigres Tristes* by Gustavo Vinagre, *Las Malas* by Camila Sosa Villada). These works negotiate their specificity and utopian potential (Muñoz 2009). There are also fictions that challenge and reshape types of traditionally heteronormative relationships such as parenthood or nuclear family (with authors such as Constance Debré and Eva Baltasar). The protagonists are often feminist or queer characters who are shown within the difficulty or even impossibility of living authentic relationships. These challenges are staged by preferentially recurring to the tragic mode, which is particularly suitable for modeling a struggle against fatal structures of oppression, the identificatory mode, which can create understanding and solidarization, the comic or camp mode, which harbor critical and transgressive potential, and the metafictional mode which prevents discrimination from being repeated at the level of the literary or filmic work. Natural symbols as fire (*Las cosas que perdimos en el fuego* by

Mariana Enriquez, *Viendra le temps du feu* by Wendy Delorme), water/waves (*A felicidade delas* by Carol Rodrigues), storms or animals (»Felina« by Guadelupe Nettel) often prepare or accompany the relationship emphasizing the intention to go beyond cultural (anthropocentric) limitations and expressing fluidity, dynamism and expansion beyond the logics of reproduction. In terms of genres, there is a tendency towards utopia/dystopia, fairy tales, science fiction, fantasy and crime novels. These are currently popular genres that are being taken up by feminist and queer activists or authors in order to appeal to the readership, they are genres with a fantastic component that have the potential to create alternative worlds, genres that are historically closely linked to the construction of alternative societies.

Even though the construct of a relationship plays such an important role in contemporary queer and feminist fictions and their reception, it has been only taken into account in a limited form to this day. In research the focus is often set on one particular woman or queer person, presenting them as exceptional in relation to the social category to which they belong, and arguing that they should be highlighted precisely for their exceptionality and pioneer status, a term rightly decried by researchers such as the art historian Eva Belgherbi. According to her, there are certain research practices that help to avoid this pitfall. Reading and re-reading the researchers, who have theorized on these issues since the 1970s, reading and quoting the work of young researchers, and thinking in terms of »networks« rather than »heroines«, are just a few examples (Belgherbi 2023).

The contributions to this anthology provide a colorful mix that studies modalities of – friendly, amorous, sexual, political, militant, artistic – queer and feminist relationships within and around cinema and literature in Romance cultures in the 21st century. Based on the perspective of literary studies, film studies and the general sociology of literature and film they focus on different countries and artistic fields.

The articles of this anthology begin by analyzing works in which traditionally heteronormative relationships are critically examined and recast from feminist and queer perspectives. In »Make Kin, Not Babies: Human-Animal Proximity, Queering Kinship and Embodied Choice in Guadalupe Nettel's ›Felina‹«, Vera Wurst shows how Nettel's text questions motherhood by developing a deep bond between the protagonist and its pet, by differentiating the traditional alignment of women with a wild and threatening nature, and by conceptualizing nature as a feminist space. In »Nomadic Motherhood: Constance Debré and Eva Baltasar Resignifying Queer-Feminist Kinship

Through Impediment«, Gabrielle Jourde reflects on how normative modes of parenthood transform the relational ethics of filiation in the novels of the two contemporary authors showing how an imaginary of nomadism and queer aesthetic contributes to undermine established notions of heteronormative love. In »Virginie Despentes: Vernon's Failing as a Way of Literary Queering«, Michaela Rumpikova demonstrates how community in *Vernon Subutex* functions as deconstruction of fundamental patriarchal, capitalist order and explains how perspective taking, non-linearity, transgressive ruptures in spatiotemporal frames and more specifically, the use of dialogue contribute to this intention. In »Negative Affects, Futurity and Queer Relationality in and around *De la terreur, mes sœurs!* (Alexis Langlois, 2019)«, Pierre Niedergang analyzes the mentioned movie as affirmation of a futuristic perspective against the anti-relational and no-future positions currently enjoying great publicity in queer intellectual discourses in France. In »Love as Crisis? The Promises of Queer Feminist Cinema in Contemporary Chile, Argentina, and Brazil«, Alkisti Eftyhmiou carves out that several contemporary Latinamerican films deal with intimacy as a collective form of queer resistance, showing how alternatives worldings of live articulate critiques of neoliberalism. In »›You Cannot Confine Imagination‹ – Contemporary Corona Fictions Embracing Lesbian Relationships«, Julia Obermayr analyses how LGBT+ communities and characters and their relationships are represented in the Corona Fictions and which metaphors, symbols and narrative strategies are used to depict relationships and matters of identity. Utopias and dystopias seem to have a special potential for questioning existing forms of relationships and designing alternative ones. In this direction Anna Langewiesche and Arthur Ségard argue in »The Poet's Choice: Céline Sciamma's Lesbian Utopias« that the impossible love stories in *Pieuvres* et *Portrait de la jeune fille en feu* initiate processes of resignifying underlining how precisely the instability and precariousness of utopias allow to criticize the heteropatriarchal order. In »The Making-With of Queer Dystopia – Entangled Relationships in Wendy Delorme's *Viendra le temps du feu*«, Audrey da Rocha works out the dystopian staging of the heteropatriarchal system in the aforementioned novel and makes clear how the concept of nomadic subjectivity forms an alternative to it.

However, queer and feminist relationships are not only found on the diegetic level of literary and cinematic works, but also on the theoretical and sociological spheres of literature. Processes of authorship and reception imply numerous decisions that are made in conjunction with other people, as well as collective action. Queer and feminist contemporary fictions explore the possibilities of replacing traditional creation processes with alternatives that are based on connectedness. In »Let's Kill the Author: Cristina Rivera Garza and Collective Authorship«, Stefanie Mayer demonstrates how Cristina Rivera Garza deconstructs the topos of the author as an individualistic writing genius by modelling writing as a collective practice that enables othered subjects to situate themselves as authors. In »Citation as/and Relation: Chronic Pain, Autotheory, and Horizontal Writing in Jennifer Bélanger and Martine Delvaux's *Les allongées*«, Hannah Volland presents relationality as a feminist mode of thinking and writing built upon intimate and intellectual relationships among writers, artists, and activists, by giving examples of filiation, collective writing practices and uses of intertextuality.

In »Exploring the *Intersectional I* in Transgender Autobiography: A Study of Camila Sosa's Early Works«, Juan Zapata shows how the mixture of genres and audiovisual media, as well as the play with the writing of physical performances that characterize the work of Camila Sosa create a literature that is capable of transcending traditional classifications.

In »Fighting to Exist in a World Where You Don't Belong: Forms of Relationships and Struggles in Lauren Delphe's *Faite de cyprine et de punaises* (2022)«, Alex Lachkar analyzes how the lesbophobia and ableism suffered by the novel's narrator lead her to flee the world and to explore relationships with both authors of lesbian literature and fictional characters, and to set up a lesbian life far from society's expectations. Similarily, Alexandre Antonlin shows in »›D'autres femmes continueront, elles réussiront‹. Réception de l'œuvre Violette Leduc dans Colza d'Al Baylac, Fiévreuse plébéienne d'Élodie Petit & Au temps du sublime de Louise-Amada D.«, the extent to which the intertextual reference to Violette Leduc is understood as a community- and tradition-building act that helps the lesbian writing community to gain visibility and identity. With regard to alternative forms of relating to literary and cinematic works as recipients, Anna Lévy analyses in »Literary Performance Festivals as a Space for Feminist and Queer Sociability« how literary performance festivals contribute to reducing the distance between authors and readers and allow for alternative sociabilities.

With these contributions, the anthology hopes to contribute to highlighting the importance of community building for making queer and feminist concerns visible, to making clear its contribution to identity construction beyond heteropatriarchal attributions, and to understanding the relational on an intra-diegetic as well as on a production and reception aesthetic level as a characteristic of current fictions. Against this background, contemporary fictions are seen as direct actions in an attempt to construct a new form of coexistence.

Bibliography

Armstrong, Cory L./Mahone, Jessica (2023): »*#Metoo* in Practice. Revisiting Social Media's Influence in Individual Willingness to Mobilize Against Sexual Assault«, in: Feminist Media Studies 32.1, pp. 185–198.

Belgherbi, Eva (2023): »Contre-canons. Contre une histoire de l'art des héroïnes, pour une histoire de l'art des réseaux«, in: un carnet genre et histoire de l'art, https://ghda.hypotheses.org/2946#more-2946 [21.06.2024].

Bradway, Teagan/Freeman, Elisabeth (2022): Queer Kinship. Race, Sex, Belonging, Form, Durham: Duke University Press.

Cavitch, Max (2022): »Everybody's Autotheory«, in: Modern Language Quarterly 83.1, pp. 81–116.

Duncan, Petti (2023): »Transnational Feminist Movement(s), Solidarities and Analyses«, in: Feminist Formations 35.2, pp. vii-xiii.

Falconí Trávez, Diego (2019): »Autorías comunitarias en los Andes. El caso de Julieta Paredes y la Comunidad Mujeres Creando«, in: Aina Pérez Fontdevila/Meri Torras Francès (eds.): ¿Qué es una autora? Encrucijadas entre género y autoría, Barcelona: Icaria.

Moraga, Cherrie/Anzaldúa, Gloria (2021): This Bridge Called my Back. Writings by Radical Women of Color, NY: New York Press.

Muñoz, José Esteban (2009): Cruising Utopia. The Then and There of Queer Futurity, NY: New York Press.

Renn, Ines Tabea (2019): Vom Hashtag zum Protest. Repräsentation von Hashtagaktivismus in den österreichischen Medien. Eine diskursanalytische Untersuchung anhand des Fallbeispiels *#metoo*, Wien: Magisterarbeit.

Turbiau, Aurore/Leïchle, Mathilde/Islert, Camille/Hertiman, Marys Renné/Gauthier, Vicky (2022): »Introduction«, in: GLAD! 12, http://journals.openedition.org/glad/4607 [22.06.2024].

Zaytun, Kelli/Ezekiel, Judith (2016): »Sisterhood in Movement. Feminist Solidarity in France and the United States«, in: Frontiers. A Journal of Women Studies 37.1, pp. 195–214.

Make Kin, Not Babies
Human-Animal Proximity, Queering Kinship and Embodied Choice in Guadalupe Nettel's »Felina«

Vera Lucía Wurst

> Viens, mon beau chat, sur mon cœur amoureux
> *(Charles Baudelaire)*

1 Human-Animal Ties

»Los vínculos entre los animales y los seres humanos pueden ser tan complejos como aquellos que nos unen a la gente« (Nettel 2013: 63). With this meditation begins »Felina«, part of Guadalupe Nettel's *El matrimonio de los peces rojos*, that collects shorts stories where animals coexist with humans in an intimate domestic space and serve, as stated by the Mexican author, as »a mirror that reflects emotions or hidden behaviors that we do not dare to see« (Nettel 2013 in Gálvez Cuen/Lámbarry 2020: 67/ Wentworth: 2021: 241). This work joins a Latin American literary trend, which, since the 1960s, according to Gabriel Giorgi's observations, has moved away from cultural traditions that associate the animal with a constitutive flaw (cultural, racial, historical) (2014: 11), and delves, instead, into »a new contiguity and proximity to animal life« (ibid.: 11). Giorgi refers, in this sense, to an animality that begins to break into the interior of houses and cities in more and more insistent ways »above all, wherever the body, its desires, its illnesses, its passions and its affections are questioned, wherever the body becomes a protagonist« (ibid.). This is the case in Nettel's tale of a woman who reminisces about a time in her student years when she unexpectedly becomes pregnant at the same time as one of her two cats, while preparing for her graduate studies abroad. These circumstances lead her to develop a deepening connection and a growing closeness with her pet as she vacillates between having an abortion and changing her future plans.

This analysis seeks to explore the themes of animality, kinship, choice and embodiment present in the story through a Gender and Animal Studies perspective, that approaches human-animal relations, or rather the relationship between human and non-human animals, from an interdisciplinary and non-anthropocentric perspective. This viewpoint derives from an academic and cultural shift towards the acknowledgement of the interconnectedness and interdependence of all living beings as part of a non-hierarchical continuum in what is now known as the *animal turn*. Below, we will discuss concepts such as the *fall of animal metaphor* (Julieta Yelin), the *community of the living* (Florencia Garramuño), the *animot* (Jacques Derrida), the process of *contiguity* to *passage* (Gabriel Giorgi) and the call to *make kin, not babies* (Donna Haraway), as we study the coexistence and cohabitation of the human and the animal through the relationship between »Felina«'s characters.

2 Literary, Animal and Gender Studies Meet

In the literary field, following Julieta Yelin, the *animal turn*, may be understood as the »fall of the animal metaphor as the primary symbolic construction of the human« (2015: 178–79). Since classical fables, language and thoughts have been projected onto animals to portray them as allegories of the human. In the literature representative of the *animal turn*, however, we can witness a weakening of the symbolic potentiality of the animal (ibid.: 178) to instead explore, on the one hand, »the possibilities of the figuration of the [...] animal and, on the other, imagine new ways of approaching and experimenting with animal interiority« (ibid.: 179).

Yelin goes on to clarify that »[these] experiences display the difference between man and animal« (ibid.: 117), but also show »a common and transitional zone (ibid.): »Whether in a crossing of glances, in a metamorphosis, in the experience of the terrifying or the sinister, the human-animal link is thematized and something of the order of the animal appears intimately linked to the human« (ibid.). This consists of »[a] position towards the animal that, distrusting the success of fetishistic or psychologizing relationships, stages a possible encounter with the animal as such« (ibid.: 116–117),[1] or as Giorgi would put it, with an animal without a precise form, that is contagious and no longer submits to the prescriptions of metaphor and figurative language in general (cf. 2014: 13). Florencia Garramuño clarifies:

> It's not a question of an animalization of the human or the humanization of the animal. It is rather an indistinction between the animal and the human, a sort of equivalence and interchangeability between words, names and actions that could define the human or the animal indistinctly, which shows a community of the living, which neither supposes nor needs similarity, but suffices itself with the shared exposure to the forces of life (Garramuño 2011: 3).

It is vital to remark that the departure of the understanding of the animal as »the absolute other« (Derrida 2008: 11) of the human constitutes a paradigm shift with far-reaching social implications. Giorgi elaborates:

> That animal that had functioned as the sign of a heterogeneous otherness, the mark of an outside unassimilable for the social order – and on which racial, class, sexual, gender, cultural hierarchies and exclusions had been projected –, that animal becomes interior, close, contiguous, the instance of a closeness for which there is no precise »place« and that dislocates mechanisms that organize bodies and meanings (Giorgi 2014: 13).

In other words, by questioning the opposition of humanity and animality, other distinctions »that had ordered and classified bodies and forms of life, and had sustained ethics and politics« (ibid.: 13) such as civilization versus barbarism, desire versus instinct or nature versus culture, among others, are also challenged (cf. ibid.).

The contestation of this last opposition is particularly relevant to the reading of »Felina« from a gender perspective. As Sherry B. Ortner explains in »Is Female to Male as Nature Is to Culture?«, women, due to their bodies' reproductive functions and the social roles that have traditionally been assigned to them, have historically been perceived as closer to nature, and therefore inferior to men, who are, in turn, identified with culture (1972: 13). Now, it is not

---

1 Cf. Garramuño 2011 for a description of the Derridean critique of the concept of »as such«.

the intention of our analysis, nor, we believe, Nettel's, to perpetuate or reproduce these types of biased and reductionist gender frameworks, rather to denaturalize and subvert them. »Felina« thus proposes to look beyond binarisms to attempt »to bridge the entrenched gap between human and nonhuman« (Wentworth 2021: 257), and conceive all living beings in »an organic, affective, material and political continuum« (Giorgi 2014: 13). Throughout this study, we will examine how this short story navigates the complex intersections between humans and animals, beginning with their shared occupation of a common space.

3 A Domestic Community of the Living

»Felina« portrays the communal domestic life of the autodiegetic narrator with her two cats, Milton and Greta: the trio accompany each other in their everyday lives, share experiences and support each other through their crisis. According to Garramuño, these kinds of stories

> bring the human and the animal closer to the highest degree of intimacy possible, placing at times animals and humans on the same level of protagonism, making the distinction between animal and human a sort of constantly mutating fold where a logic of the multiple escapes from both similarity and analogy to place itself in the description of a common and shared region between the animal and the human (Garramuño 2011: 1).

In this tale, the narrator's home is the shared and common space where human and animal come together. This means that animality is no longer located in the perimeter or related to exteriority: the animal is a character like any other in the story, and, as we shall discuss, is not only a roommate but also a mirror and next of kin.

In the story, the narrator shows a perspective that considers the heterogeneity of animals present in the continuum of the living and does not assume any knowledge based on preconceptions or generalities. For example, she begins the story by making a case for cats who have long suffered from »una reputación de egoísmo y exceso de independencia« (Nettel 2013: 64) and calls into question the classic dog versus cat debate, which sets up the former as ›man's best friend‹:

No comparto en absoluto esa opinión. Es verdad que los gatos son menos demandantes que los perros y que su compañía suele ser mucho menos impositiva, a veces casi imperceptible. Sin embargo, sé por experiencia que pueden desarrollar una enorme empatía hacia los seres de su especie, así como hacia sus amos. En realidad, los felinos son animales sumamente versátiles y su carácter cubre desde el ostracismo de la tortuga hasta la omnipresencia del perro (ibid.: 64).

The distinction that the narrator makes between animals' different traits is reminiscent of the Derridean neologism of *animot*, proposed by the philosopher to raise »his objections to the singular hegemonic reference to the animal, rather than the multiplicity of nonhuman life forms« (Armstrong/Simmons 2007: 5). In the same vein, animals in »Felina« are »best recognized not as an abstract category, but as heterogeneity and variation« (Colanzi 2017: 41) and illustrate the complexity within the community of life forms.

Throughout »Felina«, we can also appreciate the destabilization of the human-animal distance and the exploration of a new type of proximity. The narrator displays both an approximation to and engagement with animals that is based on curiosity and affection and is devoid of an intention to exert control. She focuses instead in her pets' very own particularities, refers to them by their first names and differentiates between their personalities. Hence, she christens them Milton and Greta – »un poeta y una actriz« (Nettel 2013: 66) – and later prides herself of picking names that »no podían quedarles mejor: el macho reveló un temperamento huraño pero también una generosidad increíble y la hembra actitudes de diva consciente de su belleza« (ibid.). While the naming of the cats and the narrative perspective through which we learn about their experiences imply a certain hierarchy, the narrator does not »[intenta] un contacto forzado con ellos« (ibid.). Instead, she employs an ethological perspective to observe the actions and behaviors of her cohabitants with curiosity and imparcialidad.

The narrator asks herself »¿Qué tipo de realidad conciben los animales o, por lo menos, qué tipo de realidad concebía mi gata con respecto a mí?« attempting to discern their emotions through observable cues, yet refraining from assuming access to their inner thoughts. Furthermore, as we will delve into later, she does not claim to have a complete understanding of her own inner world either. As elucidated by Liliana Colanzi, »there is no taxonomic eagerness in the descriptions of the human who observes the animal from the outside with the aim of exercising control over it, it is a look of someone who senses in the animal something of themself, without the need to project traits of human culture onto it« (2017: 41). By inhabiting this community of the living, the narrator and her pets are able to approach one another, in a dynamic that, as we shall study below, brings the animal and the human closer and closer.

4 From Contiguity to Continuity to Contagion to Passage

Moreover, it is possible to detect in the narration the representation of »an animality that can no longer be precisely separated from human life« (Giorgi 2014: 11). Her, Milton and Greta share a domestic space and with it, their most intimate moments. The narrator also does not differentiate between her pets and other people with whom she has cohabitated. When describing her living situation, for instance, she recounts that she rented an apartment »que compartía de cuando en cuando con otros estudiantes y, más tarde, con dos gatos« (Nettel 2013: 64). We can observe that, even in her syntax, she does not separate human and non-human animals, which is why she later goes on to specify: »Ahora que lo pienso, los compañeros de piso cumplen en ocasiones el papel de las mascotas y el vínculo con ellos es igual de complejo« (ibid.). The borders between animals and humans are thus porous: »the joint and adjacent figuration of the animal and the human draws borders of passage that make the coexistence between the animal and the human a way of exploring the living, beyond any distinction« (Garramuño 2011: 4).

These lines of contiguity and continuity do not, however, preclude differences between animals and humans, or as Garramuño (2011: 3) would put it, do not even suppose nor need similarity, rather it is the recognition of differences within the common space they inhabit that makes a genuine encounter possible (cf. Yelin 2015: 117). For example, at one point, the narrator mentions on the same breath the biological characteristics that differentiate her and her pets and those they have in common:

> El desarrollo animal es más veloz que el de los seres humanos. Durante el año que pasé con los gatos, seguí siendo prácticamente la misma. Ellos, en cambio, cambiaron considerablemente. De ser dos cachorros escuálidos y asustadizos, se convirtieron en adolescentes y, luego, en dos adultos jóvenes, en la plenitud de su belleza. Las hormonas empezaron a dominarlos de la misma manera en que lo hacían conmigo durante los periodos menstruales (Nettel 2013: 68).

This example – one of the many times in which the narrator compares herself to animals or considers her own biology, as we will examine in our later analysis of hers and Greta's parallel pregnancies – illustrates how in Nettel's work »the presence of other species implies the observation of codes of coexistence in which the domestic animal represents an otherness with which, in addition to sharing a space, it is possible to experience aspects in common physiologically and mentally« (Gálvez Cuen/Lámbarry 2020: 67).

The relationship of contiguity between the narrator and Greta becomes one of contagion when their reproductive cycles match up.[2] It starts when the cat goes into her first heat and her overexcited moans take over the apartment. This sparks a conversation between the narrator and a temporary roommate, Ander, and, infected by the »insoslayable celo de Greta« (Nettel 2013: 70), they end up having a sexual encounter – »[q]uizás para hacerle honor« (ibid.) – that results in a surprise pregnancy. Continuing with this instance of fluctuating contagion, Greta then also becomes pregnant after the narrator refuses to follow the veterinarian's advice to spay her, which fosters a series of parallels and mirror images[3] between the two expecting females that bring them closer in proximity. Namely, after talking to the veterinarian she tells herself that »ninguno de los dos éramos nadie para elegir por ella. Tenía derecho a ser madre, por lo menos una vez. Qué otra misión […] puede haber en la vida de los animales sino reproducirse« (ibid.: 69).[4] And later, when she ultimately decides to keep her pregnancy, it is after she asks herself if she »también tenía una misión en la vida« (ibid.: 75) while rubbing Greta's swollen belly. Furthermore, she remarks that the doctor that she consulted about terminating her pregnancy, reminds her of Greta's veterinarian: both of them interchangeable

---

2   This occurrence is evocative of the widespread myth that people with wombs who live in close proximity or spend much time together might eventually experience a synchronization of their menstrual cycles. Although this myth has been debunked, it is worth mentioning for the notions of contiguity, contagion and interconnectedness of the living that it invokes.

3   It is worth to keep in mind Isabelle Wentworth's clarification on the subject of mirrors in Nettel's work, who »rather than interpreting this ›reflection‹ as an image of the human reflected off the opaque surface of the animal« (2021: 241), – that is, as a representation of our animalistic natures or an echo of humanity's primitive evolutionary past –, reads it as »a portrayal of how our embodied minds elide the boundaries between self and other, human and animal« (ibid: 247).

4   This statement about animal rights also extends the pro-choice argument to include the animal realm.

stand ins for the male doctors who have historically tried to control and limit female reproductive choices.

Subsequently, after she miscarries because of a fall on the way to Greta's veterinarian, contagion morphs into a passage between bodies. For instance, the cat »[adquiere] la costumbre de ponerse en mi regazo a todas horas. Como si instintivamente intentara cubrir con su cuerpo la ausencia del bebé que antes llevaba en el vientre« (ibid.: 78). The miscarriage also causes her to reflect on her own animality – »Finalmente, me gustara o no, yo también era un animal y tanto mi cuerpo como mi mente reaccionaban a la pérdida de mi descendencia de la misma manera en que lo habría hecho Greta si hubiese perdido a sus gatitos« (ibid.: 77). And finally, in an act that crosses the threshold of the human and the animal, Greta gives birth between the narrator's legs, which, according to Berit Callsen, hints at a human-animal unity in which the narrator comes to feel the effort of childbirth as her own (2020: 114). This symbolic act exemplifies the passage of the animal from the exterior to the interior of the human realm – and the human itself – and traces from there new horizons of interrogation (cf. Giorgi 2017: 87),[5] such as the porous confines of kinship, as discussed below.

5 Queering Kinship

It is important to note, as well, that while reproduction is a prominent theme in »Felina«, the bonds in the story are part of a larger living network of interrelationships and interdependencies that could be better described as kinship.[6] In this manner, the trio, due to their living in close proximity, give new meaning to the expression *next of kin*. The three of them live in a pleasant equilibrium (cf. Nettel 2013: 67) that they zealously protect from any potential »intruso [que] cambiara el ambiente que había dentro de la casa« (ibid.). This is evident, for instance, when the cats involve themselves in the roommate selection process and demonstrate their disapproval of possible candidates by showing their fangs or urinating in their shoes (ibid.). The narrator thus sees them as »un equipo« (ibid.) where each of them contributes in their own way: »Yo aportaba una energía pausada y maternal, Greta la agilidad y la coquetería y Milton la

---

5   This event could be further analyzed with the concept of *becoming animal*, coined by Deleuze/Guatarri 1987.
6   Cf. Butler 2022 for a detailed examination of the concept of kinship.

fortaleza masculina« (ibid.). After the narrator's pregnancy, the cats offer their support and affection by purring in her ear and lying on her lap. Of course, we are not employing the concept of kinship in a traditional sense of the hetero-limited nuclear family, rather we are offering a queering of it, a »kinship beyond the bloodlines« (2022: 25), in Judith Butler's words.

Butler proposes Christopher Roebuck's redefinition of kinship: »Kinship [is] a means through which humans go about forming a network of relations constituted by practices of obligation, support, and care with significant and beloved others as well as offering the language through which humans give meanings to these practices« (Roebuck 2013, cited in Butler 2022: 41). This last point is important, because the narrator still sometimes uses the language of the biological family to refer to the kinship bonds she develops. For instance, she declares that Marisa, who takes over the correspondence concerning her graduate studies – and, most importantly, refers her to a doctor able to perform a clandestine abortion –, »[m]ás que como una directora de tesis o una amiga, se portó conmigo como una madre« (Nettel 2013: 78). This queer kinship in particular thus entails a redelineation of roles based on gender solidarity and sorority and brings to mind the feminist underground networks that facilitate access to abortion in the Latin American countries that prohibit it.

Donna Haraway notably queers the notion of kinship even further and »relies on the language of kinship while radically redefining it in posthuman and multispecies terms« (Bradway/Freeman 2020: 22). With her call to »Make Kin, Not Babies!«[7] (Haraway 2016: 102) she proposes a reconfiguration and expansion of »modes of kinship that cross species« (Butler 2022: 41)[8] with the purpose »to make ›kin‹ mean something more than entities tied by ancestry or genealogy« (Haraway 2016: 102–103): »I think that the stretch and recomposition of kin are allowed by the fact that all earthlings are kin in the deepest sense, and it is past time to practice better care of kinds-as-assemblages (not species one at a time)« (ibid.). In »Felina«, a queering of kinship takes place through interspecies and feminist relations, that take precedence over family ties[9] and are reshuffled throughout the tale: Marisa, for example, is the one who gets the

---

[7] She later changes her slogan to »Make kin not population«. Cf. Clarke/Haraway 2018.
[8] Another useful term from Haraway is *companion species* which defines the »co-constitutive human relationships with other critters« (2008: 73).
[9] Notably, no blood relatives are involved in the narrator's reproductive dilemma. She does not discuss her situation with any family members or even with Ander, with whom she conceived.

narrator to adopt Milton and Greta, and later is prepared to take them in to, as she states, »llenar el vacío« from her leaving (Nettel 2013: 80). Already seen as a maternal figure by the narrator, her choice of words, which portrays her as an empty nester, shows she shares this view. Haraway's slogan of »Make Kin, Not Babies!« also takes on additional meaning when reading »Felina« in light of the narrator's abortion discussed below.

6 Pro (Animal) Choice

»Felina« deals with the question of choice in humans and animals, a subject of philosophical and scientific inquiry, and reframes it as a question of reproductive choice. When the narrator learns of her pregnancy, she is faced with the dilemma of whether or not to have the child, an event that Mary-Joan Gerson (1990, cited in Gutierrez: 2021: 95) calls »the first stage in the experience of motherhood«. Her internal struggle illustrates an experience of the greatest intensity where women are expected to solely carry the weight of cultural and moral expectations (cf. Chaneton/Vacarezza 2011: 71). In this context, the narrator recalls a scientific study which claims that »[los humanos] no decidimos. Todas nuestras elecciones están condicionadas de antemano« (Nettel 2013: 77) by our cultural environment and genetic history, which leads her to ponder if our actions are motivated by choice, predetermination or animalistic instinct.

Although she does not elaborate on it, we as readers, cannot help but consider the factors and material conditions that might influence the narrator's own decision regarding her potential motherhood. As an independent and educated middle-class woman, she possesses a degree of freedom of choice that is not dictated by necessity, cultural obligations, or genuine fear for her life: she is financially capable of providing for a potential offspring; less susceptible to conditioning cultural and ideological factors that push a patriarchal reproductive imperative; and, most importantly, she may be able to avoid the risks commonly associated with clandestine abortions. She is in the position to choose, albeit one of her options falls into the realm of the clandestine. However, her indecisiveness seems to paralyze her, leading her to look to her cat, Greta, for answers.

Isabelle Wentworth explains that the human-animal bond in Nettel's work »creates bodily and affective resonances« which can guide the characters »unconscious behaviour and conscious decision making« (2021: 257–258). In this way, the narrator confesses that »siempre [le] ha costado decidir« (Nettel 2013:

72), and considers her indecisiveness in contraposition to Greta, who seems perfectly content with her gravidity. This brings her to argue that »los gatos, a diferencia de nosotros, toman ciertas decisiones« (ibid.: 78). The narrator also cannot determine, even in hindsight, if her miscarriage, caused by a fall, can qualify as accidental or as unconsciously desired, – »no puedo decir si fue un accidente o un acto fallido« (ibid.: 76) – in other words, if it was a literal or a freudian slip.[10] While the conventional assumption might suggest that animals, driven by instinct, lack free will and decision-making abilities, unlike humans who, guided by reason, are capable of making informed decisions, the point of the story is quite the opposite. Through the retrospective viewpoint of its irresolute narrator, human reason, even her own, is depicted as an enigma: whether deterministic, unconsciously driven, or potentially obstructive, it remains shrouded in mystery despite the passage of time.

In this regard, Wentworth points out that *El matrimonio de los peces rojos* challenges the notion of reason as a defining characteristic that sets humans apart from animals:

> the identification between humans and nonhumans in the anthology destabilizes the binary concepts used to divide them. Each story, in its own way, dissolves barriers of intelligence vs instinct, civilized vs primitive, self-aware vs non-self-aware, determinism vs free will. Reason as a distinguishing factor between humans and nonhumans is disrupted: as the anthology's epigraph attests, ›all animals know what they need, except for man‹ (Plinio el Viejo) (2021: 256–257).

This assertion echoes Giorgi's previously mentioned perspective that the interrogation of the human-animal dichotomy leads to question other entrenched hierarchical distinctions (cf. 2014: 13). In this instance, the narrator's indecision regarding her reproductive fate highlights the notion that reproduction is not inherently ›natural‹, but rather significantly influenced by culture. This prompts a denaturalization of reproduction, thereby contesting the deep-seated opposition of nature versus culture.[11] »Felina« thus offers a reconfiguration of the animal that »challenges assumptions about the specificity and

---

10 In the English version of the story, the narrator's comment is, in fact, translated as »But still, I can't say if my fall that evening was an accident or a Freudian slip« (Nettel 2014: 75).
11 I thank my colleagues, Teresa Hiergeist, Stefanie Mayer and Alex Lachkar, for this observation.

essence of the human« (Giorgi 2014: 15) and reevaluates notions related to hierarchies, behaviors and, as detailed below, embodied experiences that play a part in the continuum and community of the living.

7 Make Embodied Choices, Not Babies!

The process of pregnant embodiment is experienced by the narrator as a loss of control. Her pregnancy makes her corporality manifest and she grows apprehensive when she sees the dramatic changes in her cat as an impending mirror image: »Mientras observaba a Greta moviéndose con dificultad por el suelo de madera, paladeé todas las formas de la impotencia. Como el suyo, mi cuerpo cambiaba vertiginosamente« (Nettel 2013: 72). But while Greta »[disfruta] de su embarazo y de la embriaguez que producen los estrógenos« (ibid.: 73), the narrator charges on with the arrangements of her graduate studies abroad and researches »toda clase de información sobre el aborto que, en aquel entonces, aún estaba prohibido por las leyes de esta ciudad« (ibid.). In this sense, Colanzi refers to the body as »the space where the struggles over the human and the animal become visible« (2017: 8–9), as a

> place traversed by power and by the articulations of the political; it is also the space where the Self is disintegrated and fragmented, the site of unknown instincts, pleasures, suffering, illness, strength, weakness, and desires that cannot be apprehended through reason alone (ibid.: 9).

The notion of the body as a locus of contention is markedly exemplified by the case of abortion. In »Felina«, the narrator not only has to grapple with the loss of control of her physical body due to gestation, but she also has to find a way to circumvent the State mechanisms that seek to control that body and constrain her reproductive autonomy.

However, at the same time, the narrator's miscarriage can also be interpreted as an embodied choice, namely as a bodily manifestation of her unconscious desire. Even though she tentatively decides to keep her pregnancy, this desire is never fully verbalized, because the thesis advisor does not answer the phone when she wants to share the news. She then miscarries due to her tripping on the steps while holding Greta's cage in both hands to prevent it from crashing to the ground (cf. Nettel 2013: 76). That is, her possible freudian slip occurs in a moment when she shows an obligation to Greta and prioritizes her wellbeing over that of herself and her fetus: to rephrase Haraway, she chooses to make kin and not babies (cf. 2016: 102).

In the same vein, July Chaneton and Nayla Vacarezza address the subject of abortion by distinguishing between ›to decide‹ and ›to make a decision‹ – in Spanish, ›tomar una decisión‹, which would be literally translated as ›to take a decision‹, as in to hold it in one's hand – to draw attention to »the presence [...] of a power of the will located in one's own body« (2011: 71). Also, keeping in mind that the narrator regards Greta as a bastion of decision-making, her holding her cage could be read as a figurative demonstration of Chaneton and Vacarezza's concept of holding a decision in one's hands, which would open further possibilities of contagion between the animal and the human »wherever the body becomes a narrator« (Giorgi 2014: 11). In this way, the narrator, even if unconsciously, uses the forces of her body to unlock new possibilities of life (cf. ibid.: 19).

8 Cats Do Decide

The end of the story demonstrates that the animal can cross in both directions the eroded barrier between domestic interiority and natural exteriority, when the two cats disappear, having left the house with their kittens just before the narrator moves abroad. Mónica Cragnolini makes a series of observations that are relevant to the interpretation of this conclusion:

> Cats have traversed much of the history of Western thought and culture in defiance of the human-animal boundary, being domesticated but remaining, in part, alien to domestication. [...] »made« to the ways of the house, »educated« to be part of it, cats remain always, and at the same time, strange and wild. They make evident the paradox of domesticity, of the desire to transform a way of being other than one's own, and of the perception of the constant failure of this attempt (Cragnolini 2016: 184).

It is, in fact, not unusual for a cat to come and go and move freely into and out of the domestic space, but the narrator interprets this as proof that »[l]os gatos sí que deciden« (Nettel 2013: 81) and feels like »una estúpida por no haber[s]e dado cuenta« (ibid.: 81). While one interpretation of this ending could frame it as an ultimately failed attempt at human-animal proximity, we could also read it as providing valuable insights into the themes of human-animal contiguity, queer kinship and embodied choice within our analysis. We can think of Greta as making her own embodied choice of distancing herself from the human and domestic space, changing, once again, »the conception of the limits and distributions between interior and exterior« (Giorgi 2014: 98) to potentially explore other forms of kinship within the continuum and community of the living.

In sum, in our reading of »Felina«, we have touched on issues of domesticity, pregnancy and abortion, usually addressed by Gender Studies, and we have integrated them with Animal Studies to try to deepen the cultural discourses, discussions and debates around them and show them on a new light. Thus, we have analyzed the story's portrait of a domestic community of the living, that illustrates an ever-increasing proximity of cat and woman from contiguity to passage, which interrogates the porous barriers of the human-animal divide and of queer kinships through the narrator's embodied choice to make kin, not babies. However, the story does not aim to provide definitive answers; instead, it raises questions until the very end, and strives to find original ways to address these themes through a novel figuration of the animal, only possible through literary expression.

Bibliography

Armstrong, Philip/Simmons, Laurence (2007): »Bestiary. An Introduction«, in: Philip Armstrong/Laurence Simmons (eds.), Knowing Animals, Leiden: Brill, pp. 1–24.

Bradway, Tyler/Freeman, Elizabeth (2022): »Introduction. Kincoherence/Kin-aesthetics/Kinematics«, in: Tyler Bradway/Elizabeth Freeman (eds.), Queer Kinship. Race, Sex, Belonging, Form, Durham: Duke University Press, pp. 1–22.

Butler, Judith (2022): »Kinship beyond the Bloodline«, in: Tyler Bradway/Elizabeth Freeman (eds.), Queer Kinship. Race, Sex, Belonging, Form, Durham: Duke University Press, pp. 25–47.

Callsen, Berit (2020): »Cuerpo y mente extraordinarios. Formas de inclusión y concepción de figuras en la obra cuentística de Guadalupe Nettel«, in: Susanne Hartwig (ed.), Inclusión, integración, diferenciación. La diversidad funcional en la literatura, el cine y las artes escénicas, Berlin: Peter Lang, pp. 105–120.

Chaneton, July/Vacarezza, Nayla (2011): La intemperie y lo intempestivo. Experiencias del aborto voluntario en el relato de mujeres y varones, Buenos Aires: Marea.

Clarke, Adele/Haraway, Donna (2018): Making Kin, Not Population. Reconceiving Generations, Chicago: Prickly Paradigm.

Colanzi, Liliana (2017): Of Animals, Monsters, and Cyborgs. Alternative Bodies in Latin American Fiction, Doctoral Thesis, Cornell University.

Cragnolini, Monica B. (2016): Extraños animales. Filosofía y animalidad en el pensar contemporáneo, Buenos Aires: Prometeo Libros.

Deleuze, Gilles/Guattari, Félix (1987 [1980]): A Thousand Plateaus. Capitalism and Schizophrenia, Minneapolis: University of Minnesota.

Derrida, Jacques (2008 [2006]): The Animal That Therefore I Am, New York: Fordham University Press.

Gálvez Cuen, Marissa/Lámbarry, Alejandro (2020): »Especismo, empatía y diálogo«, in: Iberoamericana 20.73, pp. 57–72.

Garramuño, Florencia (2011): »Región compartida. Pliegues de lo animal-humano«, in: Boletín del Centro de Estudios de Teoría y Crítica Literaria 16, pp. 1–14.

Giorgi, Gabriel (2014): Formas comunes. Animalidad, cultura, biopolítica, Buenos Aires: Eterna Cadencia.

Gutiérrez Piña, Claudia (2021): »Los relatos de la maternidad y el paradigma de la elección en La hija única, de Guadalupe Nettel«, in: Claudia L. Gutiérrez Piña/Gabriela Trejo Valencia/Jazmín G. Tapia Vázquez (eds.), Escrituras de la maternidad. Miradas reflexivas y metáforas en la literatura hispanoamericana, Guanajuato: Universidad de Guanajuato, pp. 93–112.

Haraway, Donna (2008): When Species Meet. Minneapolis: University of Minnesota.

Haraway, Donna (2016): Staying with the Trouble. Making Kin in the Chthulucene, Durham, NC: Duke University.

Nettel, Guadalupe (2013): El matrimonio de los peces rojos, Madrid: Páginas de Espuma.

Nettel, Guadalupe (2014 [2013]): Natural Stories, New York: Seven Stories.

Ortner, Sherry B. (1972): »Is Female to Male as Nature Is to Culture?«, in: Feminist Studies 1/2, pp. 5–31.

Wentworth, Isabelle (2021): »Embodiment and the Animal in Guadalupe Nettel's *El matrimonio de los peces rojos*«, in: Catedral tomada. Revista de crítica literaria latinoamericana 9.16, pp. 239–277.

Yelin, Julieta (2015): La letra salvaje. Ensayos sobre literatura y animalidad, Rosario: Beatriz Viterbo.

Nomadic Motherhood
Constance Debré and Eva Baltasar Resignifying Queer-Feminist Kinship Through Impediment

Gabrielle Jourde

1 Introduction

> Je ne suis pas une mère. Bien sûr que non. Qui voudrait l'être? À part celles qui ont tout raté. Qui ont tellement échoué dans tout qu'elles n'ont trouvé que ce statut pour se venger du monde. Il y a des gens qui croient que c'est comme ça. Des femmes qui se disent qu'elles sont mères parce qu'elles ont des enfants. Des hommes qui pensent la même chose des femmes, pépères les pères. Ou bien des pères qui veulent être mère, comme Laurent, pour se venger des femmes qui ne sont pas des femmes, comme moi. Mère c'est quelque chose de pire que femme. C'est un peu comme domestique. Ou chien. Mais en moins bien (Debré 2020: 93).

Following her coming out as a lesbian and the publication of her first novel, French writer Constance Debré was faced with the legal system depriving her of custody of her son, born from her former husband Laurent. In an interview following the publication of *Love Me Tender* (2020), the writer responded to a journalist who questioned whether this passage was misogynistic, given the comparisons of the mother with a servant or a dog, both domestic figures who take on a degrading meaning here. Debré explained that she didn't see a problem with »being someone's mother« but rejected the condition of »being a mother« (Debré 2020). In the latter expression, ›mother‹ is an identity, a status, a social role, while ›being someone's mother‹ implies a relationship.

This comparative study examines the novels of two lesbian authors, Constance Debré and Eva Baltasar, to highlight the ambivalent relational aspect of queer antimaternalism.[1] The novels problematize the incompatibility between the role of mother and the life of a queer individual, addressing a queer-feminist issue that is resolved through the literary figuration of a nomadic motherhood. I will demonstrate that the characters endorse a queer critique of reproduction, aligned with the antinormative queer theses,[2] and are facing a dilemma: they are radically queer but have had children or are imposed with children. From this antimaternal position, how can queer motherhood be narrated and lived? I will argue that they resignify motherhood in a queer way through a journey from antinormativity towards relationality, with one of the stages being motherhood impeded by queer desire. This figuration of queerness through the motif of nomadism allows for the resignification of motherhood as a relationship rather than an identity, thus extending queer theory towards relational futures.

Constance Debré and Eva Baltasar both published their first novels in 2018 followed by subsequent releases in 2020. Debré, a former criminal defense attorney whose social origin stems from French high society, left her career to pursue writing after coming out as a lesbian. Her autobiographical trilogy, starting with *Playboy* (2018), explores her departure from heterosexuality: she leaves her husband, transforms her body through sports and sexual exploration and endeavors to shed her legacy of upper-class privilege. In her second novel, *Love Me Tender* (2020), she alternates between the narrative of her romantic relationships and the story of her legal and intimate battle for her son's custody. The book explores the dynamics of relationships and affective bonds amidst the experience of severe lesbophobia. In her novels, *Permafrost* (2018) and *Boulder* (2020), Catalan author Eva Baltasar, who lives as a nomad

---

1   Referring to queer ›antimaternalism‹, I draw on Susan Fraiman's thesis on a rejection of motherhood in queer theory. Fraiman argues that this rejection creates an otherization of women in general in queer discourse, based on the reduction of mothers »to biology, heterosexuality, traditional family, coercive normativity« (Fraiman 2003: 120).

2   I refer to the shift in queer theory from the early 1990s towards an ontological exploration of queerness as a potential to disrupt the heteronormative framework. More precisely, I refer to Lee Edelman, who criticized »reproductive futurism«, aligned with a negative and anal sexual ethics as theorized by Leo Bersani. Edelman argued that the non-reproductive nature of queer sexuality becomes a political force against the heteronormative matrix. According to this view, reproduction and having children are complicit with the capitalist and heterosexist order, a manifestation of reproductive futurism opposing the present-focused subjective practices of queer politics and thus a betrayal of an antinormative lifestyle (Edelman 2004; Bersani 2010).

between Barcelona and its surrounding countryside, infused her prose with poetic imagery, associative thinking and autobiographical elements.[3] Unlike Debré's autofictional character, Baltasar's first two novels feature different lesbian protagonists. *Permafrost* follows a disillusioned and suicidal narrator who rejects her family, represented by her mother and sister, and narrates her obsessive love for two other women, Veronika and Roxane. Her desires are intense but thwarted by her struggle to form attachments, her existential fear of commitment, and latent maternal anxieties. In *Boulder*, the protagonist is a ship's cook who falls in love with Samsa, a Swedish woman who symbolizes capitalist professional success. As her lover becomes increasingly absorbed in her desire for children and the pursuit of assisted reproduction, which necessitates the adoption of a normative, sedentary, and anxiety-inducing lifestyle, the narrator distances herself and reverts to her nomadic way of living.

The proposed examination of nomadic motherhood will be conducted in three stages. First, I will explore the ways in which queerness generates an impediment to motherhood for both characters. This will be achieved by focusing on the anxiety of homonormalization that they describe, which turns the status of mother into a repellent identification. I will then demonstrate that the queer antisocial thesis evolves to a literary form through two figurations: the cowboy and the sailor. These two queer figures embody both a dream of autonomy and disidentification, enabling the characters to access a nomadic way of thinking about gender identity and motherhood. Finally, I will argue that this nomadic figuration of motherhood enables us to reconsider attachment between queer adults and children and, consequently, to resignify motherhood through relationality within a queer-feminist framework.

---

[3] Baltasar identifies with her characters, explaining that the story aligns with her own experiences, albeit with small lies (Galo Martin 2018).

2 Against »Reproductive Futurism«: an Impeded Maternal Identification Due to Queerness?

The stories of our two authors first reveal an anxiety about homonormalization,[4] which, in this context, takes the form of a complete rejection of marriage for same-sex couples or homoparentality:

> Mon programme, c'est le moins de propriété possible. Avec les choses, avec les lieux, avec les êtres, avec mes maîtresses, mon fils, mes amis. Je pensais que c'était ça aussi, l'homosexualité. [...] Un papa une maman, j'ai donné. Une maman une maman, ça m'ennuie pareil (Debré 2020: 97).

> »You know I cannot marry you. We are lesbians!«, exclamo. La Veronika somriu. »Of course we can! Since 30th January!« Oh, Lord! Legalitzar el matrimoni homosexual ha estat una gran cosa, no ho discuteixo, però a mi ja m'anava bé, abans. El matrimoni, com la serpent de corall, no sempre és verinós però és preferible no acostar-s'hi, per si de cas (Baltasar 2018: 61).

The characters distance themselves from any form of institutionalization of their love and family relationships that might mimic the heterosexual family model. Marriage is described as boring or as a ›poisonous‹ victory, a neoliberal trap which sums up the criticism made by radical queers of the incorporation of bodily subjectivities into the project of national citizenship, directing bodies towards reproduction and maximum productivity (Edelman 2004, Puar 2007). This way of life is rejected in favor of an antisocial standard, which involves redefining one's sexuality through technologies of the self and of the body.

However, this opposition between queer lives, particularly in their sexual dimension, and motherhood is not just a political anxiety for queers but is also institutionalized in homophobic state policies. This is what happens to Constance Debré when her custody of her son is taken away due to her being a lesbian.

---

4   The term ›homonormalization‹ is borrowed from Pierre Niedergang who suggests it as a replacement from ›homonormativity‹, introduced in 2002 by Lissa Duggan to describe the enrolment of queer bodies in neoliberal sexual politics. This term emphasizes that the risk lies not in inventing new norms from queer positions but in allowing queer specificities, particularly sexual ontology, to dissolve into heterosexual normalization (Niedergang 2023 and Duggan 2002: 175–194).

> [...] la juge fixe le tatouage qui dépasse de ma manche, me demande pourquoi j'écris un livre et sur quoi, pourquoi j'ai parlé de mon homosexualité à mon fils, elle dit que ça ne regarde pas les enfants ces choses-là, elle dit qu'on ne parle pas de droit, là, qu'on parle de morale, que je peux comprendre, que je suis intelligente (Debré 2020: 21).

> Si je m'étais contentée d'aimer les femmes, à mon avis, ce serait passé. Lesbienne mais avocat, avec la même vie, avec le même pognon, avec la même apparence, avec les mêmes opinions, avec le même rapport au travail, à l'argent, à l'amour, à la famille, à la société, à la matière, au corps, à l'idéal. Si j'avais gardé le même rapport au monde, j'aurais eu moins d'emmerdes (Debré 2020: 34).

More than homosexuality, it is the assertion of dissidence from the capitalist and heterosexual moral order, especially through the body, as evidenced by her tattoos. It is not just her romantic or sexual orientation that has changed, but her entire ›relationship with the world‹, signifying her entry into a queer politicization of her existence.

Yet, the heterosexual norm also takes on an anxiety-inducing aspect that threatens acquired freedom of queerness. This is the case with Eva Baltasar when the narrator of her second novel, nicknamed Boulder by her lover, experiences a detachment from the vitality of their shared desire at the moment when the woman she loves expresses a desire for a child:

> I passa. Allò que no té res a veure amb la meva vida ni amb el perímetre quilomètric de vida que m'havia de protegir de les lleis inesborrables, atemporals, les que desafien la contingència. Arriba a casa com un convidat mortal. Inesperat i infaust. La malaltia que afectava només els altres. Vull un fill, diu la Samsa, un fill nostre. Teu. Ho diu i no sento res, com si hagués begut arsènic. Només sé que estic glaçada. [...] Acull dins seu un desig que no li dono i fa que circuli pels passadissos del seu cos com un fantasma (Baltasar 2020: 28).

Samsa's desire for a child is a desire that the narrator ›does not give her‹ because it does not belong to their queerness but falls under the domain of the timeless laws of heteronormalization for Boulder. The lexical field of illness and morbidity is in stark contrast to the idea of an unborn child as vitalism; the child to come is a poison that will drain the passion from Samsa and Boulder's story without Boulder being able to articulate that she does not want a child. Samsa's body, previously the site of an intense hunger for desire, suddenly appears as if a ghost is passing through it, heralding the end of desire to come, the narrator's coldness echoing her complete rejection of motherhood. Antimaternalism is indeed a way to resist the domestication that awaits cisgender women in heterosexuality, and which tends to reproduce itself in lesbian couples who have children. However, the heroines of Debré and Baltasar share a commonality in building a nomadic way of life in resistance to heteronormativity, which aligns with the demand for freedom within queerness.

3 Nomadic Figuration: the Cowboy and the Sailor, from Detachment to Melancholy

The constant movement of the bodies of our authors, driven by a queer desire that engenders their subjectivity, extends into space. They adopt and appropriate two literary figures of nomads, the Cowboy and the Sailor, two characters with queer potential. In her nomadic thought of a non-unitary subject arising from feminist theory,[5] Rosi Braidotti is interested in feminist metamorphoses less as metaphors than as figurations understood as »social locations« and »new cartographies of power« (2005: 14). Nomadic figurations become lines of flight that break the linear representation of subjects to propose »figural modes of expression that displace the vision of consciousness away from the dominant premises« (ibid: 36). I will argue that by appropriating the masculine gay imaginary of nomads, Debré and Baltasar employ a strategy of disidentification from the feminine gender and assignment to domesticity through nomadic thought, opening up the possibility of a new attachment to motherhood.

First, Constance Debré, by leaving her life as a heterosexual marked by class property and a geographic base in the upscale neighborhoods of Paris, embarks on a project of detachment from material goods, which makes her a nomad.

---

5   Rosi Braidotti proposes the nomadic subject as a »political fiction« that allows a »new figuration of subjectivity in a multidifferentiated nonhierarchical way« to think »the kind of critical consciousness that resists settling into socially coded modes of thought and behavior«. She is interested in the ways in which feminists can affirmatively engage with different forms of subjectivity arising from sexual difference in order to account for women's agency in history. Her definition of nomadism as the displacement of the signifier of difference enables her to consider strategies for the re-essentialization of gender, such as the masculine figuration of our lesbian female characters (Braidotti 1994: 4, 146, 5).

She discards her old clothes and books, changes apartments, no longer having her own home, and presents herself to the reader as leading an adventurous life in Paris, romanticzing precariousness from its privileged origins.

> Des studios, des chambres, des appartements, des canapés, des lits, à droite à gauche, rive droite, rive gauche. Rive droite surtout. Le 3e, le 4e, le 9e, le 11e, le 18e; le 19e. Avant je ne connaissais que la rive gauche, j'ai élargi le périmètre, je maîtrise mieux le territoire. [...] Je suis devenue nomade sans traverser le périph, je vis en cavale (Debré 2020: 129).

In this material detachment, the writer definitively breaks away from the condition of a domestic woman, a mother who, in order to take care of her family, has to renounce her individual autonomy. At the moment when the French judicial system takes away her child, she radicalizes this act of detachment and embarks on a perpetual geographical movement. Nevertheless, this nomadism is not meant to be taken literally and holds an ironic dimension: she became a »nomad without crossing the péripherique [ring road]«, on the scale of her city. This nomadic life corresponds to an identification with the figure of the cowboy:

> Je n'ai plus besoin de vivre ici, je n'ai plus besoin d'un lit pour lui, de ces objets, ses affaires et les miennes. De toute façon je ne paye plus le loyer. Balancer tout ça. Dégager d'ici. Qu'est-ce que je peux faire d'autre que persévérer, accélérer, que continuer à vivre comme un mec, un jeune homme, en célibataire, en solitary man comme dit Johnny Cash. À partir de maintenant je suis un lonesome cow-boy (Debré 2020: 25).

The cowboy is a central figure in American colonial culture, typically a cattle herder on horseback during the westward expansion. However, his appropriation by American cinema has made him a romantic yet ambivalent symbol. On one hand, the cowboy embodies American-style liberalism (a white, virile man exerting dominance over colonized people), but on the other hand, the cowboy is a nomad who sings of his sorrow and his inability to attach himself to a place (and often to a woman) because he's condemned to just passing through. In Debré's narrative, the cowboy is ›lonesome‹ because he is melancholic, driven to solitude in his constant pursuit of an ideal. The reference to Johnny Cash's song, describing a man unable to maintain a lover, reinforces this ambivalent identification with the value of freedom. The English title of the novel, *Love Me Tender* refers to Elvis Presley's song produced for the western of the same name (USA, 1956, Director: Robert D. Webb), and expresses a demand that is the antithesis of the narrator's performance of emotional detachment: »Love me tender/Love me sweet/Never let me go« (USA, 1956, Singer: Elvis Presley). This nomadic figuration allows Debré to turn her own life experience into literary material as she mentioned in an interview that her model for literary action is Ulysses: it is the »arrogance of leaving« from the Homeric character (just as she had the arrogance to leave heterosexuality) that »makes him a hero« (Debré and Myles 2022). At the same time, however, the impossibility of the cowboy to form emotional bonds is the basis for the dramatization of his romantic figure and a persistent demand: to find forms of love from his nomadic freedom.

The same ambivalence can be found in the metaphor of the sailor in Eva Baltasar's *Boulder*. Once again, the sailor is a literary image that refers to a masculine imaginary, that keeps the character at a distance from heterosexual femininity and is closely connected to the expression of desire. Although Boulder is a cook, she is employed on cargo ships, and the metaphor of the navy and navigation follows her throughout the novel, right down to the title *Boulder* which refers to the »les grans roques solitàries que hi ha al sud de la Patagònia« (Baltasar 2020: 18), the region where Boulder's boat used to sail before she went to live with Samsa in Iceland, much to her despair. Unlike Debré's narrative, which moves towards nomadism, nomadism is the way of life that Baltasar's narrator is forced to abandon for a sedentary existence. However, from Reykjavik, Boulder rediscovers an imaginary of individual freedom in the fantasy of returning to maritime adventure: »Quan la Samsa se m'asseu a sobre, amb els pits alçats en la nit com litorals, la llum de les espelmes la reflecteix en aquesta aigua i em sembla que sóc un galió a punt d'enfonsar-se, que ella és el meu mascaró« (Baltasar 2020: 19). Samsa is like the siren that sinks the ship, arousing a wild desire that condemns the sailor. But resisting the siren, allowing oneself to be taken over by desire while still being able to continue your journey, has been the particularity of heroes since Homer. Faced with a relationship crisis, the protagonist recounts that she hasn't given up on finding a maritime bay, an »inlet« to wait with her ship while she figures out a way to avoid the impending disaster: »Estimar la Samsa em fa ser prudent. Necessito una badia, necessito temps« (Baltasar 2020: 26). This metaphor allows Baltasar to draw the allegory of the boat as a body that carries the soul from English Romanticism.[6] The sailor faces the abyss of the ocean in the closed world of the ship, saturated with rituals and superstitions, and his freedom is, like that of the cowboy, haunted by a sense of flight or pursuit, as if he were condemned to keep traveling, far from the people he loves, who remain onshore. This aspect of the ship as both confinement and protection from danger reveals an ambivalent view of motherhood, with a surprising metaphor of the maternal womb at the beginning of the text:

> A bord es pensen que estic guillada, que sóc l'ovella negra d'una família aristocràtica i algú em va matar els pares i els germans. [...] Deixo que ho pensin perquè són cordials, perquè en el fons som més germans que els fills d'una mateixa mare. El vaixell ens cova dins del seu líquid, ens estima, ens nodreix, fa que ens mirem. Jo em deixo dur, la vida creix sense sobrepassar-me, es concentra en cada minut, implosiona, la tinc a les mans. Puc renunciar a qualsevol cosa perquè res és decisiu quan et negues a tancar la vida al calabós dels relats (Baltasar 2020: 11).

The reader knows nothing about the protagonist's life before her maritime adventure in *Boulder*. However, the protagonist's traveling companions formulate the nomadic hypothesis of an ambivalent detachment: her family may have been murdered, condemning her to forced solitude. But, at the same time, it made her the black sheep, rejected by the community from the start. This romantic trope of abandonment, which the narrator ironically acknowledges, aligns with the idea that nomadism is a way to break free from heteronormative family life. Paradoxically, in Baltasar's work, the family seems to be organically reconstituted in a metaphor of the boat as a maternal womb. The passengers become brothers and sisters, and the hull seems to be filling with water (perhaps foreshadowing the shipwreck of motherhood) as if with amniotic fluid, in which the children allow themselves to be carried before birth. The narrator ›holds in [her] hands‹ life, which ›develops‹ during the journey, following a fluid path that suggests a comforting and maternal agency opposing to the anguished vision of motherhood she exhibits in her life with Samsa.

---

6   In »The Rime of the Ancient Mariner«, Samuel Taylor Coleridge conjures up a sailor, haunted by the sins of his past, who travels through remote territories as if in a metaphysical experiment. The sailor betrays the albatross, a Christ figure that guided him out of the storm, by shooting it. Having committed this crime, he is haunted by his sins throughout the rest of the ballad, which condemns him to obsession and remorse (Coleridge 1991: 9–36).

What are the implications of these nomadic figurations for Debré and Baltasar in terms of gender? Beyond the mere appropriation of two traditionally masculine nomadic literary figures, the two lesbian characters identify with gay male archetypes. Cowboys and sailors both lead nomadic lives where proximity encourages the blurring of boundaries between homosociability and homosexuality. Far from the confines of marital domesticity, in command of the natural elements surrounding them and their respective horses and ships, depictions of gay cowboys and sailors are a reworking of certain codes of hegemonic masculinity in order to eroticize homosexual virility. In late 19th century New York, »fairies« awaited »trade«, sailors or soldiers, seen as an »ideal sexual partner« or a »real man« (Chauncey 1994: 16). From Melville's *Billy Budd, Sailor* (2008) to Genet's *Querelle de Brest* (2010), the figure of the sailor has become central to gay mythology, with homosexual desire associated in both novels with criminal guilt. Conversely, masculine gay cowboys, such as those depicted in *Brokeback Mountain* (USA 2005, Director: Ang Lee), desire each other, leading historian Chris Packard to designate them as quintessential figures of queer disidentification: »[…] when a cowboy desires his partner, he desires himself, destabilizing an essential given in male/female constructions of desire rooted in oppositions« (Packard 2005: 9). In all cases, idealizing cowboys or sailors is a means of radically distancing oneself from codes of femininity and domesticity, even within queer subculture. I argue, however, that the nomadic specificity of this literary figuration is primarily concerned with a detachment from identity, prioritizing the freedom to construct life practices over forms of gender assignment. In »The Straight Mind« Monique Wittig concludes her critique of the heteropatriarchal system with the phrase ›lesbians are not women‹ (Wittig 1992: 32). The explosion of lesbian desire faced by our characters propels them into a nomadic journey beyond identity, a journey of queer disidentification. Cowboys and sailors here are ›lesbians‹, an adjective that moves the body beyond the prescribed plasticity of sexual difference, making the phallic performance of hegemonic masculinity a transferable property (Chetcuti 2012). These figures are reimagined as lesbians to assert a distinct notion of nomadic motherhood: it is possible to be queer and to be a mother, beyond the confines of heterosexual domesticity. Indeed, the freedom gained through the subjectivation of anti-normative practices does not preclude the expression of a desire for relationality, connection with others and emotional relationships. Nomadic motherhood facilitates a queer practice of detachment, which also enables and necessitates reattachment and the reconfiguration of relationships. Like queer disidentification, feminist nomadism represents a movement from identity and motherhood that permits a departure from the notion of a true place, without truly departing, thus opening up the possibility for new forms of attachment.

4 Resignified Nomadic Motherhood: An Alliance of Queer Adults and Children

The forms of parental bonding that are ultimately put forward by our characters are born of relationality and ultimately take the form of a political alliance between queer adults and children. In *Permafrost* the niece of the narrator falls ill, and the protagonist gets closer to her by spending time in the hospital:

> El seu somriure, llavors, em fa venir unes llàgrimes sobtades, calentes i grosses, fantasmes d'avantpassats indòmits i desconeguts que em couen a les galtes com metall roent. [...] Ploro com plora l'excés de sucre la fruita penjada massa temps a l'arbre. Em fonc. M'abandono (Baltasar 2018: 122).

The metaphor of hardness that runs through Baltasar's geologically themed titles (*Permafrost* and *Boulder*) is broken by the connection to the child in the act of caring. Emotion is revealed in the tears that flow, and the layer of ice that has been solidified for so long melts in a play of textures. Far from abandoning sensuality in her attachment to the child, the narrator accumulates sensations, from the warmth of tears to the sweetness of fruit, following the ›intuition‹ of the queer theorist Eve Kosofsky Sedgwick according to whom »particular intimacy seems to subsist between textures and emotions« (Kosofsky Sedgwick 2003: 17). In *Permafrost*, this act of caring forms the basis of the true family bond between the narrator and her niece, as shortly afterward, the sister dies, and the narrator becomes the adoptive mother of her niece. Similarly, in *Boulder*, the narrator's motherhood becomes nomadic when she eventually returns to work on a ship, but it is first revealed in her intimate relationship with the child. While dancing in her kitchen with her daughter, Tinna, Boulder describes how maternal attachment, after being completely rejected, emerges from the materiality of the relationship, from Tinna's laughter, which transforms her into a unique person: »Tenir la Tinna així em fa sentir nova i estranya. Em fa pensar en paraules crescudes com herbes o com tanques sobre meu. Entre elles una d'incòmoda, la més antiga, la paraula Mare« (Baltasar 2020: 75). The word ›Mother‹ appears as a motherhood redefined through a sensual bodily experience with the child. The narrator imagines a motherhood emancipated from normalization, in which she and her daughter could set out, far from the safe and regulating norms, to »navigate« (ibid.: 96) together in continuation of the affirmed nomadic figuration. The heroine eventually leaves alone, leaving her daughter with Samsa, from whom she separates, but concludes normatively that her vision of motherhood involves relationality, movement:

> Veig la Tinna quatre o cinc dies al mes i en tinc prou. És cert, en tinc prou. No em cal fer-li de mare, almenys no de la manera com la Samsa entén que és una mare. No em preocupa la gran xarxa d'intendència que captura la Tinna, només m'interessa ser amb ella, tractar-la (Baltasar 2020: 80).

This final rejection of the role of ›a mother‹, echoing what Constance Debré asserted, does not prevent thinking of an ethical relationship to the child, based on care. The character wants to *tractar-la*, which means ›to be with her‹ but also to care for her, to treat her with respect.

In *Playboy* a scene involving a child who is not her own exemplifies a child-adult relationship that resists normalization. After a critical description of her first female lover's motherhood, Debré narrates a moment of connection with her child that goes against the grain of the authoritarian and exhausting march dictated by Agnès, who is embodying a hegemonic maternal norm:

> Soudain elle veut marcher, il y a un enfant avec nous, elle marche très vite, elle ne s'arrête pas quand il doit refaire ses lacets, je reste avec lui, elle ne ralentit pas, on tente de la rejoindre, on ne connaît pas le chemin lui et moi, elle marche toujours vite, je pense aux amoks, ces courses folles, mais il y a cet enfant, cet enfant qui tente de la suivre, qui tire sur ses jambes, qui pousse son corps sans rien dire, qui pleure sans rien dire, qui s'effondre enfin. Moi-même je n'en peux plus, elle vient vers lui, lui dit de se relever, elle repart, n'attend pas, elle dit qu'il va faire nuit, je regarde l'enfant, on ne dit rien, je lui prends la main, on finit la marche (Debré 2018: 74).

Beyond the language that would render this child to his mother, Agnès, Debré forges a silent alliance between the lesbian narrator and the little boy. More than an adult holding a child's hand, a partnership emerges between the one who pushes his body to conform to the norm and the one who has rejected it since childhood. The body that bends, ›pushes‹, ›cries‹ and ›collapses‹ takes on a concrete dimension in Debré's description. Attention to the child's vulnerability, in the face of a mother who ›doesn't slow down‹ to accommodate his fragile body, is a way of protecting his integrity and creating an alliance.

5 Conclusion

For Baltasar and Debré, being a mother is part of an identity assignment that endangers the freedom of queer bodily subjectivities who construct themselves through resistance to heterosexualized femininity and domesticity. The two characters gain autonomy through nomadic detachment, which is a practice of queer disidentification, and thus a redefinition of motherhood. Antinormative queer approaches cannot evade the need to build a sense of community and the necessary relationality that structures subjectivity. Motherhood here is nomadic, because it is based not on identity but on an ethic of responsibility between two subjects brought into a relationship during the process of queer disidentification beyond the heterosexual family. It is in this departure from the notion of familial kinship as a unitary concept that one can find an antifundamentalist approach to motherhood, which is not an identity but a relationship. That is why, when my characters are mothers, they are also non-biological, through adoption or as stepmothers.

As the queer-feminist writer Maggie Nelson affirms during a discussion with Constance Debré and Paul B. Preciado, »I believe that any form of attachment that doesn't also honor detachment doesn't work« (Kaprélian and Perreau 2022: s.p.). Whether it is attachment to an identity or to another being, the practice of nomadic figuration against homonormativity allows for a fluid relationality in mother-child relationships. Through their exploration of queer motherhood through nomadic thought, Debré and Baltasar establish a familial community rooted in relational dynamics and directed toward the future. This future orientation is characterized by a departure from reproductive futurism and embraces a concept of queer commonality.

Bibliography

Aparicio, Galo Martin (2018): »Eva Baltasar, la anticuada contemporánea«, in: El Salto 15.12.2018, https://www.elsaltodiario.com/literatura/entrevista-escritora-eva-baltasar-novela-permafrost [30.04.2024].

Baltasar, Eva (2021 [2018]): Permagel, Barcelona: Club Editor.

Baltasar, Eva (2022 [2020]): Boulder, Barcelona: Club Editor.
Bersani, Léo (2010 [1987]): »Is the Rectum a Grave?«, in: Léo Bersani: Is the Rectum a Grave and Other Essays, Chicago: University of Chicago Press.
Braidotti, Rosi (1994): Nomadic Subjects. Embodiment and Sexual Difference in Contemporary Feminist Theory, New York: Columbia University Press.
Braidotti, Rosi (2011): Nomadic Theory. The portable Rosi Braidotti, New York: Columbia University Press.
Chauncey, George (1994): Gay New York. Gender, Urban Culture, and the Making of the Gay Male World, 1890–1940, New York: BasicsBooks.
Chetcutti, Natacha (2012): »Monique Wittig et Judith Butler. Du corps lesbien au phallus lesbien« , in: Benoit Aucler/Yannick Chevalier (eds.), Lire Monique Wittig aujourd'hui, Lyon/St Etienne: PUL/PUSE, pp. 49–66.
Coleridge, Samuel Taylor (1991 [1898]): »The Rime of the Ancient Mariner«, in: William Wordsworth/Samuel Taylor Coleridge, Lyrical Ballads. William Wordsworth and S.T. Coleridge, London/New York: Routledge, pp. 9–36.
Debré, Constance (2018): Playboy, Paris: Flammarion.
Debré, Constance (2020): »Être la mère de quelqu'un, ce n'est pas être UNE mère«, in: France Inter 02.01.2020, https://www.youtube.com/watch?v=aIyFOou9lm [30.04.2024].
Debré, Constance/Myles, Eilenn (2022): »The Cost of Freedom. Constance Debré and Eileen Myles«, in: Albertine 9.10.2022, https://www.albertine.com/events/the-cost-of-freedom-a-conversation-with-constance-debre/ [30.04.2024].
Duggan, Lisa (2002): »The New Homonormativity. The Sexual Politics of Neoliberalism«, in: Russ Castronovo/Dana D. Nelson (eds.), Materializing Democracy. Towards a Revitalized Cultural Politics, Durham: Duke University, pp. 175–194.
Edelman, Lee (2004): No Future. Queer Theory and the Death Drive, Durham: Duke University Press.
Fraiman, Susan (2003): »Queer Theory and the Second Sex«, in: Susan Fraiman (ed.), Cool Men and the Second Sex, New York: Columbia University Press, pp. 122–155.
Genet, Jean (2010 [1974]): Querelle de Brest, Paris: L'imaginaire Gallimard.
Kaprièlan, Nelly/Perreau, Yann (2022): »Maggie Nelson, Constance Debré et Paul B. Preciado en conversation libre«, in: Les Inrockuptibles 25.01.2022, https://www.lesinrocks.com/livres/maggie-nelson-constance-debre-et-paul-b-preciado-en-conversation-libre-435598-25-01-2022/ [30.04.2024].

Kosofsky-Sedgwick, Eve (2003): Touching Feeling. Affect, Pedagogy, Performativity, Durham: Duke University Press.
Melville, Herman (2008 [1924]): Billy Budd, Sailor, London: Penguin Classics.
Niedergang, Pierre (2023): Vers la normativité queer, Toulouse: blast.
Packard, Chris (2005): Queer Cowboys. And Other Erotic Male Friendships in Nineteenth-Century American Literature, New York: Palgrave Macmillan.
Puar, Jaspir K. (2007): Terrorist Assemblage. Homonationalism in Queer Times, Durham: Duke University Press.
Wittig, Monique (1992 [1980]): The Straight Mind in The Straight Mind and Other Essays, Boston: Beacon Press, pp. 21–32.

Filmography

BROKEBACK MOUNTAIN (2005) (USA, D: Ang Lee).
LOVE ME TENDER (1956) (USA, D: Robert D. Webb).

Virginie Despentes
Vernon's Failing as a Way of Literary Queering

Michaela Rumpikova

1 Introduction

> [Virginie and Coralie] are two dogs without a master, barking at the pack of liberals who are denouncing the sexual violence of the protagonists in the film. When I tell them that Nadine and Manu are heroines for a potential queer revolution, they look at me expressionlessly. Nobody knows what the word queer means at this point in France. Mainlining gender, class, and race terrorism – now, that kind of thing speaks to them.
> *(Preciado 2013: 83–84)*

Despentes has been globally recognized as radical feminist, be it for her eloquent depictions of deviant sexuality (Sauzon 2012) and unbridled desire (Fayard 2005), for her revolting and subversive women protagonists (Hollister 2004; Schaal 2013), or for her political reflections on rape, sex work and pornography (Fleckinger 2012; Simonin 2015; Edwards 2012). As a part of third wave feminism,[1] she has drawn from subcultures and anti-austerity movements to create more inclusive and fluid spaces in French literature and in other media. While insisting on overlapping inequalities, she has dismantled repressive identity politics and subverted our commonplace notions about masculinity and femininity outside sexual binarism. This standpoint undoubtedly situates

---

1   See: Schaal 2017; Schaal 2011: 39–55.

Despentes, as Preciado predicted back in 2001, within the context of queer movement.

Over the last decade, some studies have aimed to apply queer theory to Despentes's novels. Among (not so) many others, I could mention Lara Cox's article on Despentes' movie *Bye Bye Blondie* (2012), which highlights the subversiveness of the heteronormative matrix of drag (2016). Another specialist on Despentes' work, Lucas Hollister proposes a queer reading of her crime fiction (Hollister 2012). However, perhaps the most prominent study to date that has helped shed light on Despentes' relation with queer theory, is Thomas Muzart's »Queer Displacements: Minorities, Mobilities, and Mobilizations in French and Francophone Literature«. His detailed analysis underscores various aspects of her work that could be considered as queer. First, Muzart demonstrates the author's subversive and deconstructive processes of the category of »woman« in *Baise-moi*. Then he develops the idea of »becoming-lesbian« in *Apocalypse Bébé*. Last, but not least, Muzart offers a reading of *Vernon Subutex* as queer »ethical commitment through which it is possible to envision a future ›living together‹« (2020: 202), by applying Deleuze and Guattari's concept of »becoming-minority« and Hard and Negri's notion of multitude.

With this paper, I would like to contribute to these discussions. By considering queer as a process, I understand the act of queering not only as a »radical move« that »goes beyond a simple insertion of a gay subject in an existent society« (Nigianni, Storr 2009: 24), but also both as a political and theoretical method that »breaks down oppositions imposed by state thought and its various representatives (family, school, law or army)« (Nigianni, Storr 2009: 25). Using this definition of queering, as a process of deviation, I would like to briefly elaborate on the concept of unbecoming in Despentes' *Vernon Subutex 1*. I argue that as Vernon fails to become a normative subject, we could read his failing as a key mechanism for »peripheral mode of undoing« (Butler 2004: 15). In *The Queer Art of Failure*, Jack Halberstam embraces failure as »a refusal of mastery, a critique of the intuitive connections within capitalism between success and profit, and as a counterhegemonic discourse of losing« (2011: 11–12) and attempts to study the circumstances of »failing, losing, forgetting, unmaking, undoing, unbecoming« (2011: 2) as a way of being in the world. Halberstam also understands failure as a part of other queer affects[2] (2011: 89). Adopting these

---

2   Other political affect we consider queer are for example shame, love, mourning, fear. To go further, see: Kosofsky Sedgwick 2003.

queer lens allows us to see Vernon's various failures as (un)becoming (Deleuze, Guattari 1988; Braidotti 2011 and 2014), unfixing (Halberstam 2011), or undoing (Butler 2004). Butler argues that »if gender is a kind of a doing, an incessant activity performed [...] it is not for that reason automatic or mechanical« (2004: 1), it can be also collectively undone. Throughout linear reading, I will examine Vernon's failing as a narrative process of undoing, unbecoming, or even as a form of disidentification, that Butler defines as the »experience of *misrecognition*, this uneasy sense of standing under a sign to which one does and does not belong« (1993: 219). This experience allows the subject to orient oneself differently and gives rise to unexpected forms of sociality and relationalities (with one's identity, others, objects, or places). In other terms, failure can be understood in terms of displacement and »disorientation« (Ahmed 2006: 10) within the (hetero)normative schemes. Thus, reading Vernon's trajectory from a queer perspective means to probe into his relation to these schemes. If Vernon stands for a sign, a cisgender straight white man, he at the same time fails to be one.

2 Failure as a Cataclysmic Event

In her article, »Writing as a Nomadic Subject«, Rosi Braidotti defines becoming as »opening it out to possible encounters with the ›outside‹« (Braidotti 2014: 171). Following this train of thought, Vernon's journey could be examined as a way of becoming. If we speak from a literary perspective, we could understand this process as initiation. From this standpoint, *Vernon Subutex* displays some characteristics that could be associated with the *bildungsroman*, formative novel or *roman initiatique*. Yet this time, the protagonist is neither an adolescent, nor an aspiring hero who tends to integrate within high-status social circles. On the other side, we could argue that Vernon undergoes a social disintegration. Hence, it would be preferable to use more appropriate terms such as novel of un-formation, novel of unbecoming, »l'apprentissage de la dépossession« (C.D. 2017) or even failed *bildungsroman*. While Sarah Graham argues that »a classic bildungsroman concentrates on a protagonist striving to reconcile individual aspirations with the demands of social conformity« (Graham 2019:1), Aleksandar Stević contends that »failure is seen as a problem because it contradicts the purpotedly affirmative logic of the ›true‹ bildungsroman« (Stević 2020: 8). Nevertheless, French *bildungsroman* incorporates various failing subjects as its protagonists and Vernon, as an antithetical representation to the successful socialization, could be viewed as one. Despentes, »with [her] broader sympathy for losers of all stripes« (Hollister 2021), refuses the traditional parvenu plot of hero-reproduction as a mode of social accomplishment and decides to write a story about a person struggling and living outside social conformity. More of a Frédéric Moreau than a Rastignac, Vernon is a misadventurer. Neither sympathetic nor likeable, a little clumsy, misogynist, he is not only a type of »everyday, normal, half-unaware« but he is also manifestly »unheroic« (Moretti 2000: 12). As an emblematic protagonist of failure, Vernon, with a »pseudo pourri«[3] (ibid.: 108), occupies marginal societal position. He is literally a »vieux loser« (Despentes 2015: 104) and after having lost his vinyl record store »Revolver« (ibid.: 13), he also loses »son RSA« (ibid.: 10), »cent euros au poker« (ibid.: 11) and »la solitude l'[emmure] vif« (ibid.: 20). Materially dispossessed, he lives with bitter echoes from old good days, »avec le souvenir de la fille qui est partie« (ibid.: 16). He remains to live within a nostalgic temporality, failing to adapt to the present times. From the narrative perspective, the novel therefore breaches the engine of progress conventionally associated with *bildungsroman*. His portrayal is written as a blend of passivity and indifference. Accordingly, he is committed to fail to have a dynamic »romanesque« destiny:

> Il avait trop à faire sur Internet. Il jetait encore un œil aux gros titres, sur Internet. Mais il était surtout sur des sites pornos. Il ne voulait plus entendre parler de la crise, de l'islam, du dérèglement climatique, du gaz de schiste, des orangs-outangs malmenés ou des Roms qu'on ne veut plus laisser monter dans les bus. Sa bulle est confortable (Despentes 2015: 28–29).

With a sarcastic tone, the narrator depicts Vernon as an apathetic subject to the troubling outside-world. He is living outside the schema of traditional temporality of family or labour/leisure, in other terms, outside of the daily temporality of the capital. Temporally and spatially disengaged, the protagonist fails as a social participant and a productive subject in the economic system. However, Vernon is caught red-handed once »on sonne à sa porte« (ibid.: 39) and we witness an »interpellative scenario« (Butler 1993) when he is brought into being by the normative order (the State):

---

3   Vernon Subutex is protagonist's nickname meaning »springlike« or »alder grover« referring to the preparation of a baby for the dream of the French countryside, and Subutex, which signifies Buprenorphine. He stands outside political space of national identity by rejecting a surname assigned by the state, as Rancière would put it, by *police*. See: Rancière 1999.

> Il lit d'un ton neutre, sur une tablette numérique – lalali domicilié au lalala vous êtes monsieur et lalala le locataire des lieux [...]. L'huissier lui recommande de rassembler les affaires dont il a besoin dans les jours à venir, et de quitter les lieux. [...] Les deux costauds qui n'ont pas prononcé un mot se campent au milieu du studio et lui conseillent, sans la moindre hostilité, d'obtempérer au plus vite (Despentes 2015: 40–41).

The interpellative process produces Vernon's »compliance and obedience to the law« (Butler 1993: 122). It is a paradoxical moment when he is visibilized by the system as someone who fails to pay his rent, and at the sime time he is silenced as a political subject and he has to voicelessly comply with the order. After losing his home, his marginalization is completed. This moment constitutes however a progressive shift within the narrative structure. The homelessness accounts for the unpleasant cataclysmic event and paradoxically, moving out of the apartment with a »lourd sac« (Despentes 2015: 42), triggers off an alternative trajectory. Vernon's unwilling departure with a rucksack on his back could be read as a metaphor for a »romanesque adventure«. While his journey of exploration might be unchosen, it still implies journeying somewhere. He is somehow reconfronted with the outside world, »mis dehors« (Despentes 2015: 40) and forced to leave his homogeneous life in the bubble of his room. In other words, from his chair, he is pushed into a (social) mobility. Vernon »il se fraye un chemin, son sac sur l'épaule« and »il fait le mec qui va quelque part« (ibid.: 64). Put into the world to encounter its spaces, the protagonist wanders somewhere between places and temporalities where the past seems to be too distant, the future yet to be shaped and new proximities are yet to come. There is a symbolic dimension to this wandering as it is going to be both formative and un-formative of Vernon's identity.

3 Failing (Hetero)Normative Scripts

To be in contact with the outside world and to be a part of it, as indicated by Vernon's journey, implies being phenomenologically receptive to this world. The novel is transformed into a »living map of places« (Braidotti 2011: 10) Vernon has been and is going to be. Moving from one couch to another, from one street to another, his journey accounts for an expedition to different social worlds where »relationship[s] with the social totality« (Moretti 2000: 23) could be formed. On this journey, he encounters old-new friends (Emilie, Xavier,

Patrice, Laurent, Olga), love and desire (Marcia), conflicts (Kiko) as a typical *bildungsroman* hero would. Without dwelling on character-development as something static, Despentes juxtaposes Vernon's life with several others to see how their stories converge and diverge. Thus, the journeying also happens on the narrative level of the novel as we move away from Vernon's voice to the world of voices the protagonist encounters. But these voices do not eclipse Vernon's own. Rather, the enactment of the narrative is a »process of composition and the artful juxtaposition of voices generate a unique amalgamation of singularity« (Amar 2023). This process could be applied to Vernon's identity as well – as his voice is juxtaposed with other voices, it allows us to explore how his voice (co)exists with the world.

His encounters with his old male friends seem to be essential for our understanding of his position vis-à-vis traditional masculinity and its (hetero)normative schemes. If the reproduction seems to be the most insistent framing of »man's life«,[4] Vernon stands for »the failure of such [a] signifier« (Butler 1993: 191). The moment when his old friend Xavier »viril et démonstratif, serre Vernon contre son cœur« (Despentes 2015: 81), gives us an overview of who Xavier is and who Vernon is not. Xavier, we understand, »est papa, un homme marié, un homme adulte« (ibid.: 73). Vernon, who in contrast, is childless, single, unemployed and homeless, stands for a failed (re)productive subject in comparison to the traditional masculinity embedded in patriarchal reproductive right. And he is interpellated as such by Xavier's brosplaining »on n'a plus vingt ans, il faut construire« (ibid.: 93); or by Xavier's wife: »T'as pas fait d'enfant, toi?« (ibid.: 82). The fact of not being active, not actively participating in the social structuring (i.e., job, family, social and political interests), not having a »purposeful« and »reproductive« life, excludes Vernon from expected ways of being in the social world. »Un vieux mec sans domicile sans argent sans amis sans boulot« (ibid.: 361) does not have many prospects. Vernon appears as deception for the normative.

Vernon's interaction with Patrice is another encounter with normative masculine subject. Once again, this moment is accompanied by interpellative naming of Vernon as a failure: »Comment ça se fait qu'un mec comme toi est

---

4   Ivan Jablonka defines a loser of masculinity as »the man without any virile qualification, the one who has failed at one of the four masculinities of domination: he is cowardly, whining, nerdy, bespectacled and lame« (Jablonka 2023: 397). While Vernon does not necessarily fail all these four masculinities, his way of being in the world certainly destabilizes our traditional conception about masculine identity.

pas casé depuis des années? Tu devrais avoir des gosses et tout le tremblement« (ibid.: 320). The normalizing phrase »tu devrais« brings us again to the concept of family as »the heteroreproductive unit« (Halberstam 2011: 38), which is presented as an accomplishment of adult life. But there is one more aspect that exposes Vernon as a »flawed man«. During their dialogue about Vernon's failed amourous affairs, Vernon shares with Patrice his previous relationship with a transgender woman, Marcia:

- C'était pas un travelo, au moins?
- Non, une trans. Super belle. Super classe.
- Tu plaisantes?
- Non. Tu me demandes, je te réponds...
- Oui, mais moi je demandais ça pour faire de l'humour, tu me dis brésilienne je te demande si c'est un travelo, mais c'était une vanne, pas une question qui appelait une réponse sincère (ibid.: 320–231).

Here, Patrice engages in discursive practice of transphobia as the offensive term »travelo« confirms. To him, a trans woman is a »mec en jupe« (ibid.: 323). Patrice feels as invaded by, according to him, Vernon's inappropriate response. He also feels »destabilisé« et »choqué« (ibid.: 321, 322). Despentes uses these affective responses (i.e., uneasiness, anxiety) to demonstrate how Vernon's revelation induce feelings of threat to Patrice's masculinity. The fact that »[Vernon] le claironne, haut et fort: j'ai couché avec un trav« (ibid.: 321) confronts Patrice with something he does not want to hear about, with the borders he does not want to cross. From this perspective, Vernon failed to »stay in the closet« and follow the compulsory script (to be a »real« man, to have sexual relationship with cis-gender women and to have a wife and kids). Vernon's other-than-normative corporeal experience with Marcia could be viewed as another failure of reproductive coupling.[5] While this sexual and affective experience does not make Vernon queer, his desire, as this narrative event confirms, has been »disoriented« (Ahmed 2006: 179) from the normative sexed bodies. Conventional heteronormative expectations are therefore not met. Despite not conforming to traditional masculinity in Patrice's eyes, Vernon embraces this »failure« by responding: »Je n'ai pas honte« (ibid.: 322). And it is this affirmation of »the slippage«, »the failure of identification« with prescribed beings in the world that

---

5 As Heather Love argues in *Feeling Backwards. Loss and the Politics of Queer History* »same-sex desire is marked by a long history of association with failure, impossibility and loss« (Love 2007: 22).

can be »the point of departure for a more democratizing affirmation of internal difference« (Butler 1993: 219). Despentes enacts this fluid, yet unsettling, process, which seeks to destabilize dominant understandings and underlying assumptions about masculine identity and the category of man through this experience of »patriarchal failure«. Thus, failure can be used as a technique to »negate«, to »undo« the subject rather than to form it. In other terms, failing could be read as Vernon's way of un-becoming the universal »man«.

4 Protagonist Becoming Undone

Failure is therefore a state of repetitive experience. Vernon's failing desacralizes the deals built by a dominant system that requires rational and heteronormative mode of living. As he does not settle on a singular, straight(forward) subject category, we track Vernon in becoming an alienated outsider. If, for Butler, to undo the subject »there needs to be an interrogation of the terms by which life is constrained in order to open up the possibility of different modes of living« (Butler 2004: 4), in Despentes' novel, we witness Vernon's dialogical (un)becoming through various interactions and proximity with others. The presence of the Other from the past is somehow complementary to Vernon's identity. The temporal aspect seems important here because the persons from Vernon's past differ from his present time. This transcending of time produces a reflection upon his own relation to the present and allows the protagonist to experience change and the variations of the self. This aspect is exemplified by Vernon's first encounter with his old friend Emilie, which functions as the bittersweet nostalgia, as both »la surprise et la déception« (Despentes 2015: 54). He misrecognizes her as he misrecognizes himself. The scene functions like a mirror that reflects the gap between a bygone past and the present. Seeing who Émilie has become is »le truc le plus triste qu'il ait jamais connu« (ibid.: 65) and the colourful past of the posters of their youth has transformed into »murs peints en blanc« (ibid.: 54). Figuratively speaking, living outside these normative walls generates feelings of non-belonging to this kind of present. His life as a stretched life narrative of adolescence stands in contrast with the society dominated by the cult of success and liberal self-realization, where »les cadeaux de Noël, la petite école, regarder dix fois le même DVD, les jouets, les goûters, les rougeoles, les légumes, les vacances en famille… et devenir parent« (ibid.: 82) seems to be the most expected social trajectory: grow up and settle down. Additionally, the enumeration itself highlights this linear optics of one's becoming adult and parent.

Undoubtedly, Vernon's failure goes in hand with capitalism which »must have winners and losers, gamblers and risk taker« but we can also recognize »failure as a way of refusing to acquiesce to dominant logics of power and discipline and as a form of critique« (Halberstam 2011: 88), and thus think of failure as a »happy and productive« being in the world. Symbolically, by leaving all these places (Emilie's, Xavier's, Patrice's apartments), he can disidentify with the normative and »escape a hypocritical, normativising majority« (Nigianni/Storr 2009: 27). This break constitutes another step towards his identity unfixing that could be read a »nomadic becoming«, defined by Braidotti as a »process [...] unhinged from the binary system that traditionally opposed it to Sameness« (Braidotti 2014: 171). By getting back on the streets, the protagonist does not follow »social integration and success« (Graham 2018: 3) but he rather opts for social disintegration. The distinction between inside/closed – outside/open dimensions coincides with Deleuze and Guattari's understanding of spaces as striated (sedentary) or smooth (nomadic) (Deleuze, Guattari 1988: 474). In this way, the topographical landscape in the novel stands for both space and time which »transpires into an already-there that is at the same time not-yet-here, a simultaneous too-late and too early« (ibid.: 262). Becoming homeless and becoming nomadic subject, Vernon is entering the smooth space, the »space of Go«, an »open-ended« territory (ibid.: 353). By the end of the novel, he flows back to the beginning of his journey. There is where the novel circles back to the point of departure.

While the old acquaintances remind him of what he has not become and will not become, the new encounters imply some potentiality. His journey reorients him towards new relationalities where he can »reconstruct [his identity] a posteriori as a set of steps on an itinerary« (Braidotti 2011: 40). Braidotti suggests the term, »figuration« that could be applied as well to the transformative formation of oneself outside the majority. The multitude of encounters on the street allows him to exploit new meanings of oneself outside the majority. New social bondings already emerge from Vernon's encounter with another clumsy character Olga, who has »gestes d'enfants« (Despentes 2015: 411) and »cacahuètes salées et chocolat noir de cuisine« (ibid.: 370) are her preferred diet. Olga is an outsider, interpelled as »folle«, »mûre pour l'asile« (ibid.: 366). If, as Halberstam puts it, »failure loves company« (Halberstam 2011: 121), Olga and Vernon's encouter produces an unusual kind of affinity, a »cooperation, collectivity, and nonheterosexual, nonreproductive behaviour« (ibid.: 38):

> Elle le veut comme ami. Maintenant, elle partage sa nourriture. Il mange de bon appétit, ça fait plaisir à voir. [...] Elle aime bien s'occuper des autres. Quand ils se laissent faire. Elle cherche à le faire rire. [...] Vernon rigole. Elle aime bien son prénom. Elle aimerait qu'ils traînent tout le temps ensemble. Ils feraient une équipe. (Despentes 2015: 371)

Outside of »the machine of the couple« (Deleuze, Guattari 1988: 206), Olga wants to bind Vernon to herself, »elle aimerait glisser sa main sous son bras, juste pouvoir le toucher, comme s'il était son meilleur pote « (Despentes 2015: 378). She stands opposite to the State and its golden neoliberal rule »éliminer ton prochain« (ibid.: 11). Together with Vernon, they can »challeng[e] the position they are inhabiting in the social sphere through a becoming-minority« and, as Muzart elaborated in his study, »participate in a collective elaboration of self-governance« (Muzart 20: 198). This affective relationality enables to spread the networks of relations based on a different »ethics of Eros« (C.D. 2017) and to open different kinds of proximities. This is also why their friendship becomes the cornerstone of the queer community in the subsequent volumes of the trilogy.

5 Conclusion

If Balzac and Despentes have something in common, it is probably their »fascination with mobility and metamorphoses ends up dismantling the very notion of personal identity« (Moretti 2000: 8). While a traditional »*bildungsroman* attempts to *build* the Ego« (Moretti 2000: 11), Despentes writes a trilogy where the Ego is getting unbuilt and undone. Vernon's act of failing and of deforming are two aspects that nourish one another and allow the »transformation principle« (Moretti 2000: 7) to happen. One could say there is no linear trajectory with a straight closure, Vernon's maturing is inconsistent and incessant in time and space. Yet we cannot speak about a failed initiation, the aspects of development and growth remain. Rather than being, he is constantly becoming which does not sustain, and therefore challenges the conventional binary logics. This process allows us to think beyond identity as static and fixed. Taken together, failing could be viewed as a way of making visible »queer cracks in the heteronormative façade« and of »decentering those regimes of ›normal‹ being in the world« (Green 2002: 522). Accordingly, considering Vernon from a queer perspective, we might argue that failing can be regarded as a form of queering that destabilizes his relation to (hetero)normativity. To fail is his response to normalisation. While we could say that everyone around Vernon is somehow failing, we could also confirm that Vernon is »failing well, failing often, and learning [...] how to fail better« (Halberstam 2011: 24). Failing for him means to engage with other forms of contestation and to resist the hegemonic societal structures and schemes. Failing this system seems to be a way to disengage the bonds of blood, of privacy, of companionship and to »produce becomings that go beyond normative couplings to invent new connections be it with humans, animals, vegetals or machines« (Nigianni/Storr 2009: 25). Queering should be therefore understood as a relational process through which one is formed and most importantly deformed:

> Et malade. Mais content, putain, content comme un dingue, content comme un dément. Il découvre en face de lui une vue dégagée, il voit tout Paris d'en haut. Je suis un homme seul [...]. Je suis Diana [...] Je suis Marc [...]. Je suis Eléonore [...]. Je suis un adolescent [...]. Je suis la pute arrogante [...] je suis la vache à l'abattoir [...] Je suis l'arbre [...] je suis un clodo sur un banc perché sur une butte, à Paris (Despentes 2015: 427–429).

Reading this final part of the text, could we not eventually examine Vernon as a *personnage conceptuel*?[6] As such, he represents the impulse of the text and functions like a mediator through whom we access the ethical thought of the novel. Vernon encounters the world, and the world engages around and through Vernon. Just like the trilogy itself, Vernon, too, stands for the rhizomatic relatedness, for the becoming everybody.

Bibliography

Ahmed, Sarah (2006): Queer Phenomenology. Orientations, Objects, Others, Durham: Duke University Press.
Braidotti, Rosi (2011): Nomadic Subjects, New York: Columbia University Press.

---

6   *Personnage conceptuel*, which is translated into the English as ›conceptual personae‹, is Deleuze/Guattari's philosophical concept introduced in *What is Philosophy?* (chapter 3), which could be simply explained as an aesthetic and formal device enabling us to think about philosophical concepts. For more, see: Deleuze/Guattari 1994.

Braidotti, Rosi (2014): »Writing as a Nomadic Subject«, in: Comparative Critical Studies 11.2/3, pp. 163–184.
Butler, Judith (1993): Bodies That Matter, New York: Routledge.
Butler, Judith (2004): Undoing Gender, New York: Routledge.
C.D. (2017): »Lire *Vernon Subutex* 1, 2, et 3 de Virginie Despentes. Compte rendu, compte tenu d'un état d'urgence«, in: L'Homme et la société 203.4, pp. 249–60.
Cox, Lara (2016): »Bye-Bye to Betty's Blues and ›La Bonne Meuf‹. Temporal Drag and Queer Subversions of the Rom-Com in *Bye Bye Blondie* (Virginie Despentes, 2011)«, in: Fiona Handyside/Kate Taylor-Jones (eds.), International Cinema and the Girl, New York: Palgrave Macmillan, pp. 97–106.
Deleuze, Gilles/Guattari, Félix (1988 [1980]): A Thousand Pleateaus. Capitalism and Schizophrenia, London: University of Minnesota Press.
Despentes, Virginie (2015): Vernon Subutex (vol. 1), Paris: Grasset.
Edwards, Natalie (2012): »Feminist Manifesto or Hardcore Porn? Virginie Despentes's Transgression«, in: Irish Journal of French Studies 12.1, pp. 9–26.
Fayard, Nicole (2005): »Sadeian Sisters. Sexuality as Terrorism in the Work of Virginie Despentes«, in: Sarah Donachie/Kim Harrison (eds.): Love and Sexuality. New Approaches in French Studies, Oxford: Lang, pp. 101–120.
Fayard, Nicole (2006): »The Rebellious Body as Parody. *Baise-moi* by Virginie Despentes«, in: French Studies 60, pp. 63–77.
Graham, Sarah (2019): A History of the *Bildungsroman*, Cambridge: University Press.
Green, Adam (2002): »Gay but Not Queer. Toward a Post-Queer Study of Sexuality«, in: Theory and Society 31.4, pp. 521–545.
Halberstam, Jack (2011): The Queer Art of Failure, Durham: Duke University Press.
Hollister, Lucas (2004): »Revolting Women? Excess and detournement de genre in the Work of Virginie Despentes«, in: Shirley Ann Jordan (ed.), Contemporary's French Women's Writing, Oxford: Peter Lang, pp. 113–150.
Hollister, Lucas (2021): »Virginie Despentes' Queer Crime Fiction«, in: French Cultural Studies 32.4, pp. 417–427.
Jablonka, Ivan (2023 [2022]): A History of Masculinity. From Patriarchy to Gender Justice, London: Penguin.
Kosofsky Sedgwick, Eve K. (1993): Tendencies, Durham: Duke University Press.
Moretti, Franco (2000): The Way of the World. The *Bildungsroman* in European Culture, London: Verso.

Muzart, Thomas (2020): Queer Displacements. Minorities, Mobilities, and Mobilizations in French and Francophone Literature, New York: University of New York.

Muzart, Thomas (2022): Displacing Political Horizons. Queer Writing and Transnational Activism«, in: Contemporary French and Francophone Studies 26.1, pp. 23–31.

Nigianni, Chrysanthi/Storr, Merl (2009): Deleuze and Queer Theory, Edinburgh: Edinburgh University Press.

Preciado, Paul B. (2013): Testo Junkie, New York: The Feminist Press.

Ruth, Amar (2023): »Virginie Despentes' Commitment and the Polyphonic Narration of Vernon Subutex«, in: Belphégor 21.2, s.p.

Sauzon, Virginie (2012): »La Déviance en réseau. Grisélidis Réal, Virginie Despentes et le féminisme pragmatique«, in: Trans – Revue de littérature générale et comparée 13, s.p.

Schaal, Michèle (2017): Une Troisième Vague Féministe et Littéraire. Les Femmes de Lettres de la Nouvelle Génération, New York: BRILL.

Schaal, Michèle (2013): »Une nécessaire rébellion féministe. La violence féminine chez Virginie Despentes«, in: Frédérique Chevillot/Colette Trout Hall (eds.), Rebelles et criminelles chez les écrivaines d'expression française, Amsterdam: Rodopi, pp. 265–280.

Simonin, Damien (2015): »Problèmes de définition ou définitions du problème? La ›pornographie‹ dans ›l'affaire *Baise-moi*‹«, in: Genre, sexualité et société 14, s.p.

Stević, Aleksandar (2020): Falling Short. The *Bildungsroman* and the Crisis of Self-fashioning, Charlottesville: University of Virginia Press.

Negative Affects, Futurity and Queer Relationality in and around *De la terreur, mes sœurs!* (Alexis Langlois, 2019)

Pierre Niedergang

1 Art and the Queer (Anti-)Relationality Debate

José Esteban Muñoz's work teaches us how artworks can be involved in the theoretical and conceptual debates of queer theories (and minoritarian theories in general). In *Disidentifications*, Muñoz (2013) mobilizes the works of Marlon Riggs, Isaac Julien and Vaginal Davis to describe an original relationship to identity and identification, which neither rejects identification in the strict sense nor clings to the identity at stake. In *Cruising Utopia* (Muñoz 2009), Fred Herko's dance, Andy Warhol's visual work and Frank O'Hara's poetry are invoked to defend the possibility of a utopian queer future against »no-future« and pragmatist readings of queer theories, such as Lee Edelman's (2004).

In this article, I would like to explore and extend this latter tension – between futurism and no-future within queer theories – to show how French director Alexis Langlois' film *De la terreur, mes sœurs!* can serve to defend a futuristic, utopian conception *à la* Muñoz without, however, denying negative affects and their destructive/creative potential. If I am returning to this »old« debate – which crystallised before 2010 in the North American context – it's because we have now inherited the same tension in France. This concerns not only internal debates within queer theory, but also the possibility for queer politics and theories to articulate with feminist and anti-racist struggles.

On the one hand, queer theoretical positions reject the chrono-political dimension of futurity, as the future is a straight dimension existing only through reproductive futurism. This reproductive futurism is »preserving […] the absolute privilege of heteronormativity by rendering unthinkable, by casting outside the political domain, the possibility of a queer resistance to this organizing principle of communal relations« (Edelman 2004: 2). This anti-future position is thus linked to an anti-relational and anti-communal position that sees relationality as something fundamentally straight. Queer sexuality represents an anti-future force that disrupts the straight utopia, and an anti-relational force of disruption. Inspired by the Lacanian concept of *Jouissance* and the Freudian concept of *Todestrieb*, Leo Bersani, for example, argues that gay anal sex exhibits the destructiveness and anti-relationality that are fundamental to all sexuality (2010: 25–30). As self-abolition, sexuality destroys the possibility of social bonding. Edelman's proposal is a continuation of Bersani's earlier work: because queer sexuality is a rupture in straight relationality, it represents an antisocial, »no-future« force. The influence of Slavoj Žižek's political Lacanism is also perceptible in Edelman's work and should be discussed, given the transphobic and anti-feminist views of this author.

On the other hand, certain works, including those by Eve K. Sedgwick, José Esteban Muñoz, Lauren Berlant and Sara Ahmed, have put queer relationality and relational weaving at the heart of their reflections. By approaching queer bodies and realities through an affective perspective, the aim is to resist the domination of psychoanalytic concepts within queer theories, such as the concept of drive (*Trieb*) (Sedgwick 2003: 18). This »affective turn« in queer theories allows us to embrace other ways of thinking about the body, such as phenomenological (Ahmed 2006) and existentialist (Muñoz 2009) approaches. References to Maurice Merleau-Ponty, Edmund Husserl and Martin Heidegger allow us to rethink queer spaces and temporalities (Halberstam 2005). In terms of temporality, the approach based on desire as an opening of the future, and its connection to hope, makes it possible to propose an alternative to »no-future« approaches rooted in the death drive (Muñoz 2009: 186).

This tension first emerged in the North American context. Its translation and incorporation into the French context partially reconfigure the actors involved and the terms of this debate. While references to Bersani and Edelman remain important, the figure of Guy Hocquenghem, rather marginalized in the American context, emerges as an essential figure of division (Clinton 2019; Niedergang/Piterbraut-Merx 2021). The sulphurous character of Hocquenghem, close to the 1970s french paedophile group (Idier 2017: 155–167) embodies immorality, anti-normativity, anti-relationality and pessimism, defended by the »negativist« approaches of Edelman or Bersani, as a radical dimension of queer sexuality.

Resistance to »no-future« and anti-relational theories, in France and elsewhere, takes the form of inventing alternative imaginaries, visions of the future that allow us to psychically liberate ourselves from the »quagmire of the present« (Muñoz 2009: 1). Only these alternative imaginaries – found, for example, in the eco-sexual fantasies of Cy Lecerf-Maulpoix (2021: 240) or in the work of Tarek Lakhrissi – make it possible to reopen the dimension of futurity and agency in the present.

In this article, I will be drawing on the work of another French queer artist, director Alexis Langlois, as their film *De la terreur, mes sœurs!* offers us an original way of addressing the tension between futurity and utopia on the one hand, and destructiveness and pessimism on the other. It seems to me that this short film is based, in terms of both form and plot, on an approach that privileges relationality and futurism, while showing how the weaving of alternative imaginary worlds depends on tensions and negative affects that, when dialecticized, become productive. It highlights the way in which the invention of alternative imaginaries against the »quagmire of the present« presupposes relational conflicts that manifest queer »normative debates« (Niedergang 2023: s.p.) around the values presiding over the creation of these imaginaries. The articulation between utopian construction and negative affect helps to prevent queer futurism from being accused of naiveté. Alexis Langlois's film emphasizes the role of negative affect in reopening the dimension of futurity.

2 The Communal Weaving of Alternative Imaginaries

De la terreur, mes sœurs! features a group of four transfeminine friends who meet in a straight bar for a drink and a good chat. The first scene depicts Kalthoum (Nana Benamer), walking down the street, dressed all in black and wearing sunglasses, enduring mockery and transphobic comments. Throughout the film, various forms of transmisogynist violence (Serano 2020: 25) are depicted:

a) In the first scene, Kalthoum is subjected to verbal abuse and street harassment.
b) The fetishization from »benevolent« cis people, such as the two bar staff (played by Justine Langlois and Félix Maritaud), or the display of fascination with trans bodies.
c) Institutional violence is depicted in a scene where Farah's payment card reveals her deadname to a very troubled waiter.
d) Psychological violence is evoked through a camp caricature of conversion therapy (to which we will return to later).

e) Physical violence against trans people is portrayed in a scene in a straight nightclub.

Kalthoum seems to be the one most affected by the pervasiveness of these forms of violence. By the time she joins her friends, on the doorstep of the bar, she seems to have given up all hope and fallen into a kind of melancholy, trapped in the »quagmire of the present«, as Muñoz puts it. Through verbal abuse, she sees herself locked into the role of the abject, the freak, despite the camouflage provided by her clothes and sunglasses (Kalthoum: »Encore une journée d'merde. [...] De toute façon c'est toujours pareil, même camouflée comme ça, ils se déchaînent tous sur moi. Qu'est-ce qu'il faut faire pour avoir la paix!«; 00:01:19).

Fig. 1: From left to right Naëlle Dariya, Raya Martini, Dustin Muchuvitz, Nana Benamer as Farah, Raya, Dustin and Kalthoum in Alexis Langlois' De la terreur, mes sœurs!

© Les films du Bélier

Kalthoum, at least at the beginning of the short film, represents the pessimism, the »no-future« hopelessness to which the straight world condemns queers, according to Edelman. She embodies »the negativity opposed to every form of social viability« (Edelman 2004: 9). This »no-future« negative and destructive dimension is encapsulated in the bomb that Kalthoum has hidden in her hair, with which she intends to blow up »straight land« and the cis-tem. What interests us is not so much the radical, terrorist nature of the use of the bomb, but the self-destructive nature of the planned gesture: Kalthoum wants to take herself to her death with the straight world. Thus, her solution is to identify with the death drive as a force antagonistic to straight communality (Edelman 2004: 3).

The first effect of the queer relationality at work between in the four characters, is to mock this self-destructive solution and thus to preserve Kalthoum from a suicidal response:

Raya, laughing: Tu vas faire quoi, tu vas cacher une bombe dans ta tignasse? *Kalthoum, disarming the bomb discreetly*: Bah non... J'sais pas encore quoi mais il faut faire quelque chose, et vite! Au lieu de pouffer, vous avez une idée vous? (00:05:05).

It is the disarming of the suicidal solution that will lead to a new process, that of weaving together alternative imaginaries. The construction of these visions of emancipation, revolt and transformation is only possible if pure and simple destructiveness (i.e., the queer identification with the death drive to which Edelman invites us) is overcome, towards a more dialectical use of the negative. The »black hole« of negativity must be avoided if the imagination of a non-lethal resistance to the cis-tem is to unfold.

The structure of the film is organized around the presentation of four scenarios, four fantasies constructed by each of the people around the table. Each of these imaginary represents a possible axis of resistance. The first scenario is imagined by Farah (played by actress and performer Naëlle Dariya). The proposed solution is what I would call »Reichian«, in reference to Wilhelm Reich, because it values the pleasure principle: »Plus de jouissance, moins de souffrance«. It is through pleasure that the limitations of gender and sex imposed on bodies will be eradicated. During a conversion therapy session, the plump cook Farah Makrout is invited to teach the »young girls« (played by transmasculine actors) how to cook. The lesson, however, degenerates into a queer orgy that drags everyone (including the »therapists«) into a demonic, de-gendered erotic vortex.

As for the interest in the dialectic of negative affects and their use to open up the future, there are two things about this scene that interest us, and we will come back to them later: First, the unsettling contrast between the tragic nature of the subject evoked (conversion therapy) and the cheerful, manic, Barbie-pink aesthetic of the scene. The use of this very camp style, completely at odds with the seriousness of the subject, can be seen as a way of »digesting« the negativity at work, of making the violence of conversion therapy both funny and pathetic. Second, as Farah narrates her scenario, Kalthoum intervenes several times to criticize the way Farah constructs her fantasy.

> *Kalthoum:* Argh... Attends, pour toi c'est Raya l'idéal féminin? [...] Et bien de mieux en mieux... C'est moi la boniche maintenant. [...] Pourquoi est-ce qu'il faut toujours que ça se termine en histoire de cul avec vous? (00:06:24).

By discussing what she dislikes, Kalthoum brings into play a pessimism that is no longer self-destructive, but a critical force that opens up the space for debate about the norms, values and aesthetics at work in the scenarios proposed by her friends.

The second scenario, offered by Dustina, consists of a cyber-activist uprising. In a queer hacker aesthetic, she evokes the constitution of an online network and the mass organization of civil disobedience practices. These trans cyber-activists burn their identity cards in order to warn and fight against the institutional and state imposition of a gendered name and identity. The argument is a defence of the fluidity of identities against bureaucratic and state rigidities. The ambivalence of digital tools is revealed when, after Dustina's proposal, Raya is subjected to transphobic verbal abuse on a dating app.

The third phantasmatic scenario is Raya's response to this online violence and is charged with the affect of rage. It is a fantasy of retaliatory physical violence and direct action. While Kalthoum is a waitress in a nightclub (»Raya... Pourquoi c'est encore moi la boniche?«), she is physically assaulted by Lélé (Félix Maritaux), one of the customers, and then by all the customers. That is when Raya, Farah and Dustina, dressed as leather superheroines, show up and beat up the customers to avenge Kalthoum. The battle of the heroines culminates in Raya castrating Lélé with her teeth. She then spits his ripped-off penis into a cocktail glass. The scene ends with the screams of Kalthoum, who once again acts as a critic of the norms and values that govern the construction of the fantasy. Kalthoum's critique focuses on the blind spots in Raya's solution, which pits trans people against »rednecks«, obscuring the fact that they are victims of interconnected relations of domination.

> *Kalthoum:* Stooop! Mais t'es horrible Raya. C'est comme ça que tu venges tes sœurs? Franchement toutes cette violence, ça sert à quoi ? C'est des brutes

oui, mais ce sont des pauvres types. Les trans et les prolos qui s'entretuent, il y en a à qui ça ferait vraiment trop plaisir... C'est complètement con (00:18:27).

According to Kalthoum, an intersectional approach to relations of domination is preferable to pitting trans superheroines against cis rednecks.

From this critique of violence, Kalthoum ultimately proposes her own solution: that of transforming representations and empowering trans people to shape their own representations. While a movie is being made by a cis director (who has a cis person playing the role of the gay liberation and transgender rights activist Sylvia Rivera), a shift is gradually taking place: Farah moves the microphone, the camera, and the lights to point them at Kalthoum. Thus, against the will of the cis director, the trans people present in the crew take power over the performance, decentring it.

The four strategies are not mutually exclusive; they represent four types of struggle that can and must be articulated: an erotopolitical struggle with pleasure at its core, a cyberactivist struggle, actions of self-defense and direct action and, finally, placing importance on representation. The fourth strategy of resistance, with which the film ends, is particularly interesting because it presents a paradox that we will have to explore: on the one hand, empowerment through representation seems to be the solution favoured by Kalthoum and, ultimately, by the film itself. One might think that the film is an effective realization of this solution. And yet, the director of the film, Alexis Langlois, may be queer, they are not a trans woman. There is a strange, cognitively troubling process taking place in which the film presents a glimpse of what might be in the future, but from the coordinates of the quagmire of the present, where the chances of a trans woman getting the funding to make a film about trans played by trans people are very slim. It seems to me that this might meet the demand made by José Esteban Muñoz in the introduction to *Cruising Utopia*:

> The here and now is a prison house. We must strive, in the face of the here and now's totalizing rendering of reality, to think and feel a then and there. Some will say that all we have are the pleasures of this moment, but we must never settle for that minimal transport; we must dream and enact new and better pleasures, other ways of being in the world, and ultimately new worlds (Muñoz 2009: 1).

Kalthoum's final proposal creates the effect of a film that is not self-indulgent but dissatisfied; a film that allows us to share a deep discontent with the present, with the current state of cinema, and with the conditions of trans peoples' lives and their representation, while offering an imperfect glimpse of a future horizon on which to situate queerness.

3 Camp and Negative Affects

This imperfect utopian glimpse, and the imaginary propositions that reopen the future in *De la terreur, mes sœurs!* do not exclude the work of negativity. These fantasies and scenarios of emancipation are the result of the queer relationality between the four friends: their deployment is made possible by the support and psychological breathing they try to provide for Kalthoum, who is locked in the prison of the here and now at the beginning of the film. But within this relationality, negative affects and critical relationships are at work. There is a relational work of the negative, embodied by Kalthoum. Dialecticized, this work is no longer self-destructive, but becomes a driving force, a stimulus for imagining other phantasmatic solutions and opening up a space for normative debate in which to discuss these »other ways of being in the world« and these »new worlds« that need to be invented.

The first set of criticisms concerns the exclusively sexual focus of Farah's scenario. It resonates historically with the disenchantments expressed in the 1970s with the idea of sexual liberation and liberation through sexuality (Foucault 1976). While arousing, this proposition is limited in that desires and pleasures are not naturally revolutionary energies, but realities produced and shaped by power (Niedergang 2023). »Décoincer les réac« (»Relaxing bigots«) through the queer use of pleasures is not the solution to ending the cissexist, transmisogynist system of domination. The second set of critiques is equally important. It questions the use of violence and then resonates with contemporary debates within minoritarian theories about the use of violence and self-defense (Dorlin 2017; Butler 2020). Kalthoum introduces into this normative debate the question of class and the demand to consider the possibilities of an intersectional struggle between trans and lower-class people. Again, Kalthoum is not fooled by the romanticism of subversion contained in Farah and Raya's scenarios.

Pierre Niedergang: *De la terreur, mes soeurs!* 69

Fig. 2: Naëlle Dariya as Farah Makrout in Alexis Langlois' De la terreur, mes sœurs!

© Les films du Bélier

Regarding the tension between »no-future« antisocial theory and utopian relational theory, Alexis Langlois's work with *De la terreur, mes sœurs!* and especially the character of Kalthoum, teaches us two lessons. The first one is that negativity must be recast in relationality in order to avoid self-destruction, a self-destruction that is the result of solipsistic negativity. Recast in relationality (through normative debate in this case), destructiveness becomes a dialectical critical force that can be used to open up the future through the construction of alternative imaginaries. Relatedly, the second lesson is that relationality and the construction of alternative utopian imaginaries do not presuppose the evacuation of tensions and critical negativity. Such an evacuation would be naive, but it would also be disempowering, because negativity is a critical power of transformation. It is one of the ways in which the normative demands of different parties manifest themselves in the common weaving of other queer possibilities for the future, for example, the refusal to see pleasure and sexuality as inherently revolutionary, or the demand for the articulation of trans struggles with proletarian struggles.

Alexis Langlois' movie also proposes another (profoundly queer) type of dialectization of negative affectivity: the use of camp humour. Describing this style of camp humour as it manifested itself in 1920s New York, Georges Chauncey (2019) defines it as »at once a cultural style and a cultural strategy [that] helped gay men make sense of, respond to, and undermine the social categories of gender and sexuality that served to marginalize them« (Chauncey 2019: 290). Founded on double entendre and gay cultural codes as well as on »a philosophy of transformation and incongruity«, camp is a »strategy for a situation«, a situation shaped by stigma (Newton 1979: 105). Camp appears as a way of deflecting and transforming social violence and stigma.

As used by Langlois, it allows for the representation of negativity in an impure, digested form. It is a way of shaping negativity through aesthetic choice, in order not to be consumed by it (nihilistic self-destructiveness). There are many scenes in Alexis Langlois' work, especially in *De la terreur, mes sœurs!*, but there are two examples that catch my attention, because they play out the dialectization of the negative. There is a kind of camp meanness against queer morality (Edwards 2021).

After Kalthoum has spoken about the psychological and physical violence inflicted on trans people, and the suicides linked to this violence, a solemn moment of silence falls between the four protagonists. This silence is broken by Farah's burp, which brings the commemoration to a brutal and disrespectful end. It is this burp, which follows a moment of grief and mourning, that creates the affective dialectic necessary for the deployment of the four alternative imaginaries that the film presents. Farah's camp burp allows us to avoid being swallowed up by grief and to begin to imagine futures other than those leading to death.

The second example, which I have already mentioned, is the conversion therapy depicted in Farah's scenario. The camp aesthetic, full of pink and glitz, is applied to the difficult subject of conversion therapy. During a lesson in the form of a musical in which the lyrics »il est naturel que le genre soit en harmonie avec le sexe biologique« are sung, psychiatric violence is depicted through the electroshock treatment of one of the participants. The camp aestheticization and ridicule of these so-called »therapies« pave the way for the re-eroticization of this space, which Farah uses as the basis for her revolutionary scenario. While Kalthoum presents us with a dialectic of the negative by recasting it in relationality, Farah presents us with a camp form of transformation and digestion of the negative that allows us to avoid being swallowed up by it.

4 The Paradox of *De la terreur, mes sœurs!* and On-Screen/Off-Screen Relationality

Finally, I would like to return to the final paradox of the film, as it draws to a close. The scenario of Kalthoum is a reflection on representation and, ultimately, on the cinematic representation of trans people. It is the articulation of a desire for self-representation, for gaining agency over representation in order to resist fetishizing or exoticizing processes. The scene highlights the material dimension of filmmaking. A movie is not just about actresses, it is also about camera operators, sound and lighting technicians. Cinematic transformation is not just the transformation of the people in front of the camera, but a profound change at every level of filmmaking. It is not just about casting trans people to play trans characters. But the transformation that this last scenario invites is the active participation of trans people in all aspects of the film industry: casting, technical roles (lighting, sound, camera), but also subsidies, festivals and so on. The transformation of representations presupposes a profound transformation of the conditions of production of the representation, and not only of the content of the representation.

Kalthoum's fantasy is the one with which the movie ends. From the movie set, the four protagonists return to the bar and find themselves on the street. Kalthoum smiles, empowered by the presence of her sisters and the weaving of imaginaries that took place in the bar. She seems to have escaped the »prison of the present«. The fact that Kalthoum's scenario concludes the film suggests that Kalthoum's lesson is the lesson of the film itself, that the film is a form of empowering self-representation by and for trans women. But the paradox is this: the film is indeed the work of a queer person, but not of a trans woman. The problem then is to what extent Alexis Langlois can prevent themselves from once again producing a fetishist representation of trans women. Is the casting of trans people in the film enough to produce an emancipatory representation?

At the heart of the film is an aporia that can only be resolved by taking into account the queer relationality behind the camera that made the film possible. We cannot assume that Alexis Langlois can avoid bias linked to their sexo-social position, because this illusion of a nullification, this pseudo-neutrality, is the very movement of the majoritarian that camouflages itself. What is possible, however, is to evoke the way in which the film is the result of a friendly and intimate relationship between the director, the actresses and the rest of the crew, and not the result of the imposition of a single vision, that of the director, on the bodies of the actresses. This aporia invites us to think about »queer filmmaking« as a way of undoing the straight figure of the all-powerful, phallic director.

Speaking about *De la terreur, mes sœurs!* it should be emphasized that this film is the result of the friendship that unites Alexis Langlois, the actresses and many members of the film crew. It is a film made by people who frequent the same queer milieu in Paris: Naëlle Dariya is not only an actress and performer, but also a party organizer. At the *Shemale Trouble* parties she organizes, you can meet Nana Benamer, also a performer, singer and DJ, as well as Dustin Muchuvitz, also a DJ, and Raya Martini (Desombre 2017). Of course, this does not mean that there are no power relations at work. But it allows us to understand this film not as an individual result (the imposition of a director's will) but as a queer communal result, including behind the camera. If the movie is so amusing and powerful, it is because the work done through the figure of the director is a communal work. As a filmmaker, Alexis Langlois is first and foremost a vehicle for communal forces that weave alternative imaginaries through them.

If *De la terreur, mes sœurs!* is a queer film, we have to consider that the lesson it teaches us is not that of a rigid identity politics that would require trans actresses, a trans director, an all trans crew, etc. for a film about the construction of alternative trans imaginaries. As I said, the film's proposal is more ambivalent: Kalthoum's fantasy is, precisely, not realized in the present. The film is merely an ersatz of what could be. This sense of dissatisfaction is deliberately created by the final gap between Kalthoum's fantasy and the reality of Alexis Langlois' film. The present in France in the 2020s remains a quagmire in which, doing a queer film is difficult, and an all-trans crew remains unthinkable, unintelligible. The movie is therefore a call for something that is not here and now, but then and there.[1]

I conclude this work by quoting Muñoz once again. Because I think that Alexis Langlois' movie *De la terreur, mes sœurs!* echoes perfectly with these lines:

> Queerness is that thing that lets us feel that this world is not enough, that indeed something is missing. Often we can glimpse the worlds proposed and promised by queerness in the realm of aesthetic. The aesthetic, especially the queer aesthetic, frequently contains blueprints and schemata of a forward-dawning futurity (Muñoz 2009: 1).

---

[1] This consideration of the difficulty of making queer films is also at the core of *Les démons de Dorothy* (Langlois, 2021). It shows the pressures (both symbolic and economic) exerted on queer filmmakers by the straight cinema world.

Bibliography

Ahmed, Sara (2006): Queer Phenomenology. Orientations, Objects, Others, Durham/London: Duke University Press.

Bersani, Leo (2010): Is the Rectum a Grave and Other Essays, Chicago: University of Chicago Press.

Butler, Judith (2020): The Force of Nonviolence. An Ethico-Political Bind, New York: Verso Books.

Chauncey, George (2019): Gay New York. Gender, Urban Culture, and the Making of the Gay Male World, 1890–1940, New York: Basic Books.

Clinton, Paul (2019): »The Trouble with Not Normal. Talk at the Paris Ass Book Fair 2019«, https://www.youtube.com/watch?v=a1FvrYnC0-Q [13.06.2024].

Desombre, Camille (2017): »Shemale Trouble, 2 ans déjà«, in: Friction Magazine, https://friction-magazine.fr/shemale-trouble-2-ans-deja/ [13.06.2024].

Dorlin, Elsa (2017): Se défendre. Une philosophie de la violence, Paris: La Découverte.

Edelman, Lee (2004): No Future. Queer Theory and the Death Drive, Durham/London: Duke University Press.

Edwards, Travis (2021): »Morality and Queerness. The Emergence of Queer Morality in Media«, in: Medium 2 02.09.2021, https://adangghost.medium.com/morality-and-queerness-the-emergence-of-queer-morality-in-media-f07826c2600d [13.06.2024].

Foucault, Michel (1976): Histoire de la sexualité (vol. 1). La volonté de savoir, Paris: Gallimard.

Halberstam, Jack (2005): In a Queer Time and Place. Transgender Bodies, Subcultural Lives, New York: New York University Press.

Idier, Antoine (2017): Les vies de Guy Hocquenghem. Politique, sexualité, culture, Paris: Fayard.

Lecerf-Maulpoix, Cy (2021): Écologies déviantes. Voyage en terres queers, Paris: Cambourakis.

Muñoz, José Esteban (2009): Cruising Utopia. The Then and There of Queer Futurity, New York: University Press.

Muñoz, José Esteban (2013): Disidentifications. Queers of Color and the Performance of Politics, Minneapolis: University of Minnesota Press.

Newton, Esther (1979): Mother Camp. Female Impersonators in America, Chicago: The University of Chicago Press.

Niedergang, Pierre (2023): Vers la normativité queer, Toulouse: Blast.
Niedergang, Pierre/Piterbraut-Merx, Tal (2021): »Violence sexuelle ou ›initiation‹? Communautés, trauma et normativité queer«, in: Glad! 10, s.p.
Serano, Julia (2020): Manifeste d'une femme trans et autres textes, Paris: Cambourakis.

Filmography

DE LA TERREUR, MES SŒURS! (2019) (France, D: Alexis Langlois).
LES DÉMONS DE DOROTHY (2021) (France, D: Alexis Langlois).

Dissolving into Love as Crisis
Queer Feminist Relationality in the Films
A felicidade delas (2019), *Trenque Lauquen* (2022)
and *Três tigres tristes* (2022)

Alkisti Efthymiou

1 »A Movie of Our Times«

Multiple femininities march in the streets of São Paulo, shouting feminist slogans and using colored smoke bombs. Among the protesters, a black woman holds a placard that reads »Kiss your black girl in the public square«, accompanied by a drawing of a female face with coily hair. A bit further away, another black woman is marching, with hair similar to that of the face in the sketch. While participating in the demonstration with their friends, the two women notice each other and exchange a couple of flirtatious gazes.

This is the first scene of the short fiction film *A felicidade delas* by Carol Rodrigues, released in 2019. Since the two women remain unnamed throughout the film, I will be referring to them by the names of the respective actresses: Tamirys O'Hanna (the first one in appearance) and Ivy Souza (the second one). The style of this first sequence of *A felicidade delas* is so realistic that it resembles a documentary: in fact, it looks like it was shot in an actual protest. The handheld camera follows the line of sight of the demonstrators, with the sound perfectly aligning to their slogans. The only punctuation element that alludes to fiction is the staged shot-reverse-shot of an exchange of gazes between the two protagonists.

After the protest is interrupted by the police, however, the initial observational tone of the film fades away. Sirens, blockades, with motorcycles, officers everywhere – both women start running. A video shot a phone breaks the sleekness of the HD image but only for a few seconds, just enough to remind us of the connection between reality and screen. Tamirys is caught by the police and, when she is about to get handcuffed, Ivy creates a distraction so that both women can escape. They manage to lose the tail and take refuge in a dark abandoned building. The authorities are still outside, we can hear them, but they remain off camera.

As the women walk through the unexplored site with caution and curiosity, the pace of the film slows down. The duration of the shots is longer and the transitions are softer, giving the impression that time is stretched. Without exchanging any words, Tamirys and Ivy absorb each other's presence by looking, breathing, touching. The blue and purple color palette blends with the dim light to reveal only parts of their bodies, whose relation we know nothing about other than what occurs in this suspended present. And then Tamirys makes her desire manifest on a graffiti she paints of two naked black women holding each other, jumpstarting the burst of female sensuality that is going to follow. The two women first stare into each other's eyes, then hold hands, and finally start making out slowly but progressively with more and more passion in the longest scene of the film. While we hear them breathing, the camera booms up from their interlaced fingers to their bellies and their faces, and then a series of increasingly fast-changing shots show details of their gestures. When the field size changes from closeup to medium, a dissolve transition marks the moment of climax: the bodies of Ivy and Tamirys, entwined in their sexual surge, burst into water and become a flood that engulfs everything in its path (Fig. 1–3). The dissolve of one frame into another and the splashing sound that slightly precedes the explosive transformation into liquid, smooth out the surprising change of states, perhaps suggesting a certain naturalness to the fantasy.

What resembled a feminist activist documentary in its start, becomes a work of lesbian erotica, confirming that these two genres are interlinked. Oscillating from the collective to the personal, from the public to the private, the film crosses the boundaries between micro and macro gestures of political resistance. Without a drop of rain, suddenly everything is wet, starting from the building where Ivy and Tamirys made out. The streets, which were once the property of uniformed men, are now thrown into the chaos of the flood, inundated by the liquid coming out of the love between these two women. A water that destroys, yes, but only to give life again. *Another* life.

Fig. 1–3: *Film stills of A felicidade delas (2019) by Carol Rodrigues.*

2 Love as Crisis

»Above all, [this is] a movie of our times, of our structure of feeling« (Mendes 2020, my translation), reads a comment on the online platform where I first saw this film. I call such structure of feeling *love as crisis*, a tug-o-war between trying to attain a love project in a world subsumed by capital and not completely giving in to this world's bio- and necropolitical demands. The neoliberal conditions of governmentality that guide the types of love that subjects become drawn towards, depend on crises to sustain themselves (Rosenberg/Villarejo 2011). Jordana Rosenberg and Amy Villarejo have claimed that crisis is »at least partly, an *affect* deployed in this moment to put into place and naturalize the intensification of exploitation, the systematic destruction of the gains of labor radicalism, and the unleashing of new, imperialist forms of violence« (ibid: 5, original emphasis). Seen under this light, crisis is both structural and ideological: it is, on one hand, the dismantling of reliable financial, social, and political infrastructure, and, on the other hand, a constructed state of exception that makes neoliberalism go on.

To the multiple interpretations of the word crisis, I would like to add that of »taking a stand«, inspired by one of its meanings in a language I speak. In Greek, *krísi* can mean expressing an opinion or making an informed criticism. This relation between crisis and critical thinking has been thoroughly explored by theorists such as Michel Foucault (1997), Judith Butler (2004), and Athena Athanasiou (2021), who accentuate the role of critique in practices and performances of resistance. If critique is thus introduced into love as crisis, social relations defined by loving and being loved can become sites of questioning neoliberal governmentality, at the same time that they are threatened by it. In other words, loving *as* crisis means to not fully succumb to loving *in* crisis, namely to the processes of desubjectivation and exhaustion that threaten the relationality needed to construct thriving life worlds.

Like other cultural forms of expression, cinema partakes in this worlding – and queer feminist cinema, in particular, often rearranges the building blocks.[1] In the words of Karl Schoonover and Rosalind Galt,

> queer cinema enables different ways of being in the world and, more than this, it creates different worlds. Cinema is always involved in world making,

---

1   I use the term worlding in the sense of ›patterning possible worlds and possible times, material-semiotic worlds, gone, here, and yet to come‹ (Haraway 2014: 31).

and queerness promises to knock off kilter conventional epistemologies. Thinking queerness together with cinema thus has a potential to reconfigure dominant modes of worlding (Schoonover/Galt 2016: 5).

Under this light, the present chapter aims to map emergent forms of love and relationality that invite alternative modes of inhabiting this world and lie at the intersection of queer feminist politics, crisis neoliberalism, and Latin American cinema.

In *A felicidade delas*, love manifests in several ways: in the gestures of complicity and solidarity among the protesters at the feminist march, in Irys helping Tamarys escape the police, in the sexual attraction between the two black women, in their sexual pleasure and their becoming-flood. The common denominator between the various forms is a disruption, however slight, in the continuity of self-sovereignty, leaving the subjects of love radically open to otherness and difference. The critique within love as crisis lies exactly in this possibility of »encounter[ing] another as *an other*, rather than absorb[ing] that other into a narcissistic fantasy of oneself or dialectically synthesiz[ing] into a third« (Brilmyer/Trentin/Xiang 2019: 218).

In the sections that follow, I will briefly describe the sociopolitical conditions that shape both love and narrative cinema in contemporary Brazil and Argentina, two countries that have been subject to multiple forms of crisis constructed by indebtedness, inflation, austerity measures, exclusionary politics, and religious dogmatism. Drawing from specific scenes in three different fiction films (*A felicidade delas*, *Trenque Lauquen*, and *Três tigres tristes*), all showing elements of queer feminist sensibility, I will suggest ways of thinking love as crisis – in other words, love as a practice that speculates about living otherwise, despite the structural and ideological threat of collapse. In my reading of the scenes I use a combination of analytical tools that pay attention to each film's semiotics, narrative, mise-en-scène, and cultural and affective framework. Central to the aesthetics of love as crisis is a particular element of cinematic punctuation: the dissolve, a transition where one frame fades into the other. Used traditionally to denominate the passage of or a break in time (Lindgren 1963: 72), the dissolve is used here to indicate the entrance to an altered state of relationality, from a love conditioned by crisis to a love that disorders this very crisis' establishment.

3 Far Right Ultraliberalism, Queer Politics, Cinematic Promises

The first scene of *A felicidade delas* poignantly reveals two antagonistic factors that contribute to setting love as crisis: on one hand, queer feminist movements demand new forms of relationality and, on the other hand, conservative backlash revolves around policing and strengthening the traditional, heteropatriarchal systems of kinship.[2] Queer feminism and far right ideologies have had a parallel rise across Latin America in recent years, from Brazil to Argentina and Chile, proposing drastically different sociopolitical rearrangements and applications of love. If »making a queer world« requires »the development of kinds of intimacy that bear no necessary relation to domestic space, to kinship, to the couple form, to property and to the nation« (Berlant/Warner 1998: 556), the opposite process insists on the necessity of relating intimacy with ownership, reproduction, the nuclear family, and the fatherland.

To start with Brazil, the presidency of Jair Bolsonaro legitimated the global rise of new conservatism and far-right politics and confirmed their fusion with the neoliberal model. A fervent admirer of Donald Trump, Bolsonaro became widely influential across the world as the first democratically elected far right ultraliberalist to govern the largest national economy in South America. During his term, he promoted extractivist development, market libertarianism, police militarism, gun violence, Evangelical fundamentalism, social conservatism, and anti-gender politics.[3] Although the left-leaning Luiz Inácio ›Lula‹ da Silva is now president, the influence of *bolsonarismo* in the political and social life of the country is still extensive.[4]

---

2   Arguments from a Latin American perspective that attest to these contradictory social processes have been made by, among others, Verónica Gago (2019: 219–241), Cecilia Macón, Mariela Solana, Nayla Luz Vacarezza (2021: 1–3), and Leticia Sabsay (2020: 179–180).

3   For an extensive study of the effects of Bolsonaro's governance in Brazilian society see, for example, the volume edited by Katerina Hatzikidi and Eduardo Dullo (2021). For a compelling analysis of *bolsonarismo* see Rodrigo Nunes (2020). For a thorough examination of the connection between Evangelicalism and conservatism in Brazil see Ronaldo de Almeida (2020). See also Alexander Zaitchik's (2019) insightful piece of investigative reporting for *The Intercept* concerning the increase of extractivist development in the Amazon during Bolsonaro's presidency.

4   To quote Rodrigo Nunes, »smaller than Bolsonaro's actual or potential electorate, Bolsonarismo is at the same time bigger than Bolsonaro himself: neither created by nor solely dependent on the individual from whom it borrows its name« (Nunes 2020: 3). For example, just a week after Lula started his tenure, echoing the US Capitol at-

In Argentina, conservative president Mauricio Macri (2015–2019) introduced strict neoliberal austerity policies in a failed attempt to reform the national economy, at the expense of both the middle class and the poorer social strata (cf. Catanzaro/Stegmayer 2019). Since 2018, Argentina is experiencing the worst inflation in its recent history, which Peronist president Alberto Fernández did not manage to cure, resulting in the country's situation being described as an »eternal crisis« (Centenera 2023) and giving rise to another far right ultraliberal figure in the region, Javier Milei, who won the 2023 presidential elections. Since his election, Javier Milei has introduced steep cuts in salaries,[5] closed down important ministries and institutions,[6] and openly showed his disregard towards social issues like gender equality and freedom of sexual expression.[7]

This far right shift in the two countries, however, is not met without resistance, particularly from women, queers, and people of color. In Brazil, numerous anti-Bolsonaro mobilizations have populated both the media and the streets over the last few years, with many of them including or specifically tackling issues of race, sexuality, and gender, such as the #EleNão women-led campaign that called voters to prevent the former president from being elected and the demonstrations following the murder of human rights activist Marielle Franco (cf. Bárcenas 2020). Similar protests have intensified in Argentina, during these years of turmoil in the country. Feminism played a crucial role in encompassing and expanding the various anti-capitalist fronts, through mobilizations such as the 8th of March feminist strike (cf. Gago 2018), #NiUnaMenos

---

tack by followers of former president Donald Trump, Bolsonaro supporters invaded the congress, presidential palace, and supreme court in Brasília. In addition, despite being blocked by the Brazilian electoral court from seeking office until 2030 due to his violation of election laws, the former president managed to amass 185,000 of his supporters to march with him in São Paulo on Feb 25, 2024 (cf. Galarraga Gortázar 2024).

5   For more information on the current Argentine president's severe austerity measures see Clara Olmos (2024).

6   One of the first actions of Javier Milei after he assumed the presidency was to shrink the former Ministries of Culture; Health; Social Development; Education; Labor; and Women, Gender and Diversity into the new Ministry of Health and Human Capital. In February 22, he also decided to close the National Institute against Discrimination, Xenophobia and Racism (Inadi) and threatened to shut down Argentina's largest state-owned news agency.

7   For more information on Javier Milei's problematic stance towards issues of gender and sexuality see, indicatively, the articles of Débora Rey (2024) and Martina Jaureguy (2024).

(cf. Sabsay 2020), and the multiple reproductive rights demonstrations, also known as *marea verde* (green tide) (cf. Palmeiro 2018).

This same green tide found its filmic expression in *A felicidade delas* and morphed into a literal flood. Cinema is one of the main aesthetic means in which the dissent and demands of disobedient bodies are expressed, as evidenced by the exponential rise in the number of films and festivals produced in the region that engage with queer and feminist issues.[8] What has also risen is the visibility of these films and festivals, both locally and internationally. Cinema has thus been following closely, and even anticipating at times, the dynamic social movements that surround it, making it a primary target of ultraliberal far right politics. Milei in Argentina, for example, has ordered to shut down the National Institute of Cinema and Audiovisual Arts (INCAA), in an attempt to »reform« the State (cf. Página 12 2024). Bolsonaro in Brazil severely cut public funding for the audiovisual sector, claiming that »the state has other priorities« (quoted in Agence France-Presse 2020).

Despite these measures, however, several filmmakers in Brazil and Argentina have continued to bring forward works that challenge conservative reactionism in the context of crisis. The three films that I have chosen to focus on in this chapter – *A felicidade delas* by Carol Rodrigues (Brazil, 2019), *Trenque Lauquen* by Laura Citarella (Argentina, 2022), and *Três tigres tristes* by Gustavo Vinagre (Brazil, 2022) – are examples of how cinema can become the site of critique towards crisis neoliberalism at the same time that it is produced within it. This critique proposes forms of relating with the other that could give rise to more just and permeable worlds.

4 For a Love of Difference in Likeness

Trenque Lauquen – released in 2022, directed by Laura Citarella, and starring Laura Paredes – is the latest installment of the Argentinean film collective El Pampero Cine. With a duration of almost four and a half hours and split in

---

[8] Many recent studies confirm this. See, for example, the volume edited by Annette Scholz and Marta Álvarez (2018) on the current status of women's cinema in Iberoamerican countries; the special issue on gender, sexuality, film, and media in Latin America edited by Kristi M. Wilson and Clara Garavelli (2021) for the journal *Latin American Perspectives*; and the two special issues on ›queer/kuir/cuir‹ cinemas and audiovisualities in Brazil and Latin America edited by Alessandra Brandão and Dieison Marconi (2020; 2021) for the journal *Rebeca*.

two parts, it combines elements of mystery, drama, fantasy, and comedy to reveal the idiosyncrasies of both Trenque Lauquen, a rural town 450km west of Buenos Aires, and Laura, an agronomist who arrives there to index the local flora. As Laura becomes more and more immersed in the town's habits, she surrenders (at the risk of inventing herself again) to a series of local legends and secrets, some of them taking physical form before her eyes. When she unexpectedly goes missing, her colleague Ezequiel and her boyfriend Rafael embark on a quest to discover what might have happened to her. Intricately weaving the different characters' points of view while letting them fuse with the magic realism of the natural Pampas landscape, Citarella complicates all efforts to pin Laura's personality down and produce a definite, satisfying answer to her disappearance. Laura, giving her own fragmentary and elliptical account of the story, responds to the men's request for clarity with opacity and fleetingness, protecting her sacred journey of self-discovery from the constant pursuit of reason and meaning.

The second part of *Trenque Lauquen* starts to illuminate the circumstances behind Laura's disappearance, as relayed through her own voiceover. The void left by the unresolved stories in the first part of the film is filled with an entirely new puzzle: that of two lesbian lovers, Elisa and Romina, who live in a farmhouse and are secretly raising a mutant creature that we never get to actually see. Their relationship reads like an allegorical take on lesbian motherhood and how society and the media often treat it: »Two women raising a child? Ah, the child will surely become a monster!« In today's Argentina, such an allegory seems to subversively play with the governing party's worst homotransphobic nightmares: Diana Mondino, the current Minister of Foreign Affairs, International Trade and Worship, has compared sexual diversity with having lice (cf. Santoro/Carbajal 2023), and president Javier Milei has made an analogy between homosexuality and zoophilia to talk about same-sex marriage (cf. Bayly 2023). Such statements have legitimated an atmosphere of tolerance towards anti-gender and anti-LGBTQIA+ actions, inciting attacks such as the one on four lesbians in Buenos Aires on May 6, 2024. A man threw a bottle filled with flammable liquid into their room and set it on fire, leaving only one of the four alive (cf. Centenera 2024). *Trenque Lauquen*, released just a year before Milei won the elections, anticipates this climate of homotransphobia that sets certain forms of love in crisis. Elisa is shunned by the local press for caring for the mutant being. She and Romina, trying to protect their livelihoods and avoid the materialization of such views on their bodies, have chosen to isolate themselves. The type of family that they have is deemed not only unacceptable but monstrous by the conservative powers that be.

Laura, however, is fascinated by the mystery that surrounds Elisa and subsequently by the life that Elisa lives with her partner. Elisa and Romina treat Laura with suspicion at first but gradually trust her, to the point of inviting her to stay with them. Laura might be disrupting the delicate balance of the protected world that the queer family has built, but Elisa and Romina look like they want to let her in, as long as she does not ask about the mutant. When she is with them, Laura is happy, in the few times that we see her enjoying the company of other people. Filmed in long, slow, naturalistic shots, she is taking care of the plants in the couple's herbarium, discusses with them on how to maintain the house, and gathers materials to create a natural habitat for the creature. The intimacy among the three women is dependent on these acts of commitment and care, as well as on keeping the existence of the being that the couple is taking care of a secret.

Meanwhile, Laura restrains herself from asking about the creature, even though she really wants to see it with her own eyes. »I sometimes fantasized about going up, opening the door and seeing it«, she confesses in her voiceover, »but I quickly understood that this was not the deal. I had to wait. In the meantime, everything was love between the three of us. I loved them more each day« (03:28:22-03:28:47). This is a love that accepts the impossibility of fully knowing the other, finding its expression in the »failure of ability« – of the ability to know, to possess, to grasp the other (Levinas 1987 [1947]: 87–88). It is also a love that expands beyond the couple form: it includes more than two, but it does so while recognizing that it can never be on a measurably equal basis.

The dynamic between the three women plays out beautifully in the following scene: Elisa is in the garden, over a sea of dead leaves, and waves at Laura who sits behind a window. Laura smiles back and closes the window, probably to go out and meet Elisa. The image of the window grid dissolves into a wide shot of Elisa walking in the garden and Romina running behind her and giving her a surprise hug. Laura enters the frame while looking up at the sky, as if she does not want to disturb the couple's intimacy. The formal elements of this progression of images suggest an interesting reading. The change in the size and framing of the shots (from medium to wide, from single character to multiple) and the dissolve (with the window grid disappearing over Elisa and Romina hugging each other) point toward an opening in Laura's world: from alone and trapped, she is now in good company and freed. Throughout the entire scene, dissolves have been used extensively to transition from the shots of

Laura in a recording studio narrating her experience with Elisa and Romina, to the flashbacks of her moments with the couple. Such a traveling in time and space is one of the most traditional symbolic functions of the dissolve (Cutting/Brunick/Delong 2011). However, in the window scene I just described, this element of film punctuation acquires another, more complex meaning, that of a change in mood and relational state: from solitude to companionship, from being an observer of a queer love project to participating in it.

The frame where Laura stays on the side, respecting Elisa and Romina's twosome moment, is crucial in understanding the nature of the three women's love. When Laura says in her voiceover earlier, »I felt I wanted to be with them. I wanted to *be* them. I *was* them« (03:28:48-03:28:56), she is not expressing a fantasy of merging but a sense of realization. She wanted to be *like* them, because she felt the way they lived their lives was much closer to how she wanted to live hers – independently, unapologetically, resisting the norms of heteropatriarchy. This is not another case of the »lesbian doppelganger trope« (Jenzen 2013), but a lesbian love that seduces a third woman into embracing queer life. For the brief time she was with them, Laura *was* them but in difference, not in sameness.

An ideal of sameness is particularly prevalent in the stereotypical notion of romantic love as the incorporation of two in one, of the fusion of the self with the other. For Lacan, this fusion in love is a narcissistic project, aiming at the annihilation of difference (Lacan 1998 [1975]: 6). Working in the imaginary register, it points to an »attempt to find oneself or one's ideal self in the other, overlooking all difference between self and other« (Fink 2016: 87). Psychoanalysis understands the self as divided, incomplete and in perpetual search for its always-slipping identities. In the same way that the self is incomprehensible to the subject, so is the other incomprehensible to the self. In all forms of relationality, but perhaps more prominently in erotic love, the complete understanding of the other – and by extension of the self – will always be a matter of slippage, and the subject has to learn to live with this difficult acceptance.

A side effect of such an acceptance is what Alain Badiou identifies as the radical potency of love: it can start from something that is simply an encounter and grow to encompass the construction of a world from a point of view other than that of one's mere impulse to re-affirm their own identity (Badiou 2012: 25). Echoing Levinas, Badiou sees in love a fundamental opening to otherness, an exposure to difference that breaks the assumed solidity of the self. However, he considers love not as an »experience of otherness« (Levinas 1969 [1961]) but as an experience of the world on the basis of difference – the former approach is structured around the experience that the self has of the other, still using the self as the source experiencing and the other as the object of experience, whereas the latter is structured around the lovers' encounter, an event with the other that remains opaque to the self and becomes only a bit more translucent in its multiple vibrations in the real world.

After their hug, Elisa and Romina look back at Laura and invite her to join them – they return to the intimacy of three. Over a wide shot of the women walking in the garden between two trees (Fig.), Laura admits in voiceover: »I lost the fear of dying, of losing myself, of being in danger, of turning into an animal, into the crazy in town. I felt that whatever they were doing, it would be okay. And I wanted to be there« (03:30:00-03:30:14). *I wanted to be them* has now transformed into *I wanted to be there*: Laura's desire of likeness is nothing other than a wish, against all odds, to be part of the same queer world, and experience it on the basis of difference.

5 For a Companionship That Resists Oblivion

Três tigres tristes, released in 2022 and directed by Gustavo Vinagre, presents another possible take on love as crisis. The film is set in São Paulo, in a dystopian future not so far from the present, where a virus is circulating that affects the ability to remember. Everyone is obliged to wear masks, much as we did during the pandemic (when the shooting of the film occurred). Three young, queer people drift through a city that is hiding its colonial and dictatorial past while normalizing the neoliberal, authoritarian shifts that are bleeding it dry. Pedro earns his money through OnlyFans and Bella is preparing for the college exams to study medicine – the two are roommates. Jonata is their guest for a few days. He is Pedro's nephew, but people think they are cousins because they are the same age. Jonata is from Minas Gerais and is HIV positive. To avoid being confronted with the discriminating inhabitants of his small town, he prefers to travel to São Paulo for his treatment. On top of the viral load, the context of crisis in the film is defined by historical denialism, authoritarian governance, and structural racism.

As the three protagonists wander around the city aimlessly, they encounter other queer people with whom they share intimate scenes, collectively remembering things that the virus makes the rest of the inhabitants forget. Pedro is still mourning the death of his boyfriend who committed suicide during the pandemic. He carries with him a printed painting of the two of them kissing, which he sticks on a city wall on top of a Bolsonaro poster. In a similar gesture of resistance through remembrance, Pedro, Isabella, and Jonata visit the Lady of the Afflicted, a chapel in São Paulo that everyone seems to have forgotten that it was built on top of a burial site for black slaves. By the middle of *Três tigres tristes*, the oneiric and supernatural aspects of the film culminate in a sequence where the three main characters come together with other social ›outcasts‹ in the salon of a singer named Mirta. They all break into a long musical scene – full of lush colors, costumes, sensuality, contact, and sexual arousal – that directly contrasts the aseptic outside world of the pandemic. Within and against the crisis, the pleasure of the unforgetful queers constitutes a critique against all forms of authoritarianism and subjugation.

In a film that is full of hard cuts and cutting on action, dissolves are employed sparingly to indicate the passage of time, reverie, or change of place, all of which are relatively common uses of this type of transition (Cutting/Brunick/Delong 2011). Only once and at the end of *Três tigres tristes* does a dissolve allude to the process of remembering, which seems particularly important for a film that deals with forgetfulness. Jonata has an appointment at the hospital to find out the results of his HIV treatment. »HIV has forgotten you«, announces the doctor. »Your viral load is undetectable now, which means you can no longer transmit the virus« (01:18:33-01:18:42). The doctor then writes him a receipt, on which she has drawn little fish. »I like shoals. They are like one single organism« (01:19:21-01:19:25), says the doctor and shows him her drawing book, full of colorful shoals of fish. The shot transitions with a hard cut to Isabella and Pedro waiting outside the medical center. Excited to see their friend, they ask Jonata how it went. He looks perplexed: he does not remember anything about the appointment. The virus has apparently affected his memory again. Then Pedro and Bella, decidedly, remind him exactly what had happened: that the doctor said his HIV is untransmittable and that she showed him her kaleidoscopic shoals of fish. »And when you were leaving, she said...« Jonata's close-up dissolves into one of the doctor's drawings: »Shoals never collide, unlike humans, who are always bumping into one another« (01:20:20-01:20:27). »Wait, how do you know this?« Jonata asks Pedro off-camera. After the dissolve, the drawings of the little fish transition again with a hard cut to a medium-wide shot of the three friends in the street, where Isabella and Pedro say goodbye to Jonata, who in the next shot walks away among other passers-by.

The dissolve suggests that the memory of the fish drawings (and of the fact that his viral load is no longer detectable) returned in Jonata's mind by way of his friends' reminder. This seems practically impossible: Pedro was not physically present at the meeting of his friend with the doctor. Then how did he know what happened? The punctuation of the film provides once again a possible answer. The dissolve and the hard cuts between shots of the friends and the shoals of fish create an analogy of queer sociality. Jonata, Pedro, and Bella are like fish in a shoal, having the ability to behave as if they were one single organism, albeit made of many different parts. This organism might share not only movements but also recollections. Their »swarming shareability« is a way of »being together as ›an apartness together‹« (Ruiz/Vourloumis 2021: 30–31). In the words of José Esteban Muñoz, »feeling Brown is feeling together in difference. Feeling Brown is an ›apartness together‹ through sharing the status of being a problem« (Muñoz 2007: 444).[9] The protagonists of *Três tigres tristes*, being a problem in Bolsonaro's Brazil, are feeling Brown.

Friendship as it manifests in this film scene, also points towards an interdependent form of relationality that preserves collective memory. Forgetfulness can be worked out in community, like in a shoal of fish. There is a popular saying in Brazil, that people have short memory when it comes to politics. They forget, for example, what the previous government did when the new government comes to power. Or they forget the consequences of the dictatorship and colonialism. *Três tigres tristes* comments on and subverts this common misconception. Even though the virus affects people's memory, and most characters in the film have moments where they look confused, lost, as if they don't know what they are supposed to be doing, Pedro, Isabella, Jonata, and their chosen family make constant efforts to remember, and remind those who do not.

Falling over the busy street that Jonata took, the credits of the film are accompanied by a song that resembles a catchy children's tune.[10] The melody changes from happy to sad, from a major to a minor key, and back again. When it is sad, the lyrics talk about a lonely tiger in crisis: »A tiger wanted to

---

9 The notion of ›being a problem‹ was approached by W.E.B. Du Bois in the first two pages of his seminal book *The Soul of Black Folk*, which José Esteban Muñoz expands on. In Muñoz's words, »feeling like a problem is about feeling apart, feeling separate. However, in the spirit of African American studies' interest in the nature of double-voiced discourse and Du Bois' own theory on double consciousness, one can also ruminate on the ways in which feeling like a problem is a mode of minoritarian recognition« (Muñoz 2007: 441).

10 The song, called »Pratos de trigo«, was composed for the film and sung by Cida Moreira, Nash Laila, Caetano Gotardo, Gustavo Vinagre, and Marco Dutra. The music was written by Marco Dutra and the lyrics by Caetano Gotardo.

dance the mambo/A tiger wanted to bark/A tiger wanted no Where and no When/To be, yes, but no longer to exist« (01:21:57-01:22:10). But when it shifts to major, the tigers are three, and together they lovingly manage their troubles in the world (01:22:15-01:23:01):

> Three tidy tigers don't know where to cry
> Three tidy tigers don't know when to fly
> Three tidy tigers tell a pretty joke
> So as not to choke – Woke
> [...]
> Three tidy tigers walk right into you
> Three tidy tigers play with kangaroos
> Three tidy tigers buy seven bookshelves
> To read themselves – Elves
> So many friends
> Weeping and woe
> Big fields of fig
> Buildings and clothes
> Lovely wheat dishes
> Three lovely beasts
> That finally dream
> That finally dream – Scream

6 Epilogue

The three films that were analyzed in this chapter exemplify ways in which queer feminist politics spill into filmmaking and give form to love as crisis, to love (whether expressed as companionship, romance, or friendship) that challenges the prevailing modes of relating and proposes alternative attachments to the present world. In *A felicidade delas*, feminist solidarity transmutes into queer eroticism that dissolves into water engulfing an entire city. In *Trenque Lauquen*, a couple involving three women create a family whose love is not based on fusion but on difference. In *Três tigres tristes*, a group of queer friends fights against institutional amnesia by living (in) each other's memories. In every one of these works, an element of cinematic punctuation – the dissolve – has given form to the transition from one state of love to another, proposing expanded queer feminist relationality as a tactic for survival within and despite of crisis.

Fig. 4: Film still of A felicidade delas (2019) by Carol Rodrigues.

In *A felicidade delas*, when Tamirys and Ivy explore the abandoned building, they stop for a moment to look at the graffiti that Tamirys had just painted, of two black women making out (Fig. 4). They move away from the wall to look at the work and then at each other. When a police siren is heard, they run out of the frame and make out in the following shot. Tamirys and Ivy are spectators of themselves, and we are spectators of themselves being spectators. After looking at the graffiti, i.e. the image of the rupture that their love is making in space, they make it happen, despite the lingering threat. The filmmaker seems to be inviting us here to turn from spectators to a counterpublic: a queer feminist flood.

Bibliography

Agence France-Presse (2020): »Brazilian Film Booming, but Vulnerable under Bolsonaro«, in: France 24 08.02.2020, https://www.france24.com/en/20200208-brazilian-film-booming-but-vulnerable-under-bolsonaro [11.06.2024].

Athanasiou, Athena (2021): »Taking Sides as Taking a Stand: Critical Conditions of Co-Implication and Im-Possibility«, in: Elke Bippus/Anne Ganzert/Isabell Otto (eds.), Taking Sides: Theories, Practices, and Cultures of Participation in Dissent, Bielefeld: transcript Verlag, pp. 159–169.

Badiou, Alain (2012 [2009]): In Praise of Love, London: Serpent's Tail.

Bárcenas, Karina (2020): »*#EleNão* (Él no). Tecnofeminismo interseccional en Brasil frente al ascenso del neoconservadurismo evangélico y el posfascismo«, in: Alteridades 39.59, pp. 43–56.

Bayly, Jaime (2023): »Entrevista a Javier Milei: un hombre y un elefante«, in: La Nación 12.11.2023, https://www.lanacion.com.ar/opinion/un-hombre-y-un-elefante-nid12112023/ [11.06.2024].

Berlant, Lauren/Warner, Michael (1998): »Sex in Public«, in: Critical Inquiry 24.2, pp. 547–566.

Bilmayer, S. Pearl/Trentin, Filippo/Xiang, Zairong (2019): »Introduction. The Ontology of the Couple«, in: GLQ 25.2, pp. 217–221. doi: 10.1215/10642684-7367703

Brandão, Alessandra/Marconi, Dieison (2020): Cinemas e audiovisualidades queer/kuir/cuir no Brasil e na América Latina, in: Rebeca – Revista brasileira de estudos de cinema e audiovisual 9.2, pp. 13–19.

Brandão, Alessandra/Marconi, Dieison (2021): Cinemas e audiovisualidades queer/kuir/cuir no Brasil e na América Latina (Special Issue), in: Rebeca – Revista brasileira de estudos de cinema e audiovisual 10.1, pp. 13–15.

Butler, Judith (2004): »What is Critique? An Essay on Foucault's Virtue«, in: Sarah Salih (ed.), The Judith Butler Reader, Oxford: Blackwell, pp. 302–322.

Catanzaro, Gisela/Stegmayer, María (2019): »The New Neoliberal Turn in Argentina«, in: Critical Times 2.1, pp. 133–158.

Centenera, Mar (2023): »Argentina: la crisis eterna«, in: El País 09.09.2023, https://elpais.com/economia/negocios/2023-09-09/argentina-la-crisis-eterna.html [11.06.2024].

Centenera, Mar (2024): »›Las mataron por lesbianas‹. El asesinato de tres mujeres quemadas vivas conmociona a Argentina«, in: El País 15.05.2024, https://elpais.com/argentina/2024-05-15/las-mataron-por-lesbianas-el-asesinato-de-tres-mujeres-quemadas-vivas-conmociona-a-argentina.html [11.06.2024].

Cutting, James E./Brunick, Kaitlin L./Delong, Jordan E. (2011): »The Changing Poetics of the Dissolve in Hollywood Film«, in: Empirical Studies of the Arts 29.2, pp. 149–169.

De Almeida, Ronaldo (2020): »The Broken Wave. Evangelicals and Conservatism in the Brazilian Crisis«, in: HAU. Journal of Ethnographic Theory 10.1, pp. 32–40.

Fink, Bruce (2016): Lacan on Love. An Exploration of Lacan's Seminar VIII, Transference, Cambridge and Malden: Polity Press.

Foucault, Michel (1997): »What is Critique?«, in: Sylvère Lotringer/Lysa Hochroth (eds.), The Politics of Truth, New York: Semiotext(e), pp. 23–82.

Gago, Verónica (2019): La potencia feminista o el deseo de cambiarlo todo, Madrid: Traficantes de Sueños.

Gago, Verónica/Ni Una Menos (2018): »Critical Times/La tierra tiembla«, in: Critical Times 1.1, pp. 178–197.

Galarraga Gortázar, Naiara (2024): »Bolsonaro lidera una gran marcha y proclama su inocencia ante la investigación por urdir un golpe«, in: El País 25.02.2024, https://elpais.com/america/2024-02-25/bolsonaro-lidera-una-gran-marcha-y-proclama-su-inocencia-ante-la-investigacion-por-urdir-un-golpe.html [11.06.2024].

Haraway, Donna (2016): Staying with the Trouble. Making Kin in the Chthulucene, Durham and London: Duke University Press.

Hatzikidi, Katerina/Dullo, Eduardo (2021): A Horizon of (Im)possibilities. A Chronicle of Brazil's Conservative Turn, London: University of London Press.

Jaureguy, Martina (2024): »Gender policy in the Milei Era. Five Months of Dismantlement and Misogynistic Attacks«, in: Buenos Aires Herald 03.06.2024, https://buenosairesherald.com/society/social-movements/gender-policy-in-the-milei-era-five-months-of-dismantlement-and-misogynistic-attacks [11.06.2024].

Jenzen, Olu (2013): »Revolting Doubles. Radical Narcissism and the Trope of Lesbian Doppelgangers«, in: Journal of Lesbian Studies 17.3/4, pp. 344–364.

Lacan, Jacques (1998 [1975]): The Seminar of Jacques Lacan (vol. 20): On Feminine Sexuality, the Limits of Love and Knowledge (1972–1973), New York: Norton.

Levinas, Emmanuel (1969 [1961]): Totality and Infinity. An Essay on Exteriority, Pittsburgh: Duquesne University Press.

Levinas, Emmanuel (1987 [1947]): Time and the Other, Pittsburgh: Duquesne University Press.

Lindgren, Ernest (1963): The Art of the Film, New York: Macmillan.

Macón, Cecilia/Solana, Mariela/Vacarezza, Nayla Luz (2021): »Introduction. Feeling Our Way Through Latin America«, in: Cecilia Macón/Mariela Solana/Nayla Luz Vacarezza (eds.), Affect, Gender and Sexuality in Latin America, Cham: Palgrave Macmillan, pp. 1–15.

Mendes, Vinícius (2020): Comment on *A felicidade delas*«, in: MUBI, https://mubi.com/en/films/their-happiness/ratings [11.06.2024].

Muñoz, José Esteban (2007): »›Chico, what does it feel like to be a problem?‹. The Transmission of Brownness«, in: Juan Flores/Renato Rosaldo (eds.), A Companion to Latina/o Studies, Malden: Blackwell Publishing, pp. 441–451.

Nunes, Rodrigo (2020): »Of what is Bolsonaro the name?«, in: Radical Philosophy 209, pp. 3–14.

Olmos, Clara (2024): »La ›motosierra‹ de Javier Milei se ensaña con los enfermos graves«, in: El País 05.05.2024, https://elpais.com/argentina/2024-05-05/la-motosierra-de-javier-milei-se-ensana-con-los-enfermos-graves.html [11.06.2024].

Palmeiro, Cecilia (2018): »The Latin American Green Tide. Desire and Feminist Transversality«, in: Journal of Latin American Cultural Studies 06.08.20218, https://medium.com/@j_lacs/the-latin-american-green-tide-desire-and-feminist-transversality-56e4b85856b2 [11.06.2024].

Rey, Débora (2024): »In progressive Argentina, the LGBTQ+ community says President Milei has turned back the clock«, in: The Washington Times, 12.05.2024, https://www.washingtontimes.com/news/2024/may/12/lgbtq-community-in-argentina-says-president-javier/ [11.06.2024].

Rosenberg, Jordana/Villarejo, Amy (2011): »Queerness, Norms, Utopia«, in: GLQ 18.1, pp. 1–18.

Ruiz, Sandra/Vourloumis, Hypatia (2021): Formless Formation. Vignettes for the End of this World, Colchester/New York/Port Watson: Minor Compositions.

S.a. (2024): »›Hasta nuevo aviso‹. Desde este lunes el INCAA cerrará sus puertas«, in: Página 12 22.04.2024, https://www.pagina12.com.ar/730660-hasta-nuevo-aviso-desde-este-lunes-el-incaa-cerrara-sus-puer [11.06.2024].

Sabsay, Leticia (2020): »The Political Aesthetics of Vulnerability and the Feminist Revolt«, in: Critical Times 3.2, pp. 179–199.

Santoro, Sonia/Carbajal, Mariana (2023): »Una referente de Milei comparó el matrimonio igualitario con tener piojos«, in: Página 12 04.11.2023, November 4, https://www.pagina12.com.ar/613044-una-referente-de-milei-comparo-el-matrimonio-igualitario-con [11.06.2024].

Scholz, Annette/Álvarez, Marta (2018): Cineastas emergentes. Mujeres en el cine del siglo XXI, Madrid: Iberoamericana.

Schoonover, Karl/Galt, Rosalind (2016): Queer Cinema in the World, Durham and London: Duke University Press.

Wilson, Kristi M./Garavelli, Clara (2021): Gender, Sexuality, Film, and Media in Latin America: Challenging Representation and Structures, in: Latin American Perspectives 48.2.

Zaitchik, Alexander (2019): »Rainforest on fire«, in: The Intercept 06.07.2019, https://theintercept.com/2019/07/06/brazil-amazon-rainforest-indigenous-conservation-agribusiness-ranching/ [11.06.2024].

Filmography

A Felicidade Delas (2019) (Brazil, D: Carol Rodrigues).
Trenque Lauquen (2022) (Argentina, D: Laura Citarella).
Três Tigres Tristes (2022) (Brazil, D: Gustavo Vinagre).

»You Cannot Confine Imagination«
Contemporary Corona Fictions Embracing Lesbian Relationships

Julia Obermayr

1 Introduction

The cultural representation of social relations in film, TV, and web series, etc. has shifted significantly during the Covid-19 pandemic, frequently addressing physical distancing and other containment measures. Although far from being a pandemic-specific issue, the pandemic also aggravated already problematic, unsafe, or even dangerous living situations, particularly for vulnerable minorities and women living in circumstances of domestic violence. The concepts used to analyze lesbian[1] relationship representations in contemporary Corona Fictions are based on my model to approach *Female Identities in Lesbian Web Series* (Obermayr 2020), including lesbian community building and our Corona Fictions[2] approach to tackle pandemic particularities. Hereby, understanding the importance of how storytelling across media – particularly online – functions and how it plays into the ›pandemic circuit‹[3] (cf. Research Group Pan-

---

[1] The term lesbian refers to »any person who identifies herself as a lesbian, bisexual, butch, femme, androgyn, dyke, trans, queer or does not wish to be identified at all with any of the existing terms« (Curzi 2013: 5).

[2] Acknowledgments: This research was funded by the Austrian Science Fund (FWF): P 34571-G; Project team: Julia Obermayr/Yvonne Völkl/Elisabeth Hobisch. Website: www.tugraz.at/projekte/cofi, DOI: 10.55776/P34571.

[3] »With the emergence of social media and numerous streaming platforms for audiovisual content (Facebook 2004; YouTube 2005; Twitter 2006), both the pace and the multi-faceted formats have transformed consumer behaviour as well […]. [S]ocial media not only function as immediate news sources but also encourage […] narratives […] often being created [collectively] throughout the digital world, spreading across different media formats and creating hybridity by merging video, image, text, and audio

demic Fictions 2020: 322–325) is crucial. Additionally, while integrating the pandemic perspective, the focus hereby lies particularly on the portrayal of lesbian relationships, their codes, narratives, and claiming their bodies and space in contemporary cultural productions. The prevailing lack of female (and in particular LGBT+ related) relationship representations in a still heavily male dominated film and media industry on a global scale is shifting. Making use of the new technologies available, oftentimes more easily accessible,[4] and for the most part less restricted by heteronormative codes, also allows for an easier audience migration (and consequently transnational community building) regarding lesbian audiovisual content.

This combination of cultural, film, and media studies (encoding and decoding lesbian representations) merging with LGBT+[5] studies offers a useful interdisciplinary theoretical lens as well as a versatile methodological approach to identify aspects of transforming relationship portrayals represented in the Corona Fictions investigated. Based on the example of four selected hispanophone Corona Fictions from Spain and Chile called *En Casa* (2020), *Besos Al Aire* (2021), as well as, *Edificio Corona* (2021) and *Demente* (2021), this article aims to investigate in what ways they portray lesbian characters and their relationships and shifts in relationship constellations during the Covid-19 pandemic.

    content with mutual references (cf. Nünning/Rupp 2012: 15), ›transmedia storytelling‹ (cf. Jenkins 2007/2012) encourages not only a way of constructing content, but also becomes a multi-modal approach for analyzing the current Corona Fictions [...]. Due to the interconnectedness of multiple media sources and the contemporary productivity of the pandemic discourse, it is imperative to take into account a multitude of factors in order to understand and analyze the ›pandemic circuit‹ [...]. [T]he pandemic circuit describes this specific dynamic of the hermeneutic process of the pandemic meta-narrative between (early) pandemic fiction and Corona Fictions as well as media and political discourse (related to SARSCoV-2 pandemic) which in turn change the reception of previous pandemic texts« (Research Group Pandemic Fictions 2020: 323–324).

4   Nowadays, many former restrictions on TV productions and film have become less relevant (or even irrelevant), e.g., the time of broadcasting/streaming. While lesbian content on TV, for example, had to be broadcast outside of daytime television, mostly late at night, online streaming platforms accessible according to the audiences' liking have rendered time-restricted viewing somewhat outdated.

5   Due to a lens of transnational/transcultural communities rather than of intersectionality and its axes of differences regarding individual identity formation, the chosen wording (LGBT+ instead of only queer) is consistent with earlier research on Lesbian Web Series (for more details, see Obermayr 2020: 18–19).

2 Lesbian Representations and the Covid-19 Pandemic

Lesbian narratives and relationship representations, no matter the genre or format, have faced omission and censorship[6] throughout history, across cultures and media, hence the issue is twofold: on the one hand, in more traditional media, such as films and TV series, societal norms strongly translate into more restrictive[7] visual practices regarding minority identities, particularly female ones, while the depiction of couples outside of heteronormative constellations in itself holds meaning. On the other hand, LGBT+ communities are used as scapegoats for disasters.

Contrary to former censorship, today the question of LGBT+ visibility in Spanish cinema, as can be observed in numerous other countries such as Chile, is closely tied to socio-political shifts in recognizing LGBT+ identities and their relationships while simultaneously stopping sanctions on openly living or representing LGBT+ characters on-screen. In Spain, Franco's death marked this significant shift (cf. Melero 2010: 10) during the »transición« (the Spanish transition period) towards a more open, inclusive cinematic representation. However, early post-dictatorship representations predominately focused on depictions of the »erotic lesbian«. As Melero (2013/2024: 122) points out, the »list of Spanish erotic films [...] that presented lesbian relationships as a main element of their plot is long and reveals exactly how prolific was the figure of the lesbian«. Nevertheless, depicting couples and family constellations was far from common, as marriage equality was only introduced in 2005, strongly marking another shift towards more LGBT+ representations on the Spanish peninsula. Legal and social change being closely connected, it is no coincidence, for example, that marriage equality in Chile was not introduced until recently, in 2021, and that lesbian couples of different ages were shown on-screen in the series *Edificio Corona* and *Demente*, with one of them even getting married in the end. However, it must be taken into consideration that early lesbian depictions historically originate in strongly encoded cinematographic aesthetics and story-

---

6   Demonstrated, e.g., by the data collected from the Lesbian Legacy Collection in 2013 at the One Institute (former One National Gay & Lesbian Archives) in Los Angeles, the largest international LGBT+ repository (cf. Obermayr 2020).
7   In the US, besides state censorship laws, e.g., the Motion Picture Production Code of 1930 strictly »banned all mention of homosexuality in film for over 30 years« until the era of »1960s-1970s films which treated gayness as a sickness or a perversion« before »[t]he code was abolished entirely in 1968« (Innes 1995:13).

telling, often disguising lesbianism as friendly »female bonding« in the past (cf. White 1999: xxii). Besides (indirectly) questioning heteronormative relationship constellations, recent lesbian narratives in both literature and in the film and media industry increasingly embrace dynamic, complex, story-driving female protagonists, offering women a strong voice. Hence, female agency regardless of orientation/identity nowadays often replaces the former theme of female passivity.

Throughout history, crises, natural disasters, and other man-made calamities have been previously blamed on LGBT+ people (cf. UN Human Rights Office 2020/2023). Thus, assuming to gain more impact and evoke social change by educating people in the media industries about the LGBT+ community, in 1985 a group of writers founded the Gay & Lesbian Alliance Against Defamation (GLAAD) in New York, outraged by the defamatory AIDS headlines in the New York Post (cf. Innes 1995: 53). Serving as a scapegoat, LGBT+ communities have faced »stigmatization, discrimination, hate speech and attacks [...] and there are scattered reports of this happening in the context of the COVID-19 pandemic« (UN Human Rights Office 2020/2023). In this sense, the Covid-19 pandemic may be a trigger, particularly for LGBT+ communities, and is closely connected to the AIDS[8] crisis, as Jonathon Catlin (cf. 2021) proves from a memory studies perspective. Searching for terms such as »LGBT«, »queer«, or »lesbiana« in the Covid-19 report published by the Chilean government (cf. Ministerio de Salud Chile 2022/2023), however, yielded no results. Therefore, even in the process of publishing, there was no reflection on minorities and their diverse needs during a health crisis in order to include insights into this report. Consequently, LGBT+ organizations in numerous countries conduct their own investigations, for example, in the US, the Movement Advancement Project (2020–23/2024) published a *Covid Pulse Survey Report Series: 2020-2023*, pointing out the effects the pandemic had and is still having, for example, on LGBT+ organizations and funding, etc.

Both health crises have (initially) demonstrated that minorities are not only exposed to a higher risk in terms of their health (e.g., living conditions, dis-

---

8   »AIDS had a massive impact on gay life and, consequently, on queer popular culture and on how it is produced and interpreted. [...] The very name initially given to the virus, GRID (Gay related Immunodeficiency), points to the first definition of the virus as a new so-called gay plague« (Prono 2008: 3). »Novels, memoirs, testimonies, poems, and essays about AIDS and living with the virus soon became central to gay and lesbian literature« (ibid.: 6).

crimination in health care keeping people from actively seeking help etc.) but even more so that they face the blame for a spreading illness while rarely being considered in pandemic health measures. However, as Spain, for example, has proven during the Covid-19 pandemic, change is possible through awareness and the State being willing to collect data and the needs of its people (cf. United Nations (2020/2024: 14). Hence, I argue that pandemic and LGBT+ relationship references in Corona Fictions[9] must be seen as interrelated, not treated as audiovisual representations of separately occurring societal phenomena.

3 »You Cannot Confine Imagination«: Contemporary Corona Fictions Embracing Lesbian Relationships

Cultural productions in all their multimodal and cultural diversity hold the power to profoundly move their audiences. In this context, distinguishing between the identification of a spectator with a certain character and a spectator having desire for a certain character is essential to the functioning of cinematic spectatorship (cf. White 1999: xvi). The relation between the filmmaker and the spectator functions as a tacit »contract« for both parties, generating a basic emotional tension build-up while watching a film: the »human factor« (cf. Zag ²2010: 14). Hence, comprehending what I call the »lesbian code« (cf. Obermayr 2020: 113–141) requires a functioning human factor to be able to easily decode lesbian relationships even in censored or restricted depictions. Lesbian spectatorship, relationship representations, and national – as well as – transnational community building[10] (online and beyond the screen) are, therefore, strongly interconnected. More than a decade ago, the – what is now called – GLAAD media institute still demanded more accurate, positive, and authentic lesbian images within the media landscape (cf. GLAAD 2012). Corona Fictions create new, authentic role models for contemporary lesbian, but also female communities

---

9   »Corona Fictions [...] emerge during the COVID-19 pandemic and negotiate the latter in their stories, continuing in parts the tradition of creating pandemic fiction. We argue that Corona Fictions reactivate certain structures and elements in the form of metanarratives. The pandemic produced collective experiences which can be understood as transnational and transcultural phenomena translating into the crisis while simultaneously tapping into existing pandemic narratives« (Obermayr/Völkl 2022: 4).

10 Due to the scope of this article, the aspect of lesbian transnational community building in Corona Fictions is not included in the analysis but may present a valid perspective in regard to the Covid-19 pandemic in the near future.

in general, promoting female agency and a female-dictated gaze. The benefits of visual analysis not only become evident due to this multimodal genre but, moreover, it provides additional insight into the nature of female characters and applied subcultural visual codes on-screen. Today, amongst a multitude of representations in other genres and formats, the feminine stereotype of the »lipstick lesbian« seemingly dominates in the Corona Fictions investigated. As was demonstrated concerning other genres such as web series, diversity in lesbian identity and relationship representations commonly emerges over time. This is also to be expected within the genre of Corona Fictions in the near future as they primarily target a wider – not solely LGBT+ – audience.

Before giving a brief introduction on the necessary theoretical and methodological framework of analyzing (audio)visual aesthetics of lesbian identity and relationship representations in Romance languages, we will first discuss the following proposed hypothesis and questions for this article: It is assumed that subculturally typical metaphors (e.g., the mirror) and tropes (e.g., lesbian death) or the practice of subtexting (using the lesbian code) are still used as narrative strategies for depicting lesbian relationships and matters of identity. This paper asks how lesbian characters and their relationships are represented and narrated, as well as how the Covid-19 pandemic is depicted (e.g., physical distancing and bodily practices; probable changes in storytelling/visual aesthetics due to changes in production processes,[11] etc.) in the recently emerging genre of Corona Fictions.

In the context of lesbian subcultures, it can be argued that Corona Fictions, their narratives, and especially their participatory culture (cf. Jenkins 2009), similarly to film, may also be considered »not so much a separate discipline as a set of distinct social practices, a set of languages, and an industry« (Turner 1988/2006: 60–61). Thus, from a cultural studies perspective with Stuart Hall's (1997) circuit of culture and Ansgar Nünning (2012) and his colleagues' volume on narrative Internet genres in mind, the methodological approach must be adjusted accordingly. Given the online nature of most audiovisual Corona Fictions being streamed (legally or »semi-legally«, oftentimes tolerated to reach a larger international audience), the (re)shaping and transformation of LGBT+ relationship depictions in recent years are not exclusively linked to pandemic

---

11 Changes in production processes (mainly affecting work on set) refer here to health measures introduced due to the Covid-19 pandemic in the respective countries. These may also affect relationship representations due to changes in physical proximity.

restrictions but strongly related to technological advances. These transformations in terms of format, medium, and genre are also closely connected to the emergence of new ways of categorizing (or refusing to categorize) concepts surrounding sexuality and identity, relationship constellations, their legal restrictions and social norms.

Regarding the methodological approach and cinematographic techniques suited to analyze the representation of lesbian relationships in Corona Fictions, this article applies a combination of the following: a) character analyses in film (cf. Eder 2008; cf. Faulstich 2002); b) aspects of focalization[12] (cf. Gauderault/Jost 1990); and the above-mentioned c) lesbian code (especially the lesbian body in the mirror; cf. Obermayr 2020) which has already integrated a).

In short, this investigation into lesbian couples in Covid-19 related audiovisuals aims at decoding not only pandemic references but primarily (audio)visual practices (e.g., subtexting and encoding strategies of mirror narratives,[13] lesbian gaze[14] etc.; cf. Obermayr 2020) produced and used by creators of lesbian content.

The visual aesthetics and practices of lesbian narratives across different media are socio-historically strongly rooted in encoding processes. Decoding these subculturally relevant symbols and artefacts, the »lesbian code« may in this respect also be identified in Corona Fictions. It includes the aspect of visibility as identity stabilization process, elaborates on the importance of opposing the lesbian death trope, as well as explains the lesbian codes of identification, in particular the on-screen representation of lesbian bodies in the mirror (cf. Obermayr 2020: 113–141). The analyzed corpus presented – *En Casa, Besos Al Aire, Edificio Corona,* and *Demente* – does not include any typical lesbian death trope (cf. Obermayr 2020: 122f.) for women loving women even though

---

12   What or how much information is known/restricted by the characters and/or the audience within a storyline.
13   See chapter 3.2.1.
14   In short, the »lesbian gaze« may be understood as an encoding strategy as well as a socio-cultural practice, directing the spectator's gaze from a lesbian point of view. Thus, it embodies a rupturing of the (heteronormative) male gaze and its subject-object assumptions, shifting the dynamics of looking to a higher female agency while also driving forward female-based storytelling. Determining the desired object within the frame as well as the way of looking, women in this respect simultaneously represent subject and object. Commonly, the active gaze is initially understood as male (camera, diegetic gaze, spectator; cf. Hayward 2013: 175). For a more in-depth definition of the »lesbian gaze« see chapter 6.1 in Obermayr (2020: 192f.).

in episode 100 of *Edificio Corona* Rubí has a severe car accident that toys with this trope. Subculturally typical subtexting in terms of applying the lesbian code does, however, take place regarding the depiction of relationships and identity formation. In all above-mentioned early Corona Fictions, one of the women falling in love with another woman is (or recently was) in a relationship with a man. Twice, the former relationship with men includes domestic violence (both verbal and physical abuse) by men towards women and strongly contrasts the relationship with a woman later on (see *Besos Al Aire* and *Demente*). Furthermore, the female characters mainly adhere to – what may traditionally be seen as – a rather feminine bodily representation (clothes, haircut etc.), as mentioned earlier. While traditionally solely the »mythic mannish lesbian« allowed for a lesbian character in cinema to become a visible sexual agent (cf. White 1999: 14), depictions of femme-femme relationships nowadays similarly demonstrate the possibility of (sexual and/or relationship) agency, as shown in all corpus series mentioned.

The corpus investigated comprises the four audiovisual Corona Fictions representing lesbian relationships released/streamed between 2020 and 2021: *En Casa*, *Besos Al Aire*, *Edificio Corona*, and *Demente*. All lesbian relationships portrayed in the corpus investigated follow a spectator-oriented focalization (»focalisation spectatorielle«; Gauderault/Jost 1990: 38–43) which allows spectators to have a cognitive advantage regarding the characters so as not to be surprised by certain events. The characterizations (cf. Faulstich 2002: 97ff.) primarily applied include both one of the protagonist itself (from behaviour to clothes etc.) and one through characterization by the narrator/narrative (via camera position, framing, music, etc.). The series differ in the age of actresses/characters (e.g., young women in *Edificio Corona* vs. middle-aged women in *Demente*) and the usage of the lesbian code, for example, mirror narratives regarding themes of domestic violence in *Besos Al Aire* and *Demente*, while *En Casa* mainly underlines aspects of visibility in terms of friendship-relationship boundaries and of female bodies and sexuality (e.g., speaking of orgasms and vulvas). In *Edificio Corona* and *Demente*, depicting a coming out process (in a partially homophobic environment) for at least one character also highlights the importance of the visibility of lesbian relationships. It is worth mentioning that in the series from Spain where marriage equality was introduced almost two decades ago, the coming out narrative emerges merely as an internal subtle process – if at all; whereas in both Chilean series, regardless of age, the coming out process plays an essential role in how and when the relationship moves forward.

3.1 Corpus Introduction

En Casa: Así de fácil[15] (2020) is the last 22-min. episode of five different non-consecutive episodes of a Spanish TV miniseries. It was filmed on a cell phone entirely during the first lockdown in 2020 in Spain before being released by HBO.[16] This Corona Fiction between drama and romantic comedy touches upon love, friendship, female orgasm, and (homo)sexuality. It confronts two friends, Marta (Celia Freijeiro) and Nuria (Julia de Castro), with having to live together during the pandemic since Nuria was left by her boyfriend as the state of emergency (»estado de alarma«) was declared and moved out. During that time, both protagonists become even closer friends and end up discovering a different kind of love for each other. Both actresses also share a strong bond since adolescence in real life, as Celia Freijeiro (Mejia 2020/2023) commented in an interview for Lesbicanarias.

Besos Al Aire[17] (Engl. *Blowing Kisses*, 2021) is a Spanish miniseries of only two 80-min. episodes in the genre of a romantic comedy mainly set in a hospital and in an apartment building. The main storylines evolve around eight love stories during the first lockdown which include one between Nines (María León) and Luisa (Mariam Hernández), mainly in the second part of the series. Initially, Nines is portrayed as a single lesbian mother who takes in her brother during confinement, while Luisa lives in the same building with Raúl, becoming increasingly aggressive towards her due to pandemic restrictions and having to work from home. Unsurprisingly, heteronormative love stories – the one between the male nurse Javi (Paco León) and Dr. Cabanas (Leonor Watling) –

---

15 Written by Paula Ortiz, Celia Freijeiro (playing Marta), Julia de Castro (playing Nuria), and Milena Suárez, who was also responsible for camera and sound. Directed by Paula Ortiz. Production companies: HBO, Caballo Films, and Warner Brothers. When referring to *En Casa* in this article, it only regards this episode.

16 »*En Casa* has been filmed entirely during confinement in the spring of 2020 in Spain, complying with the rules imposed under the state of emergency. The episodes have been filmed without technical equipment on set, relying solely on a cell phone and some props. This episode has been directed entirely by video conference, and surrounded by the actresses who were confined together, with their neighbour and a dog« ([EnC 00:00:07-00:00:23]; translation of this introductory text before the initial scene of the episode by the author).

17 Written by Darío Madrona. Directed by Iñaki Mercero. Produced by Mediaset España and Alea Media and streamed by Disney + via Star.

are set mainly in public spaces such as the hospital, whereas the lesbian relationship is mainly shown in private spaces and rather quickly depicts both women in bed together without a larger emotional build-up within their storyline.

Edificio Corona[18] (2021) is a Chilean telenovela with 120 (about 30-min. long) episodes broadcast and streamed on Mega, telling various love stories, one of them being a lesbian one called »Rubirena«. Macarena (Hitzka Nudelman), called Maca, follows a stereotypical coming out storyline of a young woman living with her younger sister and her homophobic, religious, widowed father in the building »Edificio Corona« (title reference). She falls in love with Rubí (Vivianne Dietz), who lives in the same building's penthouse with her mother and sister – all being very active on social media as influencers (as »Cardenashians«, referencing the US-American Kardashians). Rubirena trended on Twitter, writing history due to their first lesbian kiss on daytime Chilean TV (Span. »horario familiar«). Thus, the social impact of this series on relationships regarding coming out or parents coming to understand their LGBT+ children is evident in messages from the audience to both actresses, as Nudelman stresses in an interview (cf. Meganoticias 2021/2024).

There are numerous production companies that, surprisingly, continued to produce their series (sometimes with pauses due to lockdowns) during the Covid-19 pandemic. One of them that managed not only to cross Latin-American borders but also to reach international audiences,[19] was the couple Flavia (Patricia Rivadeneira) and Javiera (Ingrid Cruz), in short »Flaviera«, in the TV series *Demente*[20] (2021), a telenovela of 140 (30-min. long) episodes from Chile with thriller elements. Her job evolving around the abduction of Flavia's nephew Mateo, female detective Javiera falls in love with Flavia, standing by her, especially when detecting domestic violence between Flavia and her husband. Although not including any overt allusions to the pandemic in the series, the production and storytelling were nevertheless affected by

---

18   Written by Daniella Castagno, Rodrigo Bastidas, Elena Muñoz, Milena Bastidas. Directed by Nicolás Alemparte and Víctor Huerta. Produced by Mega and DDRíos Estudios.
19   Audiences beyond official broadcasting countries emerge often due to fan videos of a favourite lesbian couple in the respective series on platforms such as YouTube or Vimeo.
20   Written by Pablo Illanes, Josefina Fernández, Mauricio López, Simón Soto, and Fernanda Lema. Directed by Patricio González and María Belén Arenas. Produced by Mega and DDRíos Estudios.

pandemic management. Therefore, we define this telenovela on the fringe of Corona Fictions.

3.2 Lesbian Relationship References

Keeping in mind the human factor and participatory culture mentioned earlier, cinematic films, web and television series may not only reflect the status quo during a health crisis but, moreover, offer a different perspective[21] on morals and clichés and reveal prejudices to their audiences through their narratives (cf. Newiak 2020: 20). Regarding audiovisual LGBT+ Corona Fictions this happens twofold: on the one hand, in this particular case via lesbian-related relationship references and, on the other, through direct and indirect pandemic references.

3.2.1 Lesbian Codes in Corona Fictions: Mirror Narratives and Domestic Violence

Early Corona Fictions use the mirror[22] as a central filmic metaphor to indicate change in a certain character and to highlight a shift in identity construction and/or relationship status/constellation. Furthermore, they exercise a »no lesbian erasure« policy, hence banning the lesbian death trope[23] and using visibility as an identity stabilization process. Encoding the mirror with the revelation of »truths« regarding lesbian relationship constellations annihilated the former commonly applied lesbian death trope. The following examples demonstrate how the lesbian codes of identification function using the (for lesbian narratives) typical mirror scenes, in this case, particularly in combination with domestic violence in (former) relationships with men. In *Cinematic Studies* Susan Hayward (2013: 332) argues that »[close-ups] often have a symbolic value.

---

21   »[I]n contrast to the dominating mass media discourse, many artistic expressions focused on elevating the spirits of their audiences, e.g. through uplifting music [videos, hopeful protagonists] or the production of films within the comedy genre to strengthen resilience and support social cohesion [...]« (Obermayr 2023: 285).
22   Historical, psychological, and cinematographic details of the mirror in the context of lesbian narratives, see chap. 4.3.2. and 5.3 in Obermayr 2020.
23   »Woman becomes other or object to the male's subject – she is defined in relation to his centrality [...]. As such, she is fixed as an object of his desire, but an object whose sexuality is also perceived by him as dangerous – and therefore to be punished or contained (through death – or its equivalent – or marriage, respectively)« (Hayward 2013: 328). More details on the lesbian death trope see chapter 4.2 in Obermayr 2020: 122–123.

[...] [A] character looking at their reflection in a mirror or in the water can have connotations of duplicity (what we see is not true) or death«. This not only affects sexual orientation and coming out processes but, moreover, touches upon issues of, for example, domestic violence in (former) relationships with men (in *Besos Al Aire* and *Demente*). According to the UN Human Rights Office (2020/2023), »[d]ue to stay-at-home restrictions, many LGBTI youth are confined in hostile environments with unsupportive family members or co-habitants. This can increase their exposure to violence, as well as their anxiety and depression«. While this is not only true of LGBT+ youth but also of women in general, domestic violence is hereby depicted as male driven, thus strongly contrasting male-female relationships with female-female relationships[24] in the corpus investigated.

In episode 2 of *Besos Al Aire* (2021) shortly before the mirror scene (BAL[25] 2 [00:59:51]), Nines and Luisa are shown painting together (using the colours of the bisexual flag: pink, purple and blue) in the background of an establishing shot inside Nines' living room, pointing towards the shift that is about to come. In front and center of the frame, Nines' daughter and two dogs can be seen, comfortably playing on the floor. On the left side of the chosen framing (Ger. »Cadrage«) the real Spanish president informs the audience about the latest news on the pandemic on TV. Luisa's husband Raúl interrupts this idyllic family scene, confronting Luisa to talk about their relationship in Nines' apartment entrance. He wants his wife to come home after an incident of domestic violence, angrily telling her to look at herself in the mirror, which she does in a (medium) close-up over-the-shoulder shot into the mirror (BAL 2 [01:02:00-01:02:00]). Film aesthetically this underlines the great emotional decision she is facing at that moment. Luisa literally closes the door on him as he walks out, also visually leaving him to himself outside in the hallway, having found a home in Nines' home (BAL 2 [01:02:00-01:02:35]). This mirror sequence indicates Luisa's definitive decision for change and reveals the seriousness of her feelings towards Nines beyond lockdown living situations. As she comes back into the living room, she asks Nines, her daughter, and her brother Nacho if this could really be her new home (BAL 2 [01:03:01-01:03:25]). Nines just

---

24 Contrary to Lesbian Web Series, where domestic violence was depicted between two women in the US-American *Venice the Series* in season 2 episode 12 (2011), also following up the scene with regrets by the abuser depicted in a mirror scene.

25 Abbreviations for the series: BAL (*Besos Al Aire*), EnC (*En Casa*), EC (*Edificio Corona*), DM (*Demente*).

walks up to Luisa to kiss her (BAL 2 [01:03:25-01:03:29]) in a medium close-up but Nines' daughter also quickly enters the frame, positioning herself between them mid-frame, demonstrating a family unit. Both women look at each other, not into the camera, as a male gaze would suggest.

In *Demente* (2021) Flavia lives with her psychopathic husband, who becomes increasingly verbally and physically violent towards her over the course of the 140 episodes. By befriending the lesbian detective Javiera (initially in a seemingly stable relationship with a younger female partner at the time), she is incapable of further ignoring her identity and her feelings for Javiera, who unapologetically supports her in escaping the dangerous situation. The lesbian relationship rather than presented as an alternative to a heteronormative relationship is represented as self-realization (e.g. recognizing one's identity/desires in the mirror). Even though both women in *Demente* (2021) betray their partners in monogamous relationships at the time, they are both portrayed as likeable to the audience and having every right to do so. As Flavia's husband is depicted as gradually more evil throughout the episodes – similarly to Luisa's in *Besos Al Aire* (2021) –, she decides to make a change and leave her husband. In a mirror scene, Flavia takes a long look at herself in the mirror before remembering her and Javiera having sex in her bedroom (DM ep. 55 [00:20:50-00:21:50]) beneath a Christian cross. In another one, before having sex in the closet/dressing room, Javiera is standing right behind her while both look into the mirror (DM ep. 68 [00:14:41-00:14:51]) discussing Flavia's emotional pain being married to her psychopathic husband. Her internalized homophobia due to her religious upbringing contributes to her staying even longer in this dangerous »relationship« as she is convinced that she deserves the »punishment« (abuse).

However, in *En Casa* (2020) and in *Edifico Corona* (2021) mirror scenes may also function as a positive indicator of a change in relationship status, transforming from a close friendship into a relationship of lovers. During a series of jump cuts, Marta can be seen through the reflection in the mirror looking at Nuria during the visually introduced »acceptance« phase[26] (EC ep.5 [00:14:28]) before both are seen spooning on the couch (ibid. [00:14:32]). Contrary to Maca being the first to fall in love, in her mirror scene Rubí initiates chatting via social media (Instagram) to make up with Maca after a fight while their theme song plays in the background, standing in front of a mirror in a

---

26 For more details on pandemic phases correlating with the progression of relationship phases see »Pandemic and Lesbian Relationship References«.

medium close-up (EC ep. 6 [00:21:37-00:22:45]). Both scenes serve as a crucial emotional turning point towards their lesbian relationship later on.

3.2.2 Relationship Visibility: The Lesbian Kiss

Lesbian characters in early Corona Fictions reach a healthy, stable, positive stage of identity and visible[27] relationship representation, contrary to the negative or censored images of the last decades analyzed from material obtained in international LGBT+ archives (cf. Obermayr 2020). However, a butch-femme gap still prevails. Bodily representations still favour femininity – as a Western concept of beauty – in all series investigated for this article compared with more androgynous, non-binary, or masculine depictions.

»You cannot confine imagination« (Span. »La imaginación no se puede confinar«; *En Casa* trailer; Avanza Cine 2020/2024) is true for both lesbian and pandemic narratives, highlighting the importance of visibility in art. What human relationships in non-heteronormative contexts have, from a socio-historical viewpoint, often had to endure in the past (no or restricted physical contact/PDA in public, keeping a certain distance in homophobic environments etc.) had suddenly become a reality for all kinds of human relationships in the numerous countries on lockdowns in spring of 2020 (no touching, physical distancing in public spaces, wearing masks, etc.). Confining the body to private spaces has often been a way to exercise power over minorities in the past on and off-screen, however, the Covid-19 pandemic demonstrated a new level of imposing this on the wider population.

Visibility can be exercised in different ways, however, regarding lesbian relationship depictions, kissing scenes are a popular means of achieving this and also easier to decode for heteronormative audiences. Using a strong lesbian gaze (cf. Obermayr 2020: 192–193), indicated not only by camera movement, framing or shot size but also by the actresses' ways of purposefully looking, also casts a different light on female characters and their bodies. While the male gaze favours showing, for example, two women looking into the camera (representing the male audience), the lesbian gaze uses the camera from the position of an uninvolved observer, for example, the two women look at each other

---

27   Not only within the film and media landscape but also in literary narratives, visible lesbian representations play a significant role. As María Castrejón (cf. 2009: 75–95, cf. 2008: 196–206) debates Concha García's lesbian poetics, she thus points out key aspects which also apply to currently circulating lesbian images in Corona Fictions: visibility, women's desires, and claiming their bodies and space.

instead of directly into the camera or the camera becomes one of the women looking at the other. Additionally, music – functioning as characterization by the narrator/narrative[28] – plays a significant role in *Edificio Corona*. Its theme song for Rubirena's love story »Con la miel en los labios«[29] by the Spanish singer Aitana (2019/2023) frequently plays in the background during Maca and Rubí's scenes – at a particularly high volume during kissing scenes. This song was number one in digital charts and on official selling lists in Spain (cf. Sanchez 2019/2023). Streamed in June 2021 on Chilean TV just at the beginning of Pride month, it was used to reinforce this lesbian relationship and visible kiss between two young women and meant much more to fans and the LGBT+ communities in the hispanophone world and beyond. During daytime television this »visibilidad de todo tipo de relaciones sexo-afectivos« (López 2021/2023) left a noticeable impact that many fans took to social media. At the same time, the Chilean president Sebastián Piñera urged the importance of pushing for marriage equality[30] (cf. ibid.), which finally came to fruition at the end of 2021.

3.3.3 Pandemic and Lesbian Relationship References

Lesbian relationship representations and pandemic references in contemporary Corona Fictions frequently intersect or occur simultaneously. How to portray characters through (private or public) spaces and the human body itself as well as themes of physical proximity or distance are long known strategies to narrate lesbian relationships, even outside of pandemic storylines. For lesbian characters, physical proximity, emotional closeness, and being depicted in mainly private spaces (cf. Obermayr 2020) have long been strongly interconnected, intersecting with aspects of the coming out stage of the story's characters and institutionalized homophobia. Therefore, many pandemic management strategies of physical distancing and protagonists in lockdown confined to their homes are not new social practices in lesbian relationship depictions.

---

28   Ger. »Erzählercharakterisierung« (cf. Faulstich 2002: 97 ff.).
29   Interestingly, this song was chosen for lesbian scenes while at the same time pointing towards homophobia originating in a religious mindset by mentioning keywords such as »pecado« in the lyrics: »Disfrutamos de cada pecado. [...] Nos comimos a bocados. Nos dormimos en los brazos. [...] Me pusiste la luna en las manos. Te gané sin temblar de un asalto. Nos rompimos el alma en pedazos« (Aitana 2019/2023).
30   »On December 9, 2021, the president of Chile signed into law a marriage equality bill that passed in the Senate on December 7 and the lower house on Nov. 23. Same [sic] sex civil unions had been legal since 2015« (Human Rights Campaign Foundation 2023).

Rarely does the private space function as a danger zone in lesbian narratives except for young LGBT+ characters still living with homophobic family members, as is hinted at with Maca in *Edificio Corona* (2021) when she moves out. In all three typical Corona Fictions – *En Casa*, *Besos Al Aire* and *Edificio Corona* – social cohesion is primarily established by the governmentally enforced lockdown situation: all tenants are confined to their apartment and shared spaces within their residence. In all three series, lockdown (in addition to either a breakup or a domestic violence situation, all involving male partners) functions as an initiator of a lesbian relationship.[31]

The depiction of lesbian relationships in the corpus investigated unsurprisingly indicates numerous direct and indirect pandemic references,[32] underlining their classification within the broader corpus of Corona Fictions as a transnational and transcultural phenomenon. These pandemic references must also be mentioned briefly here as they both present tendencies of either a) affecting narrative and/or b) affecting production.[33] On the one hand, *direct pandemic references* mainly concern (audio)visual aesthetics of pandemic symbols (e.g., wearing masks/gloves, disinfecting hands/objects, distance indicators, empty public spaces, people in lockdown/working remotely/on the balcony[34] clapping for essential workers etc.) and other bodily practices (cf. Hobisch/Obermayr/Völkl 2024; e.g. physical distancing, real news snippets

---

31   In *Besos Al Aire* (2021) Nines and Luisa's relationship starts developing only after Luisa experiences domestic violence in her living situation and desperately looks for another, safer place to stay during lockdown. As another neighbour initially takes her in but turns out to be infected with Covid-19 and has to go to the hospital, she is »forced« to turn to Nines, who she does not get along with in the first part of the series due to Nines' risk factor of spreading Covid-19 since she is an essential worker in a supermarket. In *Edificio Corona* (2021) Rubí and Maca have more time to spend at home in the same building and rather than meeting people outside of their residence, they interact more with people within their vicinity, including each other, due to their building being under quarantine.

32   Due to the relationship focus of the article, however, the numerous other pandemic references will not be explored in more detail, unless relevant for the representation of LGBT+ relationships.

33   Although a third category c) regarding airing Corona Fictions in movie theatres or at streaming events in public spaces exists and has been greatly affected by pandemic restrictions, it is not included in this investigation as this would be beyond the scope of this article.

34   For example, in *En Casa* Nuria screams on the balcony »Nos vamos a morir todos […] Ya todo es mentira«; EnC ep. 5 [00:06:23-00:07:23]).

integrated into fictional narratives) commonly subsumed under the term »new normal«, as well as indicators pointing towards illness (particularly coughing and flu like symptoms) or even hospital settings and medical staff in body suits in intensive care (as in, for example, *Besos Al Aire*). PCR inserts, as detected, for example, in *Demente* and *Edificio Corona*, are overt on-screen disclaimers regarding physical proximity, inserting information on the PCR testing status of actors during kissing scenes. *Indirect pandemic references*,[35] on the other hand, comprise a different set of (audio)visual aesthetics while still following the dichotomy of being either a) affecting narrative (changing storylines due, for example, to physical distancing and/or an increased usage of videocalls and visible on-screen messaging) and/or b) affecting production (e.g., changes in production processes such as regular PCR testing on set, for example, on the set of *Demente* etc.).

However similar the tendencies of female relationship representations have been in Corona Fictions, the Covid-19 pandemic has intensified the already existing discrimination and social divide, for example, when health measures introduced in 2020 and onward required physical distancing and other restrictions concerning body politics. The Spanish and Chilean governments seem to have mainly had a heteronormative monogamous relationship or traditional family[36] constellation in mind, which led to difficulties for LGBT+ couples and rainbow families while navigating lockdowns etc. (United Nations 2020/2024). Additionally, »LGBTQ+ people regularly experience discrimination and lack of cultural competence when seeking health care. As a result, many avoid or delay seeking health care even in emergency situations« (Ithaca College Center for LGBT Education, Outreach & Services 2020/2024). Interestingly, most early audiovisual Corona Fictions (besides documentaries) did not focus on illness or death (cf. Hobisch/Obermayr/Völkl 2022: 206) but rather on how to cope with lockdown and its restrictions (cf. ibid. 200). The independent expert in the United Nations report *Protection against violence and*

---

35 Due to the small scope of this paper, the focus lies on direct pandemic references.
36 According to the United Nations (2020/2024), Spain reported that »[t]he existence of diverse family units should be acknowledged, as should the community and social networks that unite LGBT persons. As expressed in one submission [by Asociación Civil Más Igualdad Perú], State support policies are usually designed around a traditional family model that does not necessarily correspond to the reality of LGBT families and the communities from which they get their support and protection«.

discrimination based on sexual orientation and gender identity Victor Madrigal-Borloz (United Nations 2020/2024) stresses that »good practice of inclusion in State response can be attributed to« various factors, one of them being »the building and nurturing of trustworthy relationships between LGBT groups and local governments over time«. This becomes particularly relevant when dealing with »the acute first lockdown shock effect« (Singer/Koop/Godara 2021: 102) at the onset of the pandemic, as presidents, prime ministers, and/or other government officials around the world declared the situation an emergency accompanied by containment measures. Similarly to the pandemic phases of denial, anger, bargaining, depression, and acceptance (cf. Žižek 2020: 47–50), in *En Casa* (2020) the filmmakers also included phases[37] of states of mind to visually separate the different stages of their evolving lockdown experience[38] using a black background and white letters (in keeping with the black-and-white style of this episode as a whole) to introduce each phase. Interestingly, two phases are added: the initial phase of shock (EnC 2020 »1. Shock« [00:01:13]) and the last phase of learning something new (ibid. »7. Nuevo aprendizaje« [00:18:37]). As the lockdown progresses, so does the relationship between Marta and Nuria, demonstrating that the pandemic phases also coincide with the phases of their relationship.

En Casa (2020) demonstrates all the typical pandemic references, beginning, for example, with filmic paratext indicating the lockdown (Span. »confinamiento« with the Spanish president's speech declaring an »estado de emergencia« (EnC ep. 5 [00:00:25-00:00:52]) accompanied by cheerful background music that detracts from the seriousness. Nuria enters the episode in medias res, telling Marta in tears that her boyfriend left her and she has nowhere to live, so she stays with Marta and her dog. The series continues by showing the obligatory transformation of bodily practices such as washing or disinfecting the hands (cf. EnC ep. 5 [00:01:32–00:01.57]) or putting on slippers shown in a close-up on the characters' feet (EnC ep. 5 [00:01:32] »ponte las zapatillas«) as a »ritual of entry« (Hobisch/Obermayr/Völkl 2024), wearing a

---

37 (EnC 2020 »2. Negación« [00:01:58]; »3. Ira« [00:07:24]; »4. Negocicación« [00:10:11]; »5. Depresión« [00:12:29]; »6. Aceptación« [00:13:55]).
38 Slovenian philosopher and psychoanalyst Slavoj Žižek (2020) points out five phases of a pandemic in his book *Pandemic! Covid-19 Shakes the World*. Based on Elisabeth Kübler-Ross' five phases of how people confront terminal illness and their own mortality (cf. Žižek 2020: 47–50), Žižek similarly observes these phases when a society deals with a traumatic rupture such as the Covid-19 pandemic.

mask, and – in the case of Spain – also putting on gloves when walking the dog (EnC ep. 5 [00:08:08-00:08:32]) or leaving the house to shop (EnC ep. 5 [00:04:50-00:05:20]). *En Casa* (2020) uses song lyrics to point out or sum up the underlying feelings of the characters in certain scenes, for example, during grocery shopping one of Julia de Castro's own songs plays in the background, starting with »El miedo paralize«. The female body and female sexuality play a significant role throughout the episode, for example, when three minutes into the episode, Nuria mentions her sexual problems with her ex boyfriend, whereas in a dialog with Nuria, Marta on the other hand indicates that she has seen more »coños« than Nuria (cf. EnC ep. 5 [00:03:15-00:04:19]). Furthermore, while both women talk via videocall with another female friend, song lyrics can be heard that point towards »un orgasmo con amor« (EnC ep.5 [00:14:12]). At the end of the episode, as both women end up in bed together, a title reference is established as Nuria comments on her first orgasm with a woman, indicating how easy it was (»Así de fácil.«; EnC ep. 5 [00:19:52]) compared to her former relationship with her male partner. Marta responds with a content face and moist lips as she repeats the title reference (EnC ep. 5 [00:20:05]).

Due to similar but varying lockdown rules and general pandemic management in Spain and Chile, the containment measures and body politics implemented during the Covid-19 pandemic arguably influenced the dynamics of production on set (e.g. wearing masks, physical distancing, PCR testing). Interestingly, series that had started production processes as early as 2019, such as the Chilean *Demente*, are now also notably situated on the fringe of Corona Fictions. Initially not intended to include any obvious pandemic references, *Demente* follows a different pattern. The series breaks the fourth wall by including inserts[39] (positioned as captions/subtitles) indicating regular PCR testing on set. Hereby destroying the fictional illusion between audience and filmmakers/creators, the mention of such testing weighs heavily on the narrated love stories since the captions are particularly inserted and visible to viewers during physically close kissing scenes. The attention is directed towards the inserts rather than towards the kiss between the lesbian couple. Completely deconstructing the fictional romantic scenario for the audience by triggering other (maybe fearful?!) pandemic associations based on pandemic management in reality, the PCR inserts add *Demente* to the list of Corona Fictions. One can only assume that this strategy was chosen since the series was not only produced

---

39 Non-diegetic inserts usually do not form part of the narrative but serve, for example, a commentary purpose (cf. Kinofenster 2023/24).

but broadcast/streamed during the pandemic and there was a need to reassure the audience that the production would take care of health precautions for the actors. While other productions chose to maintain distance and to only record videocalls (for example, the Spanish TV series *Diarios de la cuarentena* 2020) or work with different frames to make their couples look closer but refrain from physical proximity or even touch, Mega decided to take the testing route.

Kissing scenes, thus physical proximity between lesbian characters in both Chilean series, *Edificio Corona* and *Demente* on Mega mention PCR testing via inserts. Hereby, various lesbian kissing scenes break the fourth wall at a crucial moment for the audience to stay within the fictional world and the emotional build-up. Instead, »NUESTROS ACTORES GRABARON ESTA ESCENA CON PCR NEGATIVO AL DÍA« appears inserted during Maca and Rubí's scene (EC ep. 120 [00:12:02]) or while Javiera kisses her (ex)girlfriend in a close-up (DM ep. 11 [06:25:00-07:55:00]). Seemingly depending on the current governmental restrictions in Chile (cf. Ministerio de Salud Chile 2022/2023) at different times of shooting the series, Javiera's medium close-up with her later love interest Flavia, for example, does not show any PCR inserts (DM ep. 44 [00:00:03]) beneath the couple in centre frame.

Unlike the Chilean series, the Spanish *Besos Al Aire* (ep. 2 [01:12:02-01:12:15]) does not use PCR inserts during kissing scenes but points towards the pandemic, for example, by making the characters Nines and Luisa wear masks (amongst many others with masks) before pulling them down to kiss in their medium close-up shot outside in the streets during celebrations of the end of confinement with a »fiesta de desconfinamiento«.

4 Conclusion

This paper investigated the portrayal of lesbian relationships and shifts in their relationship constellations during the Covid-19 pandemic by example of four selected hispanophone Corona Fictions from Spain and Chile – *En Casa* (2020), *Besos Al Aire* (2021), *Edificio Corona* (2021), and *Demente* (2021). The investigation into the representations of lesbian relationships in the new multimodal genre of Corona Fictions touched on numerous academic discourses, thus demanding an interdisciplinary approach. A combination of character analyses in film, aspects of focalization, and the lesbian code (including the lesbian body in the mirror and domestic violence), allowed for greater insight into the intersection of lesbian relationship and pandemic references. Their representations range from coming out narratives portrayed by young women in *Edificio Corona* vs. middle-aged women in *Demente* to the depiction of *En Casa* mainly underlining aspects of visibility in terms of friendship-relationship boundaries and of female bodies and sexuality (e.g., speaking of orgasms and vulvas).

The audiences all enter a dystopian world of mandatory lockdowns, physical distancing, and other restrictions simultaneously with the fictional lesbian characters. Yet, the latter all reclaim their agency throughout the series, emotionally and physically coming close to other characters during confinement as the episode(s) progress(es) – a common process which can also be observed in more heteronormative Corona Fictions (cf. Obermayr 2022: 158–174). In lesbian relationship related Corona Fictions, however, mirror scenes, as initially hypothesized, serve as significant moments of self-realization initiating agency and change towards the formation of positively portrayed lesbian relationships. In the analyzed episode 5 of *En Casa* (2020) the pandemic phases even directly coincide with the transformative relationship phases from friendship towards a romantic relationship. As the visibility of lesbian relationships through intimate moments such as kissing are interrupted by PCR inserts breaking the fourth wall, direct and indirect pandemic references affect both narrative storytelling and production processes (e.g. PCR testing).

Undoing patriarchy by shifting the focus to subcultural minorities, using the lesbian gaze instead of an otherwise still prevailing male gaze that dominates the film and media landscape, Corona Fictions portraying lesbian characters, or even protagonists, deconstruct numerous common heteronormative socio-cultural practices and reflect the pandemic from a different point of view.

Bibliography

Aitana (2019/2023): »Aitana – Con La Miel En Los Labios (vídeo oficial)«, https://www.youtube.com/watch?v=hD4W1UktL9E [02.05.2023].

Avanza Cine (2020/2024): »EN CASA (HBO). Trailer de la serie en Español«, https://www.youtube.com/watch?v=BbHOYN-qheA [22.01.2024].

Castrejón, María (2008):…Que me estoy muriendo de agua. Guía narrativa lésbica española, Barcelona/Madrid: Egales.

Castrejón, María (2009): »La cama donde te imaginas o la poética de Concha García«, in: Elina Norandi (ed.), Ellas y nosotras. Estudios lesbianos sobre literatura escrita en castellano, Barcelona/Madrid: Egales, pp. 75–95.

Catlin, Jonathon (2021): »When does an Epidemic Become a ›Crisis‹? Analogies Between Covid-19 and HIV/AIDS in American Public Memory«, in: Memory Studies 14.6, pp. 1445–1474.

Curzi, Patricia (2013): »Lesbian Movements. Ruptures and Alliances«, in: Gloria Careaga/Patricia Curzi (eds.), International Lesbian, Gay, Bisexual, Trans and Intersex Association (ILGA), p. 71, http://ilga.org/ilga/en/article/lYwN1bs14T [28.03.2013, not available online anymore].

Eder, Jens (2008): Die Figur im Film. Grundlagen der Figurenanalyse, Marburg: Schüren.

Faulstich, Werner (2002): Grundkurs Filmanalyse, München: Wilhelm Fink.

Gauderault, André/Jost, François (1990): Le récit cinématographique, Condé-sur-Noireau: Éditions Nathans.

GLAAD (Gay & Lesbian Alliance Against Defamation) (2012): »Media Guide to the Lesbian and Gay Community«, in: GLAAD Records, Coll2012-173, Box 2, New York/Los Angeles/Portland.[40]

Hall, Stuart (1997): Representation. Cultural Representation and Signifying Practices, London/Thousand Oaks/New Dehli: Sage Publications.

Hayward, Susan (2013): Cinematic Studies. Key Concepts, London/New York: Routledge.

Hobisch, Elisabeth/Obermayr, Julia/Völkl, Yvonne (2024): »Händewaschen, Abstandhalten, Maskentragen – Pandemische Körperpolitiken und -praktiken in Corona Fictions«, in: Romana Radlwimmer (ed.), Bodies, Remedies, Policies: From Early Modern Chronicles of the Indies to Covid-19 Narratives, Berlin: De Gruyter [in preparation].

Hobisch, Elisabeth/Völkl, Yvonne/Obermayr, Julia (2022): »Narrar la pandemia. Una introducción a formas, temas y metanarrativas de las Corona Fictions«, in: Ana Gallego Cuiñas/José Antonio Pérez Tapias (eds.): Pensamiento, Pandemia y Big Data. El impacto sociocultural del coronavirus en el espacio iberoamericano, Berlin/Boston: De Gruyter, 191–211.

Human Rights Campaign Foundation (2023): »Marriage Equality Around the World«, https://www.hrc.org/resources/marriage-equality-around-the-world [24.10.2023].

---

40 Data/material collected and consulted at One Institute (former ONE National Gay & Lesbian Archives), Los Angeles.

Innes, Charlotte (1995): »Lesbian and Gay Images. An Entertainment Media Resource«, in: Gay & Lesbian Alliance Against Defamation [GLAAD], Los Angeles/New York/Portland/Washington.[41]

Ithaca College Center for LGBT Education, Outreach & Services (2020/2024): »LGBTQ People and COVID-19«, https://www.ithaca.edu/center-lgbt-education-outreach-services/resources-and-services/lgbtq-people-and-covid-19 [09.11.2020].

Jenkins, Henry (2009): Confronting the Challenges of Participatory Culture. Media Education for the 21st Century, Cambridge/London: MIT Press.

Kinofenster (2023/2024): »Filmglossar. Insert«, https://www.kinofenster.de/lehrmaterial/glossar/insert/ [20.03.2024].

López, Carla (2021/2023): »Esta es la canción de Rubí y Macarena en Edificio Corona«, in: FMDOS, https://www.fmdos.cl/espectaculos/esta-es-la-cancion-de-rubi-y-macarena-en-edificio-corona/ [02.05.2023].

Meganoticias (2021/2024): »›Rubí‹ y ›Maca‹ afirman que sus personajes son un aporte a la sociedad: ›Generamos empatía‹«, https://www.meganoticias.cl/tendencias/335562-edificio-corona-cancion-rubi-macarena-reparto-actores-vivianne-dietz-hitzka-nudelman-nex15.html [12.03.2024].

Mejia, Paola (2020/2023): »Así de fácil. El episodio de ›En Casa‹ que tienes que ver«, in: Lesbicanarias, https://lesbicanarias.es/2020/09/28/asi-de-facil-el-episodio-de-en-casa-que-tienes-que-ver/ [19.09.2023].

Melero Salvador, Alejandro (2010): Placeres ocultos. Gays y lesbianas en el cine español de la transición, Madrid: Notorious Ediciones.

Melero, Alejandro (2013/2024): »The Erotic Lesbian in the Spanish Sexploitation Films of the 1970s«, in: Feminist Media Studies 13.1, pp. 120–131.

Ministerio de Salud Chile (2022/2023): »Covid-19 en Chile: Pandemia 2020–2022«, https://www.minsal.cl/wp-content/uploads/2022/03/2022.03.03_LIBRO-COVID-19-EN-CHILE-1-1.pdf [02.05.2023].

Movement Advancement Project (2020–23/2024): »Covid Pulse Survey Report Series: 2020 2023«, https://www.mapresearch.org/2023-pulse-survey-report [21.02.2024].

Newiak, Denis (2020): Alles schon mal dagewesen. Was wir aus Pandemie-Filmen für die Corona-Krise lernen können, Marburg: Schüren.

Nünning, Ansgar/Rupp, Jan (2012): »›The Internet's New Storytellers‹. Merkmale, Typologien und Funktionen narrativer Genres im Internet aus

---

41   Ibid. One Institute.

gattungstheoretischer, narratologischer und medienkulturwissenschaftlicher Sicht«, in: Ansgar Nünning/Jan Rupp/Rebecca Hagelmoser/Jonas Ivo Meyer (eds.), Narrative Genres im Internet: Theoretische Bezugsrahmen, Mediengattungstypologie und Funktionen (vol. 7), Trier: WVT. Wissenschaftlicher Verlag Trier, pp. 3–50.

Obermayr, Julia (2020): Female Identities in Lesbian Web Series. Transnational Community Building in Anglo-, Hispano-, and Francophone Contexts, Bielefeld: transcript.

Obermayr, Julia (2023): »Corona Fictions Agents: Cinematic Representations of Hopeful Pandemic Protagonists in Early Corona Fictions«, in: Yvonne Völkl/Julia Obermayr/Elisabeth Hobisch (eds.) Pandemic Protagonists. Viral (Re)Actions in Pandemic and Corona Fictions, Bielefeld: transcript, pp. 277–301.

Obermayr, Julia/Völkl, Yvonne (2022): »*Stay Away!* Negotiating Physical Distancing in Hispanophone Corona Fictions«, in: Altre Modernità 28, pp. 158–174, https://doi.org/10.54103/2035-7680/19125.

One Institute (2024): »About ONE«, https://www.oneinstitute.org/about/ [24.01.2024].

Prono, Luca (2008): Encyclopedia of Gay and Lesbian Popular Culture, Westport/London: Greenwood Press.

Research Group Pandemic Fictions* (2020): »From Pandemic to Corona Fictions: Narratives in Times of Crises«, in: PhiN-Beihefte 24, pp. 321–344, http://web.fu-berlin.de/phin/beiheft24/b24t21.pdf [11.05.2023] [*Yvonne Völkl, Albert Göschl, Elisabeth Hobisch, Julia Obermayr].

Sanchez, Manuel (2019/2023): »Aitana habla con Togayther sobre feminismo y diversidad LGTB+«, in: Togayther, https://www.togayther.es/noticias/entrevistas/aitana-habla-con-togayther-sobre-feminismo-y-diversidad-lgtb / [02.05.2023].

Singer, Tania/Koop, Sarah/Godara, Malvika (2021): »The CovSocial Project. How did Berliners Feel and React during the COVID-19 Pandemic in 2020/21? Changes in Aspects of Mental Health, Resilience and Social Cohesion«, in: The CovSocial Project, Berlin: Max Planck Society, https://www.covsocial.de/wp-content/uploads/2021/11/CovSocial_EN_WEB.pdf [28.11.2021].

Turner, Graeme (2006): Film as Social Practice IV, Oxford/New York: Routledge.

UN Human Rights Office (2020/2023): »Covid-19 and the Human Rights of LGBTI People«, https://www.ohchr.org/Documents/Issues/LGBT/LGBTIpeople.pdf [17.04.2023].

United Nations (2020/2024): »Protection against violence and discrimination based on sexual orientation and gender identity«, in: UN General Assembly, pp. 1–25, https://documents-dds-ny.un.org/doc/UNDOC/GEN/N20/197/62/PDF/N2019762.pdf?OpenElement [23.01.2024].

White, Patricia (1999): UnInvited. Classical Hollywood Cinema and Lesbian Representability, Bloomington/Indianapolis: Indiana University Press.

Zag, Roland (2010): Der Publikumsvertrag. Drehbuch, Emotion und der »human factor«, Konstanz: UVK Verlagsgesellschaft mbH.

Žižek, Slavoj (2020): Pandemic! Covid-19 Shakes the World. New York: OR Books.

Filmography

BESOS AL AIRE (2021) (ES, D: Iñaki Mercero).
EDIFICIO CORONA (2021) (Chile, D. Nicolás Alemparte/Víctor Huerta).
EN CASA [EP. 5 ASÍ DE FÁCIL]] (2020) (ES, D: Paula Ortiz).
DEMENTE (2021) (Chile, D: Patricio González/María Belén Arenas).
DIARIOS DE LA CUARENTENA (2020) (ES, D: Álvaro Fernández Armero/David Marqués).
VENICE THE SERIES [S.2, EP. 12] (2011) (USA, D: Karen Wilkens/Susan Flannery/Maria Macina).

The Poet's Choice
Céline Sciamma's Lesbian Utopias

Anna Langewiesche, Arthur Ségard

1 Sciamma's Partial Utopias

»Utopias are not ghosts, they are based on something we actually experience, such as ecological utopias or sisterhood utopias, which I experience in reality«, said Céline Sciamma in an interview for the Italian magazine *Cinecittà News*.[1] The filmmaker often uses the terms »utopia« and »utopian« when talking about her films, but when she does so, she does not refer to the ordered worlds of classical utopia. Her use of the term is, however, in phase with modern and contemporary reshapings of the concept (Cohen/Lagrange/Turbiau 2022; Riss 2021). In this article, we will explore how Sciamma's approach to filmmaking can be called utopian, particularly in her two films that focus on lesbian love stories – *Water Lilies* (2007), and *Portrait of a Lady on Fire* (2019).

In her 1991 book *Partial Visions. Feminism and Utopianism in the 1970s*, the literary scholar Angelika Bammer neatly defines two contending understandings of utopia: on the one hand, the ideal of a state of harmony guaranteed by a rational order, and on the other hand, a second understanding of utopia as a »dream« – the »dream of a state of freedom unbounded by regulating forces« (Bammer 1992, 28). This second understanding, more capacious than the first, allows for a re-envisioning of the utopian tradition that includes a larger variety of cultural productions, including texts and artworks created by »those who have been designated Other from the perspective of a hegemonic culture« (ibid.: 3). Bammer calls for *partial* utopian visions: partial both »in the positive sense of being committed to a goal«, and »in the negative sense of being

---

[1] »Le utopie non sono fantasmi, si fondano su qualcosa che viviamo veramente, come l'utopia ecologista o quella della sorellanza che io sperimento per davvero« (Paternò 2019).

constrained by the limits of its time and place in history« (ibid.: 45). »Even as our radical theories and politics push to extend the boundaries of the possible and imaginable«, Bammer writes, »we are also always bound by and to the very structures we are trying to escape. However, as long as we think of utopia not as an antithesis, but rather as a process, a series of utopian moments within the shifting configurations of the possible, those structures will not be immutable« (ibid.: 45). Sciamma's fictions are not invested in the representation of different historical realities, better social and political structures than those of our present and past. Instead, they are historically-grounded stories of the here-and-now or of the factual historical past, interspersed with possible moments that are suffused with a »utopian impulse«. They represent the development of lesbian love and relationalities within the bounds of larger heteropatriarchal structures.

Water Lilies follows a young French teenager, Marie, as she develops desire for another girl, Floriane, who is on a synchronized swimming team and lives in the same town (the *ville nouvelle* Cergy-Pontoise in the outskirts of Paris). The film takes place during a few summer days. Floriane is unsure of what she wants. She develops a bond with Marie that can be understood in utopian terms, but which is broken when, in a decisive scene at the end of the film, she decides to abandon this alternative connection in favor of conformity to the heterosexual order (Wittig 2001: 54–55). *Portrait of a Lady on Fire*, set in 18th-century France, follows Marianne, a painter, who has been commissioned for the marital portrait of Héloïse, a young noblewoman. The two spend a few days alone on a remote island manor, accompanied only by a servant, Sophie. Their time alone becomes the occasion for an artistic, intellectual, and eventually romantic connection.

Both films can be said to present lesbian utopias that are resolutely concrete, rooted in characters' bodies and in space. Neither film represents a sustainable and fully-fledged lesbian relationship. They could both, as such, be interpreted in terms of queer negativity (Edelman 2004). The importance they place on artistic creation, however, coupled with the filmmaker's insistence on the potencies of cinema, allows these films to become objects of joyful communion and political agentivity. Within these utopias – within these counter-spaces that protagonists build for themselves, disconnected from the heteropatriarchal order – these characters are able to experiment with new forms of relationality. These utopias are precarious, unstable, and fated to end; they can, however, also be read as joyful calls to the audience for queer communion, and furthermore, as metaphors of Sciamma's cinema.

2 Physical Utopias: Grounding Desires

Céline Sciamma's filming technique focuses on her characters' bodies, on their sensations, and on their »choreographies«, to borrow a term that she often uses (Gailleurd 2016). When her film *Tomboy* (2011) was released, she said in an interview that to »look at childhood from a child's point of view is, in every sense of the word, to be *à la hauteur*«, an expression that means to be up to the task, but also to be at the same height as the character, both »in terms of camera and frame« and »in terms of feeling« (Lefort 2011). This focus on the characters themselves is even clearer in a historical piece like *Portrait*, where the broader context is left out of the frame. This difference is particularly obvious when comparing the film to other period pieces, for instance Schoeller's *One Nation, One King* (2017) or Maïwenn's *Jeanne du Barry* (2023), both of which include long shots that present ambitious historical reconstitutions and stress the political turmoil of their settings. In *Portrait* historical change is represented more immanently through the characters' sensations and experiences.

At the beginning of *Portrait*, Sciamma follows Marianne's trajectory as she travels to the island manor where her commission awaits. After the opening scene in Marianne's studio, which provides a frame story for the film, the flashback begins with a long sequence that follows her journey by boat and by foot. The sequence that shows her journey from the continent to the small island off its coast is dynamic, the camera follows the boat's rough movements on the ocean. When her canvases fall overboard, she does not hesitate to jump into the turbulent ocean to fetch them. The oars, and the boat crashing against the waves take over the soundscape. These formal choices allow the character's force and determination to become perceptible to the viewer as she braves the harsh elements. Once she arrives at the manor, she takes off her wet clothes and smokes in front of the fireplace, naked. The ease with which Marianne moves characterize her as a relatively free woman. She wanders through the house barefoot, that night, in nothing but her smock, and helps herself to bread and cheese from the kitchen's *garde manger*. When Sophie enters the kitchen and sees her eating, she says »Je me suis permis«. She grants herself freedom.

Héloïse's body is, by contrast, presented to the viewer as highly constrained. She holds herself stiffly, decorously. She is not permitted to leave the manor alone – her mother insists that she be accompanied at all times; in *Water Lilies*, Floriane, too, must be accompanied to be allowed out of the house. Important moments of liberation that Héloïse does eventually experience are embodied. When Héloïse tries to swim for the first time, the film stops on a long shot in which we see the character unlacing her stay and shedding her heavy layers of clothing on the beach, then walking into the vast open ocean in nothing but her loose-fitting shift. The character's return to heterosexual constraint later, toward the very end of the film, is marked by a change in clothing too. When Héloïse's mother returns to the manor – at the moment which marks the end of the protagonists' time spent together alone – Marianne finds her in bed wearing the same shift, warns her that »they're back«, and Héloïse proceeds to put her stay on over her shift. In the final shot that we see of the two protagonists, Marianne tightens its laces brusquely.

The lesbian utopias that take form in Sciamma's films are deeply attached to sensitive experiences.[2] Furthermore, they are also translated into space, in the compositions that she has her character's bodies create as they move through the places of the films. In *Water Lilies*, there exists an entire language of paths and lines that the protagonists trace as they walk together through Cergy. The utopian impulse materializes in two particularly striking sequences that take place in the underground garage where Floriane meets for covert dates with her boyfriend, François. The space of the garage is unquestionably the same one in both sequences, but the camera is placed slightly differently each time, and thus creates different compositions.

The first of the two sequences begins with a 12-second fixed shot that shows Marie and Floriane walking side by side toward the camera in the garage, which appears to the viewer as a tunnel. The sequence then cuts to a brutal reverse shot that shows François standing opposite them, and reveals to the viewer that the tunnel is a dead end (Fig. 2). Distressed, Marie waits inside the garage while Floriane spends time with Francois off screen. She then walks Floriane home.

---

[2] This is also demonstrated too in the sound work in her films. Drawing a parallel between *Water Lilies* and Mia Hansen-Løve's *Goodbye First Love*, Fiona Handyside notes »Part of the way they signal the cataclysmic impact of desire in through reconfiguring the soundscape, so that the girl's emotions become part of the very fabric of the film. [...] These films are alive to the very specific feelings of girlhood, its textures and emotions, and can use form to express the disjunctive, disturbing, but also profoundly touching intimacies of love and friendship« (Handyside 2016, 123).

Fig. 1–4: The first garage sequence (left) and the second garage sequence (right).

A few days later, the two girls return to the same garage, and we see them walking straight toward the camera again, in a similar fixed shot, but this time the camera is positioned slightly differently, revealing a previously obscured opening to the side. This new opening apparent in compositions of the second sequence (Fig. 3) was in the camera's blind spot in the first sequence (Fig. 1). Once the characters reach the middle of the garage, Floriane tells Marie that she will be back in an hour, but this time around Marie refuses to be instrumentalized. She tells Floriane that she will not wait, and she exits through the newly revealed opening. Floriane is left alone in the garage. Marie's movement out of the frame materializes her defiance in space – it alters the characters' dynamics and their trajectories. Within the shifting configurations of the possible for these two girls, one of them pushes back against norms of teenagehood in 2000s suburban France, *i.e.* that teenage girls cannot circulate freely outside of the family, yet that they should engage heterosexually with teenage boys, at least symbolically, in »romantic and conjugal [activities] before feeling desire« (Clair 2023). In this sense, Marie both literally and figuratively clears a new path.

This scene constitutes a pivotal moment within the film's plot – Floriane is at a literal and figurative crossroads, forced to choose between a heterosexual experience and an alternative form of relationality that Marie has just introduced. She appears troubled by the choice she must make. She varies her stance, and looks around as she deliberates. Sciamma seems to insist on slowing down on this moment. Floriane stands in the middle of the frame, and the shot lingers on her for 12 seconds. Between her contrapposto stance, the low horizon line of the shot, and the simplified background, Sciamma gives iconographic value to her figure. After hesitating and scanning the space, Floriane follows Marie's path out.

Her decision to join Marie leads her to a new space. She catches up to Marie in the street, then the two characters continue to trace a line walking together on either side of the central axis of a 3.2 kilometer site by the land-artist Dani Karavan that runs through Cergy. They stop and sit at the steps below an esplanade of twelve giant concrete columns that give out on a panoramic vista of cityscape.

Here, Floriane opens up for the first time about her sexual experiences. She tells Marie that she kissed her hawking swimming instructor in an effort to spite the other girls at the pool, all of whom have crushes on him, then recounts to Marie a moment during which this adult exposed himself to her while she was holding her breath underwater. »I guess you could say that getting hard like that in cold water is flattering«, says Floriane, which Marie rejects forthrightly. »That's gross«, she responds. Floriane attempts to shrug it off, saying »well, that's life«, and she searches for an expression of agreement on Marie's face that she does not find. That which seems to be the one and only inescapable order of things for Floriane does not appear that way to Marie. The girls take part in this intimate conversation over soft, unearthly music, as the camera slowly pans in a half circle around them, moving from Floriane's perspective to Marie's, a movement carefully synchronized with the pace of their conversation and in close dialogue with the structure of the space. The abstract nature of the site, composed of flat surfaces, straight lines, and basic geometrical shapes, removed from the entanglements and particularities of daily life in the suburbs, seems to allow the necessary distance for these characters to confront the structures they are bound to.[3] The site also allows them to intuit new possibilities. From this point on in the film, Marie begins to de-naturalize experiences that Floriane struggles to see beyond on her own.

When talking about the making of *Water Lilies*, Sciamma said that she likes to »think that homosexuality is not a subject but a journey«. When working on the film, she decided to »observe a very small moment: the awakening of the desire, the journey of that desire from the moment it is born in the stomach until it travels to Marie's consciousness« (Wood 2014, 130). She did not want

---

3   We thank Eduardo Vergara Torres for his insights and contributions to our formal analysis of the *Axe Majeur* site.

the film to express any particular thesis on lesbianism. Instead, she wanted it to follow the abdomen and the impressions of this character who is profoundly troubled by another girl. She wanted any idea about lesbianism to come from this subjective trajectory, and not the other way around. The same can be said of *Portrait*: Sciamma's films are not created as political demonstrations. They are means of experiencing sensations that allow the viewer to »inhabit new ideas, to explore other ways of living and thinking«.[4]

3 Precarious Utopias: Lesbian Suspensions in a Heteropatriarchal World

When speaking about *Portrait*, Adèle Haenel (who plays Héloïse) described »a closed world on an island«, that escapes »the general [heterosexual] order of the world«. The love story between her character and Marianne is »in suspension«: »It's in this suspension, which can only be a suspension, because we're swallowed up by the world afterwards, it's in this suspension that there's life, and in fact this is how the film is political«.[5] One of the most central and political aspects of Sciamma's cinema is the way that it presents utopian moments that undo heteropatriarchal rules but that are always precarious, in suspension, fated to end quickly. This is particularly clear in *Portrait*, since the characters are left alone for a few days until the mother comes back and Héloïse must leave for Milan, where she is to be married. Their love story is permanently haunted by its own ending. Héloïse and Marianne are always aware of the

---

4 »[Question:] Avoir un impact politique et social? [Céline Sciamma:] Évidemment! Mais pas en faisant un tract! Pas avec les codes du cinéma politique qui font chier tout le monde. En proposant des expériences, plus que des débats. En montrant d'autres visages, d'autres attitudes, d'autres rapports. En sortant de la dramaturgie du conflit, omniprésente dans la fiction. Mes films ne se veulent pas des pavés dans la mare. Il n'y a pas de démonstration, je n'assène pas des vérités. J'offre des sensations qui permettent d'habiter des idées nouvelles, d'explorer d'autres façons de vivre et penser« (Cojean 2022, 308–309).

5 »C'est une sorte de déni du monde, on a reconstruit un monde clos sur une île où l'on n'est pas confrontée, en tout cas l'espace de quelques jours, de quelques semaines, on n'est pas immédiatement confrontée à l'ordre général du monde qui nous empêche, cet ordre qui est dans le couvent, cet ordre qui est dans le mariage, etc. C'est dans cette suspension-là, qui ne peut être qu'une suspension, parce qu'on est ravalée par le monde après, c'est dans cette suspension qu'il y a de la vie, et en fait c'est en ça que le film est politique« (Simonin 2019).

passing time that brings them closer to their separation. At one point Marianne sees »the ghost« of Héloïse in her wedding dress, conflating the institution of marriage with death.

There is a tragic element to Sciamma's cinema: it is as though her characters can only escape the heteropatriarchal world for a moment before being »swallowed up« once again by it. There are several of such scenes in *Water Lilies*. For instance in the first garage scene, when Floriane's motivations in bringing Marie to this space are made clear in the reverse shot that shows François. With this simple effect, the viewer understands Marie's frustration: it turns out that Marie was not being considered as a (lesbian) subject, but rather as a means to a (heterosexual) end. Later, alone together in a locker stall before a synchronized swimming competition, Marie brushes gel into Floriane's hair, dolling her up for her performance. This moment of care is interrupted by the instructor, who enters the stall to give her »a quick massage to relax her«, and Marie's presence is no longer wanted. Then, after the competition, Floriane and Marie share another tender moment in the bus: they are removed from the other girls who sing a silly song in the background. Floriane gives the medal she has just won to Marie, and asks her if she is happy. She then asks, »will you pick me up tomorrow night? Like last time?« by which she wants to know if Marie will walk her to another date with François. This breaks the harmony of the moment, and Marie suddenly looks upset. The most striking instance, however, of a sudden break of intimate connection takes place when Marie accompanies Floriane to a nightclub, where she hopes to find a man to lose her virginity to. The two girls end up dancing together, at first in a medium shot, then in a close-up that concentrates on their intimacy, as if they were separated from the rest of the world. This proximity allows the viewer to perceive Floriane's tender, sensual gestures towards Marie: she touches her face, her hair, their faces move closer, and Marie shuts her eyes, but right as Floriane's lips get close to Marie's, seemingly preparing to kiss her, she is suddenly drawn back and Marie is left alone in the frame for a few seconds. Marie opens her eyes, and a cut to a medium shot shows Floriane dancing with a man. An intense lesbian connection is once again broken by the return of the heterosexual order.

Some scholars have compared Sciamma's work to the 1990 television film by Chantal Akerman, *Portrait of a Young Girl at the End of the 60s in Brussels*, especially because of how similar the title of this film is to that of Sciamma's *Portrait* (Reeser 2022, 208; Wilson 2021, 15–16). One scene in Akerman's film is similar to the aforementioned *Water Lilies* scene. At a party, the main character, Michèle, a teenage girl, dances in a long continuous shot with her friend, putting forward her lesbian desire for the first time. But suddenly, the music changes. Her friend starts dancing with a boy and Michèle is surrounded by straight couples. The music playing goes, »this is a man's world…«, as a close up on Michèle's face shows her frustration. One of us had the chance to meet Sciamma once, and was able to ask her whether this Akerman scene was a direct inspiration for her. She responded that she had not seen Akerman's *Portrait* before shooting her film, but that she recognized and was touched by this parallel when she did watch it later on. Although this was not a reference she had in mind when making *Water Lilies*, these two scenes were certainly arose from similar experiences of teenage frustration, she said.

4 Art as Utopia: Communion and Celebration

In *Portrait*, another memorable scene presents a utopian moment ended abruptly, about 36 minutes into the film, when the two protagonists convene around a small harpsichord. This scene begins with a powerful shared aesthetic experience. The two discuss Héloïse's plans for the next day, since she has exceptionally been granted freedom of solitary movement around the island. Héloïse tells Marianne that she will go to mass, to hear music, and Marianne responds »the organ is pretty but it's the music of the dead«. »It's the only one I know«, says Héloïse. Here, the viewer understands the extent to which this character's life has been one of sequestration spent between the family manor and the convent. We infer that Héloïse has never had access to art conceived with a purpose other than to instruct, to reinforce conformity within the interrelated orders of the family and the catholic church.[6]

Héloïse asks Marianne what an orchestra sounds like. Rather than describe, Marianne plays: she sits at the harpsichord in the room and plays notes from Vivaldi's Concerto No. 2 in G minor, *Summer, Presto*. Héloïse joins her on the instrument bench, shown in a head shot of the two sitting side by side, touching. Héloïse watches Marianne intently as she plays and tells the story of

---

6   Music at the convent would have been largely religious. A text (and film) that comes to mind is Diderot's novel *La Religieuse* (and Jacques Rivette's 1966 cinematographic adaptation of it) which exposes with *avant-la-lettre* realism the near incarceration of women sent to the convent during this period. The novel (and its adaptation) is a testament to how austere the musical repertoire was at convents during the period of *Portrait*'s setting.

the piece (Vivaldi's *Four Seasons* is an example of the kind of instrumental yet narrative music that became popular during the eighteenth century, in which a literary text, in this case sonnets, were published alongside the partition, which tells a story – in this case, the story of an approaching storm). The shot, which lasts for the whole duration of Marianne's story, creates a sense of deep intimacy, highlighting the characters' faces and showing the looks they share, as well as Héloïse's concentration and joy as she listens and smiles. This is in fact the first time we see Héloïse smile, 38 minutes into the film. What is shown here is a shared aesthetic experience that is not oriented by any utility within the dominant orders of the day: it can even be said that this is art with no utility perceivable other than itself. The moment only lasts about a minute, though. It is brutally interrupted by a reminder of Héloïse's marital future, so the return of the patriarchal order. Marianne fumbles, then says »You will hear the rest later. Milan is a city of music«, breaking Héloïse's smile and this brief moment of connection.

In *Portrait*, one character is more bound and constrained than the other. The two protagonists are from different parts of the country (rural vs. urban), and from different classes. Héloïse is a noblewoman, and Marianne is an artist who receives commissions: she can live off of her labor, so she does not need to marry. In interviews, Sciamma has herself defended the idea that one of the particularities of this historical period is the diversity in degrees of constraint for women: »This precise moment of the second half of the eighteenth century is full of possibilities, of opportunities for woman painters. I had access to a very vast corpus and to moving images produced by women«.[7] In Sciamma's words, »Marianne existed«. Unlike nineteenth-century France – a time in which it was extremely difficult for women to gain institutional recognition and sustain themselves with painting – the second half of the eighteenth century that preceded it was not devoid of woman painters. To borrow Sciamma's succinct explanation of this phenomenon, »The lid of the invention of the nineteenth-century bourgeois woman had not yet been put down« during the eighteenth. Héloïse does not have the same possibilities as Marianne, though: as a noblewoman, the only choice she has is between religious orders and the family. The meeting of the two women is made possible by the institution of

---

[7] »Cette période très précise de la deuxième moitié du XVIIIe siècle est bourrée de possibles, d'opportunités pour les peintres femmes. J'avais accès à un corpus très large et très émouvant d'images produites par des femmes« (Becker 2019).

marriage, the business of a marital portrait, but together they manage to repurpose their meeting and carve out moments of freedom and joy. Sciamma shows the characters holding onto these moments of shared joy in the form of a memory for the rest of their lives, partially by way of memorialization through artistic creation. Once the characters part, they do not go back to their lives unchanged, far from it. The film's final scene makes this clear: we see both characters attending the same performance of Vivaldi's *Four Seasons*, by chance. The movie ends with a long head shot on Héloïse's face, which displays a progression of ambivalent affects as she listens to the movement that Marianne introduced her to, this time all the way through. This is what Céline Sciamma concentrates on in the film, the hyper focus on this short, joyful interlude during which these specific, historically probable women's lives cross: and not the before or the after of their lives of constraint. It is the story of what could have happened in those intimate moments between regularly subjugated individuals, moments that rarely make their ways into archives. When asked by an interviewer why she decided to tell a story of women who seek freedom during, what in his words, was »a period when they were officially constrained«, Céline Sciamma responds that the film does not focus on the character's constraint, »we know that they are constrained«, she explains, »but our view onto them is of all their possibilities, [...] and not of their places of hindrance«. The film concentrates on moments that can take place once these characters are in private, she adds, once they are »no longer being watched, once they're [...] outside of life in society, [it concentrates on] what happens when they are alone, and when they share their intimacy«. She compares these moments to islands: »We see them in an almost insular way, like a utopia«.[8]

In Sciamma's work, music is indeed fundamental to the stories of characters coming together. In her 2014 film *Girlhood*, just like in *Portrait*, the most powerful moments of connection are enabled by what the filmmaker calls »hits« (*des tubes*): in the former, it is Rihanna's »Diamonds«, played in its entirety as the characters dance together; in the latter, it is Vivaldi's *Summer*, »a

---

8   »[I]l y a ce qu'on met dans le cadre, et [ce qu'on ne] met pas. Le film ne prends pas le temps [...] de raconter le cadre de la domination, qui est quasiment une convention de fiction du passé. On sait qu'elles sont contraintes, mais on les regarde dans tous leurs possibles, on les regarde dans leur puissance, et pas du tout dans les endroits d'entrave ou de conflit. On les regarde quasiment de façon insulaire, comme une utopie, [...] qu'est-ce qui est possible à partir du moment où on est pas sous le regard, où on est hors du protocole, hors des mondanités, qu'est-ce qu'il se passe dans la solitude, comment elles partagent leur intimité« (Richeux 2019).

classic title that is absolutely democratic, so that everyone can feel its power«.[9] There is something political about bringing viewers to share characters' emotional experiences when interacting with art. And these uses of »hits« are also a way of shifting viewer's perceptions of tunes that everyone knows. Sciamma has said that »Diamonds« »finds a new meaning« in *Girlhood*, and the same can be said for the Vivaldi movement in *Portrait*. Since 2019, this piece has become emblematic of lesbian love in a cult lesbian film, so we could say, paraphrasing Monique Wittig's call to »lesbianize the heroes of love, lesbianize symbols, lesbianize gods and goddesses, lesbianize Christ«, that Sciamma has lesbianized Vivaldi, as well as, for example, the myth of Orpheus and Eurydice, which is reinterpreted and, in a way, relived by the characters (Wittig 2022, 182).

This historical piece on a woman artist is also a way of looking otherwise at artists from this period, in particular at woman artists, who are underrepresented in both historiography and fiction. Work by scholars such as French art sociologist Séverine Sofio and American art historian Linda Nochlin afforded Sciamma the historical premise necessary for the creation of this fiction (Genand/Pavy-Guilbert/Sandrie 2023, 321–340). In *Portrait*, there are occasional references to woman artists of the past: when Marianne studies Héloïse's ear in detail, for instance. This sequence is significant in the way it offers new and unusual cinematic images by eroticizing a part of the body that is seldom eroticized. It is significant, too, for the way in which it integrates a primary historical source: the voice-over discreetly incorporates an exact passage extracted from a note in Elisabeth Vigée Le Brun's memoirs.[10]

Sciamma places herself in the legacy of woman artists who have been largely undervalued in art history, and this in turn allows her to create new representations, namely representations of lesbian desire. This link between non-canonical art history and lesbian representation is also established by the pieces Marianne and Héloïse produce to »memorialize« (Bacholle 2023) their love: drawings which, unlike Marianne's painting, are private, hidden, and

---

9   »J'avais envie de faire un geste de cinéma très fort, avec la présence d'une bande originale [...] et puis aussi la présence d'un tube, notamment une chanson de Rihanna, qui trouve là un nouveau sens« (Poncet/Dupont/Attal/Lacombe 2014). »*L'Été* de Vivaldi c'est la musique de bien de nos attentes administratives, mais c'est un tube. Et je voulais un tube, je voulais un titre classique qui soit absolument démocratique, pour que tout le monde puisse revivre sa puissance« (Erner 2019).

10 This is acknowledged in the end credits.

can only resurface in official paintings in coded forms. These sorts of coded representations are put forward most iconically in the portrait of Héloïse displayed at the Salon du Louvre at the end of the film: she is married, with her child by her side, but her finger rests on the page of her book where Marianne had sketched herself undressed – page 28, which has since become a symbol. References to or even tattoos of »p. 28« have now become part of lesbian culture.[11] The protagonists' work of »archivization« and monumentalization of lesbian love allows their story to outlive its inevitable end. This, in turn, reflects Sciamma's own artistic undertaking, her own work of monumentalization.

This desire to memorialize lesbian stories is particularly visible at the end of *Water Lilies*. Marie has just kissed Floriane at a party held at the municipal pool. They kissed in private, in the locker room, which can be understood to serve as a parallel, utopian space, removed from the main space of the party – a central room at the pool where teenagers are gathered and submitted to heteronormative social pressures; in André Téchiné's *Being 17* (2016), co-written by Céline Sciamma, the two male protagonists similarly kiss for the first time in the »counter-space« (Foucault 2009) of the bathroom, rather than in the main space of the high school halls. After the kiss, Floriane returns to the party, to the main space of heterosexual order – the viewer discovers that she has decided against a sexual or romantic relationship with Marie. In the aesthetic musical sequence that follows, Marie meets with her friend Anne and they get into a deserted pool where they are alone. A shot of Floriane dancing in the main space is intercut between shots showing these two in the pool, and the very last picture of the film is a »regard caméra« from Marie. Floriane's character is iconized as Marie loses her. The image of Floriane persists, both in Marie's memories and in the film itself. Marie's look at the camera breaks the fourth wall at the film's very last moment. It turns the viewer into a direct witness, and invites them to consider the filmic object in a reflexive way. The film itself is a monument to lesbian love and desire, a means to celebrate lesbian experiences. The film itself is a lesbian utopia. If we decide to read Marie's character as an alter-ego for the filmmaker herself (Sciamma has suggested that Marie's intrigue watching synchronized swimmers from the bleachers stems from an autobiographical episode[12]), then this last look can be interpreted as

---

11 »[J]e n'aurais jamais pensé que la page 28, par exemple, deviendrait un abri commun« (Nicol 2022, 29).
12 »Concernant la natation synchronisée, il y a une anecdote de départ qui est autobiographique. À l'adolescence, j'ai assisté par hasard à un gala de natation syn-

a filmmaker's gaze revealing itself, embracing itself, and becoming aware of cinema's powers of memorialization.

5 Conclusion

Water Lilies and *Portrait* can be viewed as attempts to create lesbian utopias that are sensory and tangible – utopias that involve the character's bodies as well as those of the viewers. These utopias are, however, fragile. They present life trajectories that may ultimately be fated to be »swallowed up« by the heteropatriarchal order, even though characters experience moments of powerful utopian impulse. They also establish new repertoires of utopian imagery. They undertake a process of memorialization and monumentalization – of communion through art, both within and beyond the film's diegesis. »The heroines of my films are the viewers, so there is a happy ending for the viewers, not a happy ending for the characters. You can provide joy to the viewers without joy necessarily winning in the film«.[13] Sciamma's characters might not make the »lover's choice«, but they make the »poet's choice«: they immortalize utopian moments they have lived by means of artistic creation rather than by attempting to sustain them directly.[14] Furthermore, we argue that this artistic gesture can, in turn, generate joy and creativity for its viewers.

»Utopia« was the name of the movie theater Céline Sciamma went to when she was a teenager in Cergy. She said something about this space that deepens our understanding of the utopian dimensions of her films: »It's not just about finding shelter in cinema, it's about how [cinema is] contagious to your own

---

chronisée qui m'avait fait une très forte impression, mais je n'arrivais pas vraiment à discerner pourquoi. J'étais persuadée que j'avais raté ma vie et que j'aurais dû faire ça. Au bout de quelques jours, je me suis aperçue que j'avais été impressionnée par des filles qui, au même âge que moi, étaient déjà dans la concrétisation et dans la prouesse. Et moi je n'étais, au mieux, qu'une promesse. Je trouvais que c'était une situation assez exemplaire de ce qu'on peut ressentir à l'adolescence, c'est-à-dire une sorte de malentendu avec ses désirs. Il y a des choses souterraines qui agissent sur les événements du quotidien« (Sciamma 2007).

13 »Les héroïnes de mes films, ce sont les spectatrices, donc c'est un *happy ending* de spectatrices, ce n'est pas un *happy ending* pour les personnages. On peut donner de la joie à des spectatrices sans forcément que la joie gagne dans le film« (Nicol 2022, 30).

14 »[Orphée] ne fait pas le choix de l'amoureux, il fait le choix du poète« (Sciamma 2019, 01:13:50).

life« (Sciamma 2020). Utopia is not a refuge, it is not a place of escapism. A film may be a shelter, but not one from which we can forget the world. To the contrary, it is from these shelters that it might be possible to rethink the world: to envision new political relationships, new gender dynamics, and to let these utopias be »contagious to our own lives«.

Bibliography

Bammer, Angelika (1992): Partial Visions. Feminism and Utopianism in the 1970s, London: Routledge.

Bacholle, Michelle (2023): »For a Fluid Approach to Céline Sciamma's *Portrait of a Lady on Fire*«, in: French Cultural Studies 34.2, pp. 147–160.

Becker, Cécile (2019): »Interview Céline Sciamma. *Portrait de la jeune fille en feu*«, in: Zut Magazine, 29/08.2019, https://www.zut-magazine.com/categorie/culture/cinema/celine-sciamma-portrait-jeune-fille-feu/ [08.06.2024].

Clair, Isabelle (2023): Les choses sérieuses. Enquête sur les amours adolescentes, Paris: Seuil.

Cohen, Judith/Lagrange, Samy/Turbiau, Aurore (2022): Esthétiques du désordre. Vers une autre pensée de l'utopie, Paris: Le Cavalier Bleu.

Cojean, Annick (2022): Nous ne serions pas arrivées là si..., Paris: Grasset.

Edelman, Lee (2004): No Future. Queer Theory and the Death Drive, Durham: Duke University Press.

Erner, Guillaume (2019): »Céline Sciamma. Portrait d'une réalisatrice en feu«, in: Les Matins de France Culture, 18.09.2019, https://www.radiofrance.fr/franceculture/podcasts/l-invite-e-des-matins/celine-sciamma-portrait-d-une-realisatrice-en-feu-7732045 [08.06.2024].

Foucault, Michel (2009): Le corps utopique – Les hétérotopies, Fécamp: Lignes.

Gailleurd, Céline (2016): »Céline Sciamma – Conversation avec Céline Gailleurd – Université de Paris 8«, online, https://youtu.be/QsgALkcXSg?si=vEUW2boxU8xPAIRS [08.06.2024].

Gallaher, Catherine (2018): Telling It Like It Wasn't. The Counterfactual Imagination in History and Fiction, Chicago: University of Chicago Press.

Genand, Stéphanie/Pavy-Guilbert, Élise/Sandrie, Alain (2023): »›Ma volonté est de créer une archive‹. Entretien avec Céline Sciamma«, in: Dix-huitième siècle 55.1, pp. 321–340.

Handyside, Fiona (2016): »Emotion, Girlhood and Music in *Naissance des Pieuvres* and *Un Amour de Jeunesse*«, in: International Cinema and the Girl. Local Issues, Transnational Contexts, New York: Palgrave, pp. 121–133.

Lefort, Gérard (2011): »Interview – ›L'identité est un terreau à fiction inépuisable‹«, in: Libération, 20.04.2011, https://www.liberation.fr/cinema/2011/04/20/l-identite-est-un-terreau-a-fiction-inepuisable_730227/ [08.06.2024].

Nicol, Lauriane (2022): »Céline Sciamma«, in: Lesbien raisonnable, pp. 28–37.

Paternò, Cristiana (2019): »Céline Sciamma, ›La mia utopia è reale‹«, in: Cinecittà News, 13.12.2019, https://cinecittanews.it/celine-sciamma-la-mia-utopia-e-reale/ [08.06.2024].

Poncet, D./Dupont, A./Attal, R./Lacombe, S. (2014): »Bande de filles«, in: 19–20 (FR3), 19.10.2014, https://www.inamediapro.com/notice/5362617_001?is_extrait=0&isNoticeMere=1 [08.06.2024].

Prendergast, Christopher (2019): Counterfactuals. Paths of the Might have Been, London: Bloomsbury.

Reeser, Todd W. (2022): Queer Cinema in Contemporary France. Five Directors, Manchester: Manchester University Press.

Richeux, Marie (2019): »Céline Sciamma. ›Plus on est intime, plus on est politique‹«, in: Par les temps qui courent (France Culture), 11.09.2019, https://www.radiofrance.fr/franceculture/podcasts/par-les-temps-qui-courent/celine-sciamma-plus-on-est-intime-plus-on-est-politique-8719230 [08.06.2024].

Riss, Laëtitia (2021): »Utopier le présent. Le rêve historique des utopies«, in: Mouvements 108.4, pp. 29–38.

Sciamma, Céline (2007): *Water Lilies* press release, https://www.hautetcourt.com/wp-content/uploads/2019/06/naissance-des-pieuvres-droits-echus-dossier-presse.pdf [08.06.2024].

Sciamma, Céline (2020): »Céline Sciamma on the Cinema Utopia, the Cinema of her Teens«, in: BFI, 22.10.2020, https://www.bfi.org.uk/sight-and-sound/interviews/dream-palaces/celine-sciamma-on-cinema-utopia [08.06.2024].

Simonin, Patrick (2019): »Adèle Haenel, Noémie Merlant, Céline Sciamma à Cannes. *Portrait de la jeune fille en feu*«, in: L'Invité, 28.05.2019, https://youtu.be/hcRNVzHNNPA?si=_p_hvhnQHx5g_dib [08.06.2024].

Wilson, Emma (2021): Céline Sciamma. Portraits, Edinburgh, Edinburgh University Press.

Wittig, Monique (2001): La Pensée straight, Paris: Amsterdam.

Wittig, Monique (2022): Le Corps lesbien, Paris: Minuit.
Wood, Jason (2014): Last Words. Considering Contemporary Cinema, New York: Columbia University Press.

Filmography

BANDE DE FILLES (2014) (FR, D: Céline Sciamma).
JEANNE DU BARRY (2023) (FR, D: Maïwenn).
NAISSANCE DES PIEUVRES (2007) (FR, D: Céline Sciamma).
PORTRAIT DE LA JEUNE FILLE EN FEU (2019) (FR, D: Céline Sciamma).
PORTRAIT D'UNE JEUNE FILLE DE LA FIN DES ANNÉES 60 À BRUXELLES (1990) (BE, D: Chantal Akerman).
QUAND ON A 17 ANS (2016) (FR, D: André Téchiné).
SUZANNE SIMONIN, LA RELIGIEUSE DE DIDEROT (1967) (FR, D: Jacques Rivette).
TOMBOY (2011) (FR, D: Céline Sciamma).
UN PEUPLE ET SON ROI (2017) (FR, D: Pierre Schoeller).

The *Making-With* of Queer Dystopia
Entangled Relationships in Wendy Delorme's
Viendra le temps du feu

Audrey da Rocha

> Quand retentit minuit
> Brûlons nos lits
> Et entrons dans la danse
> Génération qu'on oublie
> Il est temps de sortir de l'errance [...]
> Le feu nous éblouit
> Car cette nuit
> Notre vision est grande
> Sens-tu venir la folie?
> Elle nous saisit
> Et l'ancien monde tremble
> (Ysé 2021)

1 Introduction

If Wendy Delorme's novel *Viendra le temps du feu* had a soundtrack, it could aptly complement the above-mentioned musical epigraph. Despite its tangential relation to the book's narrative, this epigraph shares a profound thematic resonance, facilitating the introduction of the argument I aim to advance here: *Viendra le temps du feu* constitutes a profound exploration of queer and feminist relationships and connections, situated within networks of underground resistance and the construction of a parallel society. Both endeavours are underpinned by a shared goal of dismantling the entrenched structures of the »old world«, encapsulated in the epigraphic notion of the »ancien monde«.

Within the novel, the ostensibly »old world« reveals itself to be a newly established, dictatorial regime. Set against a backdrop of impending environmental, political, social, and racial crises, a reactionary movement emerges, giving rise to a new societal order characterized by a heteropatriarchal and technologically advanced capitalist framework. Individuals are stratified based on their utility to the system, whether in labour or reproductive capacities. Only heterosexual relationships are permitted, with mandated reproduction deemed obligatory for those in favoured social strata. Non-normative sexual orientations and gender fluidities are ruthlessly suppressed, with queer individuals facing persecution and potential death. Following the establishment of this dictatorial and dystopian regime, some elect to flee its grasp, forming a lesbian and trans community across the river. Identifying as sisters and adopting the collective pronoun ›elles‹, they forge a symbiotic, utopian existence, rekindling interpersonal connections and effectively rewriting their shared narrative. Tragically, their sanctuary is compromised by law enforcement, resulting in dire consequences. While some manage to evade capture, they are compelled to navigate the harsh realities of life under the authoritarian regime. The intentional alignment of Ysé's song with Delorme's narrative within this academic exposition underscores what I would like to discuss here: the transformative potential of intertextuality in fostering connections and relationships as a mean of feminist resistance against oppressive structures and patriarchal epistemology.

The thesis articulated herein posits that queer subjectivities within the novel are emblematic of the collective power of community, with (inter)textual elements serving as pivotal connectors between queer protagonists. *Viendra le temps du feu* emerges as a polyphonic narrative that blurs the boundaries of identity and genre, content and form, while intricately weaving intertextual connections reminiscent of an intricate anthill. As Susan S. Lanser notes: »polyphony is more pronounced and more consequential in women's narratives and in the narratives of other dominated peoples« (Lanser 1986: 350).

To a greater extent, I will therefore argue that intertextuality is crucial in shaping and influencing the ongoing process of how queer identities and subjectivities are understood and constructed, in the content but also in the very form of the novel as well. It implies that queer identities are not static but are constantly evolving through the interplay of various textual influences and references. Consequently, intertextuality emerges as the driving force in the ongoing ontological process of shaping queer subjectivities.

2 Power of the Collective

Undoing and negating female bonds and communities to ensure the proper functioning of the heteropatriarchal order is a »basic tactic of patriarchy« (Daly, cited in: Rycenga/Barufaldi 2017: 204) that peaked by the late 16th century in Western Europe. This tactic becomes even more evident when one looks at historical events, such as witch hunts (cf. Federici 2018: 35–40).[1] Lesbian existence and bonds suffered even greater repression and elimination (cf. Rich 1980: 649, 653). Female communities and sisterhood, then, must reconstruct kinship ideally within an »exodus community« (Daly, cited in: Rycenga/Barufaldi 2017: 45),[2] suggesting that female bonds can only exist outside the realm of (hetero)patriarchal society (cf. Auerbach 1978). It becomes apparent, as articulated by numerous critics (cf. Wagner-Lawlor 2013; Bartowski 1991), that the utopian genre serves as the favoured organizational framework for envisioning spaces wherein female and queer communities can potentially elude the constraints of heteropatriarchal dominance, either through its cessation or deliberate dismantlement. The link between literary utopias and feminism seems therefore particularly evident and historically ancient.[3] Utopias serve as imaginative constructs that respond to perceived deficiencies or shortcomings in contemporary society. Instead of presenting an idealized vision of humanity, utopian narratives highlight areas which the authors believe society, or specific groups such as women, are lacking in the present reality (Levitas 2001: 26; cf. Levitas 2011; cf. Sargisson 1996). Joanna Russ states for example that:

> [...] utopias are not embodiments of universal human values, but are reactive; that is, they supply in fiction what their authors believe society [...] and/or women, lack in the here-and-now. The positive values stressed in the

---

[1] See in particular p. 40: »Female friendships were one of the targets of the witch hunts, as in the course of the trials accused women were forced under torture to denounce each other, friends turning in friends, daughters turning in their mothers«.

[2] And further: »[Women] have to go out from the land of our fathers into an unknown place«.

[3] The first literary utopia in history might even have been feminist and written around 1405 by a woman, before being overshadowed in literary historiography by Thomas More's *Utopia* (1516), cf. De Pizan, Christine (1405): *The Book of the City of Ladies*.

stories can reveal to us what, in the authors' eyes, is wrong with our own society (Russ 1981: 81).

Creating a »Society of Outsiders« (cf. Woolf 1966) in Delorme's novel allows the establishment of a feminist resisting community in which the strength of the bond provides protection because the community offers a viable utopian space in which lesbianism, transgender identities, and differences can be openly lived. Where the repression of any deviation within the dictatorial regime is commonplace, the utopia created on the other side is »the concrete possibility for another world« (Muñoz 2019: 1)[4] and is nothing less than the protective cocoon of minority subjectivities and the guarantor of their survival:

> Nos amours qui partout doivent se taire, se cacher, ces amours pour lesquelles toutes nous avons dû fuir nos contrées d'origine, à cause desquelles certaines portent un sceau d'infamie brûlé à même la chair, ont vu celles qu'elles aimaient pendues, violées, brûlées, enfermées pour toujours selon la loi du lieu où elles vivaient avant, ces amours interdites, chez nous pouvaient se dire, et se vivre au grand jour (Delorme 2022: 117).

The community of sisters appears as a secure space to the violence from the other side, a place of peace where each one can live their (romantic) relationship without danger. Individual selfhood, on the other hand, only exists in relation to the communal group, tending to fade within the »cercles se formant chaque soir auprès du feu, pour que les corps se touchent et que les épidermes échangent de la chaleur« (ibid.: 30). The group serves as a powerful foundation, a rhizomatic force in which »[ê]tre un soi cohérent et autosuffisant n'est pas chose essentielle, quand on sait faire partie d'une communauté d'êtres« (ibid.: 82).

The bond and power of the group not only protect but also heal the wounds inflicted by the dominant heteronormative system, experienced by the sisters through repression of their sexual orientations or gender identity. This newfound capacity for love centers relationships and intersubjectivity in a feminist ontology, making individualism secondary. The connection with others is reparative, allowing powerful creative forces to emerge within their unity:

---

4   Muñoz (2019: 1) sees queerness almost as a synonym for utopia: »Queerness is essentially about the rejection of a here and now and an insistence on potentiality or concrete possibility for another world«.

»Elles étaient toutes brisées et pourtant incassables – Elles existaient ensemble comme un tout solidaire, un orchestre puissant, les organes noués en ordre aléatoire, un grand corps frémissant. Et j'étais l'une d'entre elles« (ibid.: 82).

The oxymoron »all broken and yet unbreakable« emphasizes that individual cannot function separately; their individual wounds are overcome by the strength of the group, within which each one becomes unbreakable. The group and the relationships it fosters create a communal sanctuary, exponentially amplifying the strength and array of possibilities for each individual.

> On aimait simplement. On n'avait pas besoin de se sentir unique. Chacune d'entre nous même la plus mutilée trouvait parmi ses sœurs de quoi combler ses brèches, et l'on pouvait hurler, se taire et ne rien dire, chanter ensemble ou danser sans fatigue jusqu'à l'aube. [...] Je n'ai plus jamais su ce qu'est la complétude depuis qu'elles sont parties (ibid.: 83).

The queer utopia of this novel, therefore, allows for the establishment of very strong individual decentred exchanges and interpersonal bonds. Furthermore, the utopia enables the symbiosis of bodies, human and non-human, in a Braidottian ethical interdependence: »A posthuman ethics for a non-unitary subject proposes an enlarged sense of inter-connection between self and others, including the non-human or ›earth‹ others, by removing the obstacle of self-centred individualism« (Braidotti 2013: 49–50).

The idea of a community composed of subjects in the process of becoming is at the core of Rosi Braidotti's nomadic philosophy. Nomadic subjectivity[5] challenges the ideals of liberal individualism and instead promotes the value of diverse connections. Additionally, it imbues interconnection with a sense of eroticism by highlighting the importance of passions, empathy, and desire as ways to engage with the social and human environment without self-centred

---

5 According to Braidotti (1994: 5), nomadism »refers to the kind of critical consciousness that resists settling into socially coded modes of thought and behavior. Not all nomads are world travelers; some of the greatest trips can take place without physically moving from one's habitat. It is the subversion of set conventions that defines the nomadic state, not the literal act of traveling«. The nomad does not necessarily need to be in physical motion. In *Viendra le temps du feu*, we find both physical and material displacement (border crossings, changes of location despite being assigned to a specific area, etc.) as well as the decentering of the modern, unitary subject, particularly through linguistic and discursive reflection and the materiality of language and text.

glorification (cf. Braidotti, cited in: Pinsart 2003: 49). According to the philosopher, the subject is constituted through a process of contact with other beings and becomes a multiple hybrid that, unlike the unitary subject postulated by humanist modernity, forms an identity through contact and interdependence with others (ibid.: 32).

The break with the patriarchal system in *Viendra le temps du feu* can only be achieved by creating a feminist and lesbian utopia in which the subjects, through the will to form a collective whole, become the embodied post-humanist and nomadic subjects of Braidotti, interconnected with each other »in the flow of relations with multiple others« (Braidotti 2013: 50). The sought-after relational ideal, through lesbian love, surpasses mere bodily contact, turning the exchange of cells and DNA into the very space of a utopia to be pursued, to be reconstructed – a utopia whose condition of existence rests on the rejection of patriarchal authority and heterosexuality:

> Il n'y aurait pas d'homme. Personne pour me dire que c'est le couvre-feu. Il n'y aurait personne faisant autorité. Celle du père, je l'ai fuie. A vingt ans j'ai rompu le pacte qui me liait aux Autres en mélangeant ma sueur, ma salive, l'empreinte de mes doigts, les cellules de ma peau, mes ongles, mes cheveux, à ceux d'une autre femme. Et je n'ai eu de cesse ensuite de chercher un autre monde possible, un territoire annexe, un peuple qui n'aurait pas de pères, et pas d'heure à laquelle se coucher (Delorme 2022: 317).

Not only is this community the sanctuary providing protection, but it is also, precisely because it revolves around connections and exchanges, a place of therapeutic care and healing, in which the human and non-human world function as a whole, cooperating and working together for survival: »notre utopie était de pierre, de bois et d'eau, de chair, de sang, de peau, d'exil, de peine, d'amour, de chants, d'espoir, de paix« (ibid.: 219).

And further on, it is a:

> Monde où la violence ne s'exerçait pas pour soumettre et dominer, seulement pour survivre. D'un monde où l'on touchait la pierre, le bois, la peau, d'une même façon, pleine et caressante. D'un monde où l'on savait que les contours des autres ne commencent pas là où s'arrêtent les nôtres, et que blesser autrui c'est se faire mal à soi. Car nous sommes un tout (Delorme 2022: 297).

3 Textual Relation – Relational Text

The utopian vision pursued in Delorme's novel, wherein liberated queer individuals depend on communal support, is not merely a thematic motif confined to the plot; rather, it permeates the very narrative structure of the text. The text itself manifests interdependencies and a perpetual blurring of boundaries. All characters depicted in the narrative are presented as individuals who are both writers and readers.[6] Through this *mise en abyme*, they are consistently involved in exchanges where the focal point revolves around characters who embody the roles of readers and authors, regardless of whether they exist within the fictional realm or in the real world. The multiple characters' voices are given equal weight and prominence, while the dynamic interplay between them as both creators and consumers of literature blurs the boundaries between fiction and reality.

This blurring of boundaries between fiction and reality, between literary genres, and between activities can also be observed in the work of the author Wendy Delorme, »figure incroyable de la nuit qui brouille toutes les pistes«, who creates »un monde où les frontières sont floues« (Pourquery 2007). Employing a pseudonym for her fiction writing, she explores a diverse array of expressive mediums, including neo-burlesque, cinema, translation, and academic research. In doing so, she establishes connections across fields and disciplines, driven by a militant commitment to feminist inquiry into issues of gender, performance, and identity. Furthermore, Delorme is part of the queer collective writing group RER Q with other queer artists and writers and experiments with collaborative fiction.[7] *Viendra le temps du feu* demonstrates characteristics consistent with this perspective of blurring tracks on the one hand and serving as a collective palimpsest on the other.

As Gayle Green (1990: 84) puts it, it appears that feminist writers are eager to challenge traditional literary and linguistic conventions:

> [...] by making their protagonists readers and writers. They make them readers who are aware of the way fiction has shaped their expectations of life –

---

6   They write in their diaries and letters to loved ones, but they also produce political tracts and historiographical mythologies. Some of these writings are fictional, while others are actual existing literature, borrowed for intertextual play, which I will analyze later.

7   For instance: Delorme/Chiarello: *L'Évaporée* (2022).

who in fact contemplate many of the same questions feminist critics do. Or they make them writers whose attempt to forge new forms in their fiction is the correlative of a search for new forms in their life. They make women's relation to the literary and cultural tradition the subject of speculation. Unlike the metafictions of ›postmodern‹ (male) novelists, their metafictions are means of investigating women's relation to the forms of the past, feminist strategies that expose systems as systems capable of being changed.

Going further, Greene (ibid.: 85) states that »[...] women's writing resembles the ›scriptible‹ or ›writerly‹ text described by Roland Barthes – a text which, by drawing attention to its processes of production from the available discourses and inviting the reader to become a part of that production, challenges the ideological complicity of conventional forms«.

Gayle Green's insights shed light on the innovative approach taken by feminist writers, who challenge traditional literary and linguistic conventions by portraying protagonists as both readers and writers. By imbuing their characters with an awareness of the influence of fiction on their perceptions and experiences, feminist authors engage in a profound exploration of societal norms and expectations. Furthermore, the depiction of characters as writers striving to forge new narrative forms not only parallels the feminist quest for new modes of expression in both literature and life but also highlights the invisibility of women in discourse production and history. *Viendra le temps du feu* accentuates this by paying homage to the lesbian continuum,[8] thematizing both the invisibilization of queer and non-heteronormative sexual desire *and* the sororal and friendly bonds among individuals. The Gentlemen's Club[9] is a former bookstore (books have been mostly forbidden by the authoritarian regime), now functioning as a tolerated nightclub and refuge for gay and trans men. It serves as a place where the resistance is organized, a space for sharing, where forbidden books are exchanged and read in circles, illicit relationships are pursued, and where »Chaque nouvel arrivé se trouvait accueilli, ils parlaient, partageaient, des pages, des sensations« (Delorme 2022: 191). Elsewhere, the analogy between physical intimacy and engagement with text and with writing is imbued with the same eroticism: »ce que je fais avec ces compagnons de nuit est une double infraction aux lois de notre époque: on s'aime et

---

8   Rich: 1980.
9   A place rightfully defined by Arthur Ségard (2022) as a heterotopia.

on lit« (ibid.: 194). This subversion of dominant discourse elevates queer characters who confront their own invisibility at a meta-narrative level. Written artifacts facilitate thematic exploration of invisibilization, fostering tangible connections between individuals. Reading is equated with physical encounters, both equally prohibited. Yet, what is at stake here is indeed a political eroticism and an act of resistance, for it concerns two essential relationships – that with the text and that with the lover – crucial to the agency and subjectivity of queer characters: the text is indeed a tool for battle and the pretext that gathers and unites:

> Ces choses inavouables, lire des livres interdits et faire l'amour entre hommes, il faut que tu comprennes, relèvent d'un seul geste: refuser de mourir, de vivre emmurés, dans nos corps, nos esprits. Une main qui se pose sur la peau nue d'un bras, une page que l'on lit, pour soi ou à voix haute, sont les seuls remèdes à notre aliénation. Les seuls que j'aie trouvés, de moins, dans cette vie (ibid.: 205).

The subversive dimension of the text is an act of survival, aiming to document queer subjectivities and counter their invisibility. Rosa, a sister in the utopian community, finds herself walled up after authorities destroyed the underground galleries. Condemned to a slow death, she writes her story and Herstory,[10] distinguished by an italic font. This act of writing gives meaning to her final moments, making the text not only a guarantee of Rosa's survival but also of the stories she puts on paper, which will outlive her (cf. ibid.: 298).

In her stone grave, Rosa »gratte sur la pierre [...] pour y laisser des noms« (ibid.: 41), those of her resistant sisters so that they are not forgotten »puisqu'ils ont effacé toute présence de nous, ils n'iront pas creuser pour exhumer nos corps, les récits de nos vies, dessins de nos visages, témoignages de notre existence en ce lieu, du monde que nous avions bâti comme un refuge pour toutes les pourchassées« (ibid.: 71). More than just writing »a mythology for the lesbian community« (Zimmerman 1990: 16), literature is defined in the novel from a political perspective where »stories can be retold, can be fashioned to fit [...] lesbian experience, and can therefore be used for survival« (Farwell 1996: 11).

Reading, writing, and storytelling, with their dual role in subversion and survival, as well as in facilitating the expression of subjectivity, serve as a link

---

10 The term was coined in 1970 by Robin Morgan, paving the way for a now essential notion in feminist historiography (cf. Morgan 1970).

between the characters, narrators, and authors. They also establish a connection between the historical experiences of sexual minorities and their subsequent transmission:

> Car écrire c'est aussi traduire l'expérience de nos corps en ce monde, quand les chairs sont muettes, que la conscience n'est plus. Remanier le langage, réinventer les mots, les rendre caressants, les faire se reproduire, et puis donner naissance à d'autres mondes possibles. Notre histoire nous survit, pourvu qu'elle soit écrite, pourvu qu'on puisse la lire (Delorme 2022: 318).

4 Writing Stories – Spinning Texts – Weaving Language – Feminist Materiality

The metareflexive dimension in Delorme's novel acts as a resistance tool, documenting the history of queer minorities. However, I propose a materialist analysis, suggesting the text not only reflects queer experiences but actively constructs queer subjectivities. This perspective offers a deeper understanding of queer complexity, emphasizing its interconnected solidarity within a network of literary echoes and resonances. The concepts of heteroglossia and dialogism as elucidated by Bakhtin have acquired a renewed significance, particularly in the context of Julia Kristeva's exploration of intertextuality. Within this framework, these notions assume a more distinctly postmodern character, wherein the traditional understanding of the text as immanent and autonomous gives way to a view that regards the text as a medium for critical reflection on the humanistic constructs of authorship and subjectivity (cf. Hutcheon 1988: 126).

Intertextuality, in that it allows a shift in the approach from the author/text connection to the interaction between reader and text, blurs the boundaries and limits between the reading subject and the writing subject.[11] Thereby, intertextuality anchors the meaning of the text within the broader context of discourse history. In *Viendra le temps du feu*, intertextuality serves a broader political project, for the discourse history in which it inscribes itself is a radical feminist and queer one. The intertextual references made explicit through bibliographical references at the end of Delorme's book, serve less to fetishize the

---

11 »derjenige, der schreibt, ist auch derjenige, der liest« and is »selbst nur ein Text, der sich aufs neue liest, indem er sich wieder schreibt« (Kristeva, cited in: Ihwe 1972: 372).

referenced authors than to produce a theoretical discourse framed in »relation to systems of representation [...] created in an active exchange process between reader/viewer, context, and text, thereby producing connections and links between groups of texts and political moments« (Melzer 2006: 9).

In *Viendra le temps du feu*, The Gentlemen's Club, owned by a character named Paul, embodies the author and philosopher Paul B. Preciado, who literally steps into the diegesis to become a fictional character. Some excerpts from his philosophical essay step into fiction and are arranged to constitute the texts of fictional revolutionary tracts created by the queer resistors, the ›Uranians‹.[12] The queer resistance movement within the dystopian regime defined as a »réseau vivant décentralisé« wants »une citoyenneté totale définie par le partage des techniques, des fluides, des semences, de l'eau, des savoirs...« (Delorme 2022: 162).

Preciado is just one example; the narrative includes texts and quotes from various real authors like Rainer Maria Rilke, David Foster Wallace, Sarah Waters, Velibor Čolić, and Monique Wittig, whose feminist epic *Les Guérillères* is pivotal. Louise, a character raised under dictatorship, stumbles upon a box of forbidden books in the Gentlemen's Club where she works. She discreetly reads from it, revealing the book to be Wittig's *Les Guérillères*. This fictional discovery is an actual artifact, reimagined by the sisterhood community to craft their creation myth and chronicle their narratives.[13] The fictional book discovered is, in fact, a real artefact, yet Wittig's novel undergoes a process of re-fictionalization. Les ›Guérillères‹ emerges from Wittig's work to metaleptically embody the queer protagonists resisting oppression in *Viendra le temps du feu*. The book found by Louise serves as a dialogue between the dystopian system in which she reads it and the utopian system it represents, all within a *mise en abyme* that blurs the boundaries between content and form, between fiction and the materiality of the text. I propose, therefore, to understand Delorme's novel in terms of its relational transfers, which lend it a materialist dimension. As Braidotti (1994: 154) puts it:

> The text must rather be understood as a term in a process, that is to say a chain reaction encompassing a web of power relations. What is at stake in

---

12 Following Preciado's book *Un Appartement sur Uranus* (2019)
13 This also encapsulates the narrative arc of Wittig's *Les Guérillères*: a utopian collective of lesbians engaged in acts of resistance and the crafting of their own mythologies.

the textual practice, therefore, is less the activity of interpretation than that of decoding the network of connections and effects that link the text to an entire sociosymbolic system. In other words, we are faced here with a new materialist theory of the text and of textual practice.

Therefore, both the materiality of the text and the materiality of language are constantly reflected throughout the novel and engage in a continuous dialogue between what to say and how to say it. Like *Les Guérillères*, a work in which Wittig continues her feminist reworking of language,[14] the queer characters in *Viendra le temps du feu* have chosen »d'user du féminin pluriel pour s'autodésigner. Comme acte politique, pour détruire dans la langue l'exercice du pouvoir qui les violentait« (Delorme 2022: 267). The characters use words from a »dead language«, and many reflections on language as being phallogocentric are scattered throughout the novel: »J'étais tout animée par la joie radicale de traverser les flots qui séparaient le monde des futurs à venir, et celui où la langue fait corset invisible à tous les corps femelles, rogne chaque jour nos ailes, fait de nous des fantômes entre les pages de livres qui ne content d'histoires que les autorisées« (ibid.: 317).

The novel's reflection on language peaks in the hidden chapter, placed after the bibliography and marked by unique typography. This section examines language's materiality and its oppressive potential, while exploring the interdependence of beings, prompting a reimagining of collective narratives. Though it may seem to be from Eve's journal, its paratextual placement gives it significance beyond fiction, highlighting blurred boundaries. Moreover, the dystopian regime in the narrative follows a society on the brink of collapse, recounted analeptically and reminiscent of our Capitalocene era (cf. Haraway 2015), where environmental, social, and migratory crises intertwine. »Les scientifiques décrivent en détail« the climate upheavals »sans que rien ne change dans la législation des grandes industries« (Delorme 2022: 152). The inspirational figure of this generation, Geia Walden, co-founder of the »Mouvement des jeunes pour la planète«, is none other than the parodic[15] incarnation of

---

14   Which she had already initiated with *L'Opoponax*. cf. Wittig 1964.
15   Parody is also an important device in Delorme's novel, and as a form of intertextuality and as the expression of »a repetition with a difference« (Hutcheon 1985: 32), parody seems to be a quintessential postmodern form in several respects, as it simultaneously embraces and subverts the elements it parodies. Furthermore, it prompts a reassessment of the concept of originality, aligning with other postmodern critiques of liberal humanist ideals (Hutcheon 1988: 11). Alongside Hutcheon,

Greta Thunberg, who is literally heard haranguing the reader with her »How dare you?«[16] while we read »Les médias moquaient autant qu'ils encensaient cette gamine frêle, qui faisait la morale aux grands hommes d'État« (ibid.: 150). Geia Walden eventually ends up immolating herself in public, followed by many other young people as a protest (ibid.: 150–153). The parodic dimension is political and reminiscent of the short story written by Mariana Enriquez (2016) »Las cosas que perdimos en el fuego« in which voluntary self-immolation as a sign of protest and resistance is staged by groups of women. These are ›survivors‹ of domestic violence who reclaim fire as a weapon to protest the treatment inflicted on them by husbands, lovers, etc.

One could also mention »la grande cathédrale de cette ville capitale qui a brûlé hier« (Delorme 2022: 168), a fire orchestrated by queer resistors. The allusion to the Notre-Dame de Paris fire in 2019 is obvious here, an event after which Paul B. Preciado (2019) had incidentally written an essay entitled »Our Lady of the Ruins«, which denounces the government priorities of political leaders in the face of social inequalities and whose dystopia by Delorme could be, in turn, the fictional parody. Pyromania, and the symbol of fire in general, thus remain at the heart of a feminist and queer intertextual network,[17] in which it is seen as a symbol of destruction but also as a tool which empowers and gives agency to once oppressed subjects. We might think here again of the musical epigraph at the beginning whose call was to gather at night, akin to a witchy Shabbat, and setting fire to the old order to create new, sustainable forms of kinship and light the »fire of female friendship« (Daly 1978: 382–4).

Overall, the textual, linguistic, and corporeal dimensions of the queer protagonists in the novel establish a foundational expression of queer subjectivities. Delorme addresses the invisibilization of sexual minorities and draws from a lineage of queer epistemology through citation and appropriation. These literary techniques illustrate relational dynamics. Thus, *Viendra le temps*

I consciously use the notion ›parody‹ here not in a pejorative way but rather as an intertextual feature of postmodern literature, which in this case functions like a femmage, with Geia Walden being presented as a very inspirational figure.

16   »»How dare you?‹ – Emotional Greta Thunberg attacks world leaders«, Youtube (23.09.2019).

17   There is a considerable array of literary texts and historical symbols that explore the affirmative association between fire and feminist or queer realities. Here is a non-exhaustive selection: Clark/Yusoff 2018; Enriquez 2016; Sciamma 2019; Rodrigues 2022. See also the women called ›Pétroleuses‹ during the Paris Commune; See also: Bachelard 1949.

du feu could be characterized as a sympoietic novel, echoing Donna Haraway's concept of sympoiesis, which is: »a simple word; it means ›making-with‹. Nothing makes itself; nothing is really autopoietic or self-organizing. [...] . That is the radical implication of sympoiesis. Sympoiesis is a word proper to complex, dynamic, responsive, situated, historical systems. It is a word for worlding-with, in company« (Haraway 2016: 58).

Delorme's narrative construction involves collaboration with pivotal figures in feminist theory, fictively portraying these scholars and engaging with their theoretical frameworks. This creative endeavour engenders a metareflexive palimpsest, emphasizing that queer subjectivities emerge from dynamic interactions with other agents and their surroundings. The novel's content and form intertwine, yielding a hyperfiction characterized by infinite interconnectedness. Authorial agency relinquishes its autonomy as a narrative structure, assuming a subordinate role within a broader hermeneutic framework aimed at exploring queer becomings in order to: »ensemble diffracter le système, le déstabiliser, y ouvrir une brèche. Et peut-être créer les conditions d'un possible futur« (Delorme 2022: 256).

Exploration of interpersonal and intertextual sympoietic connections within Delorme's work disrupts prevailing Western philosophical paradigms, which prioritize autonomous individuals. Instead, emphasis is placed on relational, cooperative dynamics in identity formation and knowledge production. Commencing with the sobering declaration »They are all dead« (ibid.: 9), the novel culminates, following a tapestry of echoes, resonances, and intertextual allusions, with the affirmative proclamation »And we are alive« (ibid.: 306). Herein lies the assertion that characters persist, deceased authors endure through their writings, and the potency of collective endeavours – be they theoretical, fictional, or human – is imperative for the realization of queer and feminist subjectivities. Echoing Haraway's sentiment: »It matters what stories we tell to tell other stories with; it matters what concepts we think to think other concepts with« (Haraway 2016: 118).

Bibliography

Auerbach, Nina (1978) [1943]: Communities of Women, Cambridge: Harvard University Press.
Bachelard, Gaston (1992) [1949]: La Psychanalyse du Feu, Paris: Gallimard.

Bartowski, Frances (1991): Feminist Utopias, Lincoln: University of Nebraska Press.
Braidotti, Rosi (1994): Nomadic Subject. Embodiment and Sexual Difference in Contemporary Feminist Theory, New York: Columbia University Press.
Braidotti, Rosi (2003): »Vers une subjectivité viable. Un point de vue féministe et philosophique«, in: Marie-Geneviève Pinsart (ed.), Genre et bioéthique, Paris: Librairie Philosophique J. Vrin, pp. 27–52.
Braidotti, Rosi (2013): The Posthuman, Malden: Polity.
Clark, Nigel/Yusoff, Kathryn (2018): »Queer Fire«, in: Feminist Review 118, pp. 7–24.
Daly, Mary (1978): Gyn/Ecology. The Metaethics of Radical Feminism, Boston: Beacon Press.
Delorme, Wendy (2022): Viendra le Temps du Feu, Paris: Cambourakis.
Delorme, Wendy/Chiarello, Fanny (2022): L'évaporée, Paris: Cambourakis.
De Pizan, Christine (1999) [1405]: The Book of the City of Ladies, London: Penguin.
Enriquez, Mariana (2016): Las Cosas que Perdimos en el Fuego, Barcelona: Anagrama, Editorial S.A.
Farwell, Marylin (1996): Heterosexual Plots and Lesbian Narratives, New York: New York University Press.
Federici, Silvia (2018): Witches, Witch-Hunting, and Women, New York: PM Press.
Goodwin, Barbara (2001): The Philosophy of Utopia, London: Taylor & Francis Ltd.
Greene, Gayle (1990): »Feminist Fiction, Feminist Form«, in: Frontiers: A Journal of Women Studies 11, pp. 82–88.
Haraway, Donna (2016): Staying with the Trouble. Making kin in the Chthulucene, Durham: Duke University Press.
Haraway, Donna (2015): »Anthropocene, Capitalocene, Plantationocene, Chthulucene: Making Kin«, in: Environmental Humanities 6, pp. 159–165.
Hutcheon, Linda (1985): A Theory of Parody. The Teachings of 20th-Century Art Forms, New York: Methuen Ldn.
Hutcheon, Linda (1988): A Poetics of Postmodernism. History, Theory, Fiction, London: Routledge.
Kristeva, Julia (1967): »Wort, Dialog und Roman bei Bachtin«, in: Jens Ihwe (ed.): Literaturwissenschaft und Linguistik. Ergebnisse und Perspektiven, Frankfurt: Athenäum, pp. 345–375.

Lanser, Susan S. (1986): »Toward a Feminist Narratology«, in: Style 20, pp. 341–363.

Levitas, Ruth (2011): The Concept of Utopia, New York: Peter Lang.

Melzer, Patricia (2006): Alien Constructions. Science Fiction and Feminist Thought, Austin: University of Texas Press.

Morgan, Robin (ed.) (1970): Sisterhood Is Powerful. An Anthology of Writings from the Women's Liberation Movement

Muñoz, José Esteban (2019): Cruising Utopia. The Then and There of Queer Futurity, NYU Press.

Pourquery, Didier (2007): »Bon genre«, in: Libération, 21.11.2007, https://www.liberation.fr/portrait/2007/11/21/bon-genre_106734/ [11.04.2024].

Preciado, Paul B. (2019a): Un Appartement sur Uranus, Paris: Grasset.

Preciado, Paul B. (2019b): »Notre-Dame-des-Ruines«, in: Libération, 19.04.2019, https://www.liberation.fr/debats/2019/04/19/notre-dame-des-ruines_1722432/ [11.04.2024].

Rich, Adrienne (1980): »Compulsory Heterosexuality and Lesbian Existence«, in: Signs 5, pp. 631–660.

Rycenga, Jennifer/Barufaldi, Linda (2017): The Mary Daly Reader, NYU Press.

Russ, Joanna (1981): »Recent Feminist Utopias«, in: Marleen S. Barr (ed.): Future Females. A Critical Anthology, Bowling Green. Bowling Green State University Popular Press, pp. 71–85.

Sargisson, Lucy (1996): Contemporary Feminist Utopianism. London: Routledge.

Ségard, Arthur (2022): »Des îles et des lunes. Hétérotopies queer dans la fiction contemporaine«, in: Genre, sexualité & société 28, https://journals.openedition.org/gss/7534 [11.04.2024].

Thunberg, Greta (2019): »›How dare you?‹ – Emotional Greta Thunberg Attacks World Leaders«, https://youtu.be/xVlRompc1yE?si=IOg70eCwhDD5618z [11.04.2024].

Wagner-Lawlor, Jennifer A. (2013): Postmodern Utopias and Feminist Fictions, Cambridge: Cambridge University Press.

Wittig, Monique (1964): L'Opoponax, Paris: Les Editions de Minuit.

Wittig, Monique (1969): Les Guérillères, Paris: Les Editions de Minuit.

Woolf, Virginia (1966): Three Guineas, San Diego: Harcourt Brace.

Zimmerman, Bonnie (1990): The Safe Sea of Women. Lesbian Fiction 1969–1989, Boston: Beacon Press.

Filmography

Fogo-Fátuo (2022) (PRT, R: João Pedro Rodrigues).
Portrait de la jeune fille en feu (2019) (FR, R: Céline Sciamma).

Let's Kill the Author
Cristina Rivera Garza and Collective Authorship

Stefanie Mayer

1 The Death and Resurrection of the Author

The title of this article may evoke Barthes' (1993) famous essay, but focusses not so much on the death of the author as a general instance, »the project of radically impersonalizing discourse« (Burke 2019: 16), but rather on questioning and refiguring a very specific type of author. What I refer to is the modern conception of authorship, which established the idea of an author as »an individual who is solely responsible – and thus exclusively deserving of credit – for the production of a unique, original work« (Woodmansee 1994: 35). In this conception of authorship, the author is a God-like creature that individually and in pure solitude creates unique masterpieces. The help of others, any training or education is unnecessary in this conception, as writing is no longer an artisanship or profession, but pure vocation: »la définition vocationnelle de l'activité artistique qui a dominé à partir du romantisme: don plutôt qu'apprentissage ou enseignement, inspiration plutôt que labeur soigné et régulier, innovation plutôt qu'imitation des canons, génie plutôt que talent et travail« (Heinich 2005: 39). What is hidden in this rather old and yet still popular idea of an author are the difficulties this conception implies for certain individuals to meet the requirements to position themselves as authors. Criteria like divinity, uniqueness, individuality and solitude render it difficult for any person who is marked as ›other‹ to position themselves as authors. By comparing, for instance, the traditional characteristics of modern authorship with the stereotypical traits of femininity, we can observe that they are in opposition to each other:

> [...] es la identificación de la mujer – en este singular general, reificante – con los términos negativos de parejas jerárquicas tales como unicidad vs. repetición, producción vs. reproducción, autonomía vs. heteronormía, singularidad vs. comunidad o interioridad vs. corporeidad, lo que nos permitirá explicar las exclusiones simbólicas que constituyen el campo literario y artístico desde un punto de vista de género (Pérez Fontdevila 2019b: 27).

Most of the features, which in this example are marked as ›feminine‹, also align with other ›othered groups‹ and the described difficulties to correspond to the image of the traditional author multiply, in an intersectional way, by each discriminated category an author might be part of. With that in mind, the request for a complete disregard of the author seems to be a welcome development. Nonetheless, the discriminatory structures of the literary field do not disappear by erasing the author, simply because the field in the 21st century continues to function by linking texts to their authors:

> [...] la idea de que una obra de arte es lo que es desde un punto de vista estético, con independencia de quien la haya creado [...] choca con una realidad hoy en día indiscutida: la importancia que actualmente se da, en el mercado del arte y en la sociedad, a quien es el autor (López Fernández 2020: 16).

Even if it may seem legit to request a »desbiologización de la letra« just as important voices in the Latin-American literary scene, such as Diamela Eltit (2021) or Fernanda Trías (2021) have done, ignoring who wrote a text, might benefit the same individuals that already have been privileged to begin with and, additionally, increase the lack of transparency. In other words »theoretically Barthes's injunctions against the (male) author might be logically and philosophically sound, politically they may contribute to or perpetuate a silencing of diverse (and the diversity of) authorial voices« (Power 2021: 3). As the erasure of the author is currently not a solution to the problem, it seems plausible to work on a refiguration of the conception of authorship in order to facilitate the positioning of discriminated authors. One author that works intensively on such a modification both trough her autopoetic and literary texts is the Mexican writer Cristina Rivera Garza (CRG). With her work, she tackles many of the characteristics of the modern author, one of them being the one linked to singularity, uniqueness and solitude. This article seeks to show how CRG's idea of authorship as a collective concept is not only to be found in her theoretical texts, such as the essay *Los muertos indóciles* (2019), but also in her literary work. In a close reading of the novel *El mal de la taiga* (2019), the article demonstrates how, by presenting writing as a collective practice in the need of others, CRG dismantles the myth of writing as a solitary activity, discloses the importance of the readers in the construction of meaning, and positions literature as a common good.

2 Singularity and Otherness in the 21st Century

In her book, *L'élite artiste*, Nathalie Heinich (2005) shows how in 19th century France a tendency that already started in the 18th century became increasingly apparent: »le régime de singularité«. By fostering a new representation of artistic excellence, being an artist came to mean adhering to the romantic conception of the inspired creator or the unrecognized genius, vocation became the key element to artistic creation and originality overruled tradition and classical rules (cf. ibid.: 67–68). This new way of thinking about artists and artistic creation continues to be in vogue, not only in France, but internationally. Nonetheless, we can observe a quite paradox situation in the current century:

> La retórica cultural de nuestra época se basa en una contrariedad, ya que, a pesar de que el panorama creativo actual tiende a la desmaterialización de la imagen y sus flujos disuelven las nociones de originalidad, propiedad, verdad y memoria, la autoría se enaltece hasta límites insospechados, por mucho que se siga especulando con su muerte o disolución (López Fernández 2020: 16).

Authors as individuals seem to be more important than ever, as the progressive festivalization and socialization of literary culture, which can be observed since the end of the last century, has one concrete epicenter: the spectacularization and professionalization of the writer (cf. Gallego Cuiñas 2023: 323). The need to stage oneself as an author, to be present and visible as much as possible, has become an important part of authorship in the 21st century and has transformed the author into a »personaje mediático«, which is both »causa y efecto del sentido de la obra« (cf. ibid.: 323–324). On the one hand, these new trends offer attractive opportunities for formerly disadvantaged authors to enter the literary field; on the other hand, they require similar qualities to those brought into the field by the regime of singularity and therefore continue to cause difficulties for othered authors, especially for those who are targeted by multiple discriminations. A simple example: even if we can notice a great increase of female authors in the Latin-American literary field (cf. Guerreiro), most of those »heroínas de un canon inverso« are neither Black nor indígena, the vast majority of them is straight and not only have the most of them attended university, but hold a degree in an Artistic Discipline and/or Journalism. Nevertheless, even as more privileged Latin American women writers, they are still disadvantaged in the global literary sphere, as their condition can be understood as »doblemente subalterna el espacio de la literatura mundial: por ser latinoamericanas y por ser mujeres« (Gallego Cuiñas 2022b: 73). The reasons for these discriminating structures are certainly multifaceted, but one important cause is precisely the way authorship remains a synonym for uniqueness, individuality and autonomy. Othered subjects by their attribution of being ›other‹ lack of those features not because they actually miss them, but because:

> [their] lack is symbolically produced by marking [them] as gendered, racialized, and ›cultured‹. [...] If women, the poor, the colored, the queer, the ones with cultures (whose cultures are denied and rendered invisible as they are seen as our mark) are deemed unfit for the public, it is because we are tainted by need, emotion, the body (Lugones 1994: 467).

As the quotation points out, art of the othered subject is not recognized as ›real art‹ in the cultural hegemony, precisely because of its close link to the ascribed corporeality. Whereas the »impartial reasoner« – an allegory Lugones introduces to illustrate a non-othered position – is »the measure of all things. He is transparent relative to his position in the hetero-relational patriarchy, to his culture, his race, his class, his gender. His sense is the only sense« (Lugones 1994: 476). This explains why a male writer is a writer, whereas a female writer had and sometimes still has to struggle with the label ›women writer‹. It also makes clear why the erasure of the author poses no problem for subjects that are not forced into othered positions. Last but not least, the attributed marks explains why othered authors are often seen as mere representatives of their respective othered group, part of a collective rather than a unique artist, which makes it difficult for them to stand out in the way the regime of singularity demands:

> Es, pues, la ausencia de autonomía de tales sujetos – paradójicamente menos sujetos en cuanto que más sujetos – lo que les condena a la heteronomía

creativa: »genderizados, racializados o ›culturados‹« (Lugones, 1999, p. 247), sus productos no llevan la firma del creador singular que, paradójicamente, permite universalizarlos en cuanto representativos del Sujeto (no sujeto) (Schaffer, 1997), sino las respectivas marcas – culturales, genéricas o raciales – del colectivo al que representan, identificadas con los estereotipos a los que las reduce en los que las inmoviliza la posición privilegiada (pp. 252–253) (Pérez Fontdevila 2019b: 38).

Given the difficulties that the current conception of authorship imposes on othered subjects, a refiguration of the image of the author seems essential, especially when it comes to its state of singularity. CRG uses her othered, yet privileged position, to tackle precisely this task by pointing out and focusing on the collective character of writing.

3 Rewriting Authorship: CRG and Collectiveness

Questions on authorship are a recurrent topic in the work of CRG. The most obvious example might be her essay *Los muertos indóciles: Necroescrituras y desapropiación*, where she openly tears down the pillars on which authorship is built in the sense of the »regime of singularity« (Heinich 2005):

> La escritura no es resultado de una inspiración tan *inexplicable* como *individual*, sino una forma de *trabajo material* de *cuerpos concretos en contacto* – tenso, volátil, irresuelto – *con otros cuerpos* en tiempos y lugares específicos. Las escrituras, en otras palabras, son *cuerpos en contextos*. En su contacto con ese *bien común* que es el lenguaje, el *trabajo de la escritura* participa de distintos procesos de producción y *reproducción* de riqueza social. La que escribe, en este sentido, no representa la realidad, sino que la presenta, es decir, la produce, *en relación a tradiciones literarias, o no*, para su futura *reproducción* en forma de *lectura* (Rivera Garza 2019b: 97–98, emphasis added).

With only a few sentences, CRG (1) negates the vocational regime, defining writing not as a product of inexplicable inspiration but as material labor; (2) refuses the myth of individuality and originality by pointing out the inherent contact to other texts, writers and literary traditions of any text and presenting writing as a combination not only of producing, but also of reproducing; and (3) tackles the question of property by highlighting those connections, by describing language as a common good and by including the readers in the production of sense. Following María Clara Lucifora's definition of the »espacio autopoético«, the essay can be interpreted as part of CRGs autopoetic space as it includes elements that refer to »el hecho artístico, como concepciones sobre la poesía, el poema, el proceso creador, el lenguaje, la obra« (Lucífora 2020: 59). Voices in favor of the death of the author, might argue that analyzing literary works based on an autopoetic texts is an illegitimate and non-scientific move. The intention of the following analysis, however is not to explain *El mal de la taiga* through the words or the biography of CRG, but rather to show how her autopositioning as an author and the associated refiguration of authorship is a complex procedure that results from an interplay of different »prises de positions« (Bourdieu 1992).

3.1 Profession Rather Than Convocation

As CRG herself is the director of the Creative Writing Program in Hispanic Studies at the University of Houston, it is obvious that the author conveys that writing is a profession that can be learned (at least to a certain degree). This conception of writing implies one or more persons that the individual can learn from and establishes writing as a labor that is linked to the market; it is, therefore, in contrast to the idea that a ›real artist‹ only needs their inspiration and can write in complete autonomy:

> L'inspiration créatrice est l'antithèse, on l'a vu, du rapport professionnalisé à l'écriture. La vocation, en effet, est indissociable de cette forme singulière de détermination de l'activité qu'est l'inspiration, qui déclenche et justifie l'activité créatrice. Elle s'oppose point par point à la régularité, à la prévisibilité, au contrôle qui gouvernent l'exercice du métier ou de la profession. Ceux-ci peuvent être dits « hétéro-déterminés », au sens où l'activité satisfait ou anticipe la demande d'autrui (le marché, la relation de service), alors que le régime vocationnel est auto-déterminé [...] (Heinich 2005: 83).

A literary text, which reflects this conviction on various levels, is the novel *El mal de la taiga*. In the narration, the autodiegetic narrator is a detective who is very bad at her actual job, but uses all her unresolved cases as source material to write novels (cf. Rivera Garza 2019a: 23). By this very detail, being a writer is presented as a secondary occupation with a certain benefit and applicability right from the beginning and the text suggests a certain similarity or at least an overlap between the two professions. This reading of a certain assimilation of writing to detective work is reinforced by the fact that the book bears the same title as the report that the detective writes for her client (cf. ibid.: 27), alluding, in this way, to a mise en abyme. By comparing writing to investigating, it is presented as a profession that demands dedication, time, and collaboration rather than an independent passion that feeds merely on talent and inspiration. Furthermore, the text presents ›being an author‹ as something that goes far beyond writing texts. As the protagonist in the novel knows, extra-literary activities are just as important for being a successful author. A tendency that has become increasingly important, where »se trata para cada escritor de adoptar una postura, no tanto para escribir como para hacerse ver, para señalarse, esto es, para existir en el campo visual de la literatura« (Diaz 2016: 157). According to Diaz (ibid.: 158), this process of »señalarse« implies playing a role. An affirmation that is taken literally in *El mal de la taiga*, since the protagonist pays somebody else to cover the extraliterary activities the job implies:

> Fue ese editor el que me ayudó, de hecho, a idear el plan para proteger mi identidad: firmaría con un pseudónimo y, para evitar la curiosidad malsana que suele suscitar el que se esconde demasiado, contrataría a una mujer más o menos de mi edad, más o menos de mis características físicas, para llevar a cabo entrevistas y presentaciones (Rivera Garza 2019a: 25).

The collective as an essential component of writing is hinted at by the fact that the protagonist hires someone to help her fulfill the requirements of the profession and the importance she attributes to her publisher. Both the necessity to »perform« authorship and the importance of »gatekeepers« such as the editor are particularities of the 21st century literary market (cf. Gallego Cuiñas 2022a). However, not only the aftermath of the writing process in *El mal de la taiga* requires and involves others but writing itself is portrayed as a collective practice.

3.2 Dependency and Reproduction Rather Than Autonomy and Originality

The equation of being a detective and being a writer implicitly presents writing as a collective and interactive process: The content of the book depends on the investigation, which in turn, depends on contacts, witnesses and traces that others left behind. Right from the beginning, the protagonist makes her dependency on others transparent:

Contacté a amigos que, a su vez, me pusieron en contacto con amigos que, poco a poco, me fueron aproximando hacia la taiga. Hacía falta, como siempre face falta, un traductor. Un informante. Y, mucho antes de llegar, mucho antes de partir incluso, tenía ya entre mis contactos al hablante de su lengua que se encargaría de ponerlo todo en mi lengua (37–38).

The emphasis on the necessity of others is also implemented stylistically, as the protagonist positions herself as a rather narrator that depends on others by highlighting her own ignorance and uncertainty. The narration is marked by verbs, which indicate her subjectivity and a variety of structures that point out her intern focalization, clarifying that her narration is rather a subjective perception than an objective retelling of events: »supongo/supuse que« (14, 34, 40, 130), »creo que« (21), »hube de imaginar« (41), »Imaginé« (50), »me sorprendió« (50), »tenía el aire« (10), »daba la impresiónv (10, 29, 134), »me pareció que« (13, 43), »parece indicar que« (33), »parecía que« (44), »no era difícil imaginarse que« (130). Additionally, she explicitly points out her uncertainty: »no sabía a ciencia cierta« (96), »es difícil saber a ciencia cierta« (9, 14), »tampoco lo sabía con exactitud« (9), »imposible saberlo con toda certeza« (88), »no pude identificar« (11), »tenía poca idea [...]. Tenía tan poca idea« (3), »Nunca supe si eso fue, alguna vez, cierto [...]. Nunca tuve idea de« (40). As she herself is incapable of knowing, she heavily depends on the other characters to tell the story, disclosing that her position as a narrator (and author) is not privileged or autonomous in any way. She is unable to originally create, but rather reproduces, which is also reflected in the recurring anaphora »Que« (9, 15, 21, 23, 27, 31, 37, 43,…), which indicates indirect speech and marks the beginning of nearly every single chapter as well as the frequent use of doubly reported speech:

[...] dijo el hombre que decía la mujer (53)
interrumpió la muchacha y tradujo, de nueva cuenta, el traductor (46)
eso quedaba claro en el resumen que había hecho el traductor de lo dicho por el niño (85)
dijo que eso le había preguntado (70)
el traductor me contaría [...] lo que le había escuchado decir al niño (72).

By this, the text strongly contradicts the idea of authorship as something that relies on singularity and autonomy, by placing the author not in the usual ivory tower, the »lugar de omnisciencia y de poder desde el cual conocer y dirigir el espacio común que se mantiene a distancia« (Pérez Fontdevila 2019a: 73), but rather among the community. One could assume that the protagonist is positioned even below the other characters due to the mentioned ignorance, but actually and as the text makes clear that »siempre se devela que nadie sabe a ciencia cierta [...] que nadie sabe nunca« (21), »[n]adie puede saber en realidad« (29), »[n]adie en realidad sabe [...] Nadie sabe« (57). If nobody actually knows, everybody can speculate, which opens the text for free interpretation and can be understood as a metafictional invitation for the readers of the text to make sense of it. The same is true for the illustrations the text includes as well as the soundtrack, added as playlist in the penultimate chapter, both adding layers of ambiguous meaning. The text itself – as detective fiction – reflects the desired inclusion of the readers via its genre (cf. Rodríguez 2022: 74) and even more so as the detective outs herself as incompetent right from the beginning. By including the readers in the production of the narration, the (fictional) author might not be killed as Barthes had implied, but at least their supremacy is negated and they become part of the text they are narrating. The strong focus on dependency and reproduction lays the groundwork for understanding literature as a common good.

3.3 Common Good Rather Than Personal Property

The final and perhaps most radical contrast to the idea of authorship as a concept linked to singularity is to position literature, not only as something collective but as a common good, which belongs to everybody. This idea is mainly established in the text by the literary genres it incorporates and corresponds to. The most present literary genre, apart from the detective fiction, is the fairy tale, which is already alluded to on the blurb: »Éste no es un cuento de hadas«. Despite this statement, the text can be interpreted as such or at least invokes the genre on several occasions. The presence of the genre is relevant because of two of its inherent features. Firstly, fairy tales are »originated within an oral storytelling tradition« (Zipes 2006: 3), and secondly, they »do not have single, stable originals that we can depend upon as source texts; they proliferate as narratives, and it is often unclear which version, if any, should have priority over others« (Teverson 2013: 4). The orality, which traditionally characterizes the fairy tale, is emphasized in *El mal de la taiga* via the already described particularities regarding the reported speech and suggests the arbitrariness of the final written text. As the protagonist herself clarifies when writing about the client, that she investigates and writes the report for:

> [...] le pediría que tomara en cuenta que nada de lo escrito ocurre nunca tal cual. Nada de lo escrito ocurre tal cual, repetiría eso o algo parecido. [...] que tomara en cuenta que había mucho tiempo entre alocución y alocución. Deténgase, le pediría. Lea como si hubiera muchos minutos, incluso algunas horas, entre las palabras pronunciadas primero y, luego las palabras escritas. Transcritas. Las frases (38).

But also when reflecting about the genre itself:

> En los cuentos de hadas el lobo siempre es un lobo feroz. [...] Aunque en las versiones benignas de la Caperucita Roja, el lobo es superado por un leñador e, incluso en otras versiones, por la sabiduría y la fuerza de la abuela misma, los cuentos originales utilizaban la figura del lobo para transmitir con todo rigor ciertas lecciones morales. [...] Pero en las versiones más antiguas, antes de que la lección moral se volviera un imperativo en los cuentos infantiles, el lobo no sólo triunfa, sino que lo hace de la manera más atroz (53).

Moreover, the possibility of different versions is put into practice in the text by using various words to describe the same facts of the case, giving the readers the option to choose for themselves the word they estimate the most adequate: »con respecto o terror« (43), »de miedo o de espanto« (70), »el silencio o el miedo« (99), »Producto de la voluntad o del deseo« (98), »dijo u ordenó« (53) »Avizoré o vi« (70), columpiarse o saltar (78), »a través o junto con« (85), as well as the frequent use of anaphoras (23, 24, 28, 59, 71, 72, 77,...) that show the doubt of the narrator to make herself understood, but also the desired doubt, which she describes as her own narrative style:

> [...] me dediqué a escribir los casos en que había participado, pero los escribía de otra manera. *No era que* resolviera en la imaginación lo que la realidad me había negado. *No era que* mi apesadumbrada figura se convirtiera, por obra y gracia de la ficción, en una heroína de opereta o una villana de poca monta. *La otra manera* consistía en contar una seria de eventos con rigor, sí, pero sin descartar el desvarío o la dubitación. *La otra manera* no consistía en contar las cosas como son o como pudieron ser o haber sido como tiemblan todavía, ahora mismo, en la imaginación (24, emphasis added).

The inclusion of doubt in her narrative style can also be read as a strategy to allow for ambiguous interpretations. Insisting in the orality, the possibility of different versions, as well as in the importance of the readers are all characteristics that put into question the dominant position of the author and highlight the collectiveness of literature.

4 Authorship in the 21st Century

As demonstrated, CRG's work conveys the idea of authorship as a construct necessarily in need of the collective and relational, leaving behind the conception of the genius author who creates unique works independently of others. In doing so, these texts not only invite us to rethink what it means to be an author, but also contrast with the patriarchal structures inherent in the literary tradition. The collective concept of authorship she calls for in her essays is reflected in her literary texts, such as *El mal de la taiga*. As has been shown, the novel transmits the idea of writing as a collective and interactive practice by portraying authorship as profession, that highly depends on others, including the readers themselves, and always partially reproduces something that already had existed, as it is made out of something that belongs to everyone and, therefore, belongs to everyone itself. With this positioning, CRG inscribes herself and her work in a tendency that Gallego Cuiñas (2022a: 38) regards as characteristic of the change from the last century to the current one:

> [el] giro colectivizador o cooperativista de finales del siglo XX, que ha propiciado la vuelta pre-capitalista a la matriz social de la literatura oral y a la reivindicación de lo literario como un bien público o bien común, democrático, compartido a través de las redes sociales y de sociabilidad que promueven las comunidades letradas.

However, it remains to be seen whether this observable change will lead to a generally accepted new conceptualization of authorship and whether this in turn will finally help to open up the field of literature for less privileged othered subjects.

Bibliography

Barthes, Roland (1993): »La mort de l'auteur«, in: id. (ed.), Le bruissement de la langue, Paris: Seuil, pp. 61–67.

Bourdieu, Pierre (1992): Les règles de l'art. Genèse et structure du champ littéraire, Paris: Seuil.

Burke, Seán (2019): Authorship. From Plato to the Postmodern. A Reader, Edinburgh: Edinburgh University Press.

Diaz, José-Luis (2016): »Las escenografías autoriales románticas y su ›puesta en discurso‹«, in: Aina Pérez Fontdevila/Meri Torras (eds.), Los papeles de autor/a. Marcos teóricos sobre la autoría literaria, Madrid: Arco/Libros, pp. 155–185.

Eltit, Diamela (2021): »Es necesario desbiologizar la letra«, in: Nexos 27.11.2021, https://cultura.nexos.com.mx/es-necesario-desbiologizar-la-letra-discurso-del-premio-fil-de-literatura-2021/ [17.06.2024].

Gallego Cuiñas, Ana (2022a): Cultura literaria y políticas de mercado. Editoriales, ferias y festivales, Berlin/Boston: De Gruyter.

Gallego Cuiñas, Ana (2022b): »Feminismo y literatura (argentina) mundial. Selva Almada, Mariana Enríquez y Samanta Schweblin«, in: Gustavo Guerrero/Jorge J. Locane/Benjamin Loy et al. (eds.), Literatura latinoamericana mundial. Dispositivos y disidencias, Berlin/Boston: De Gruyter, pp. 71–96.

Gallego Cuiñas, Ana (2023): »Autor, obra y mercado en la cultura literaria del siglo XXI«, in: Guadalupe Silva/Magdalena Cámpora (eds.), Literatura y legitimación en América Latina. Polémicas, operaciones, representaciones, Buenos Aires: Corregidor, pp. 323–331.

Guerreiro, Leila: »Algo está pasando«, in: LENGUA, https://www.penguinlibros.com/es/revista-lengua/escritoras-latinoamericanas/escritoras-latinoamericanas [17.06.2024].

Heinich, Nathalie (2005): L'élite artiste. Excellence et singularité en régime démocratique, Paris: Gallimard.

López Fernández, Elba (2020): »La autoría y la apropiación en la creación del siglo XXI«, in: Revista SOBRE 6, pp. 15–24.

Lucífora, María C. (2020): Máscaras autorales. Análisis de las autopoéticas, Mar del Plata: Editorial de la Universidad Nacional de Mar del Plata.

Lugones, Maria (1994): »Purity, Impurity, and Separation«, in: Signs 19, pp. 458–479.

Pérez Fontdevila, Aina (2019a): »Otear la comunidad desde la torre de marfil: Apuntes sobre la noción de autor como constructo inmunitario«, in: Adriana de Teresa Ochoa (ed.), Horizontes teóricos y críticos en torno a la figura autoral contemporánea, Ciudad de México: Universidad Nacional Autónoma de México, pp. 69–92.

Pérez Fontdevila, Aina (2019b): »Qué es una autora o qué no es un autor«, in: Meri Torras Francès/Aina Pérez Fontdevila (eds.), ¿Qué es una autora? Encrucijadas entre género y autoría, Barcelona: Icaria, pp. 25–59.

Power, Andrew J. (2021): The Birth and Death of the Author. A Multi-authored History of Authorship in Print, New York, London: Routledge.

Rivera Garza, Cristina (2019a): El mal de la taiga, New York: Literatura Random House.

Rivera Garza, Cristina (2019b): Los muertos indóciles. Necroescrituras y desapropiación, Ciudad de México: Debolsillo.

Rodríguez, Humberto A. (2022): La novela policíaca negra y criminal. Arraigamiento en la literatura latinoamericana a partir de la obra de Rubem Fonseca y Roberto Bolaño, Bogotá: Universidad Distrital Francisco José de Caldas.

Teverson, Andrew. (2013): Fairy tale, New York: Routledge.

Trías, Fernanda (2021): »Democratizar la letra. Fernanda Trías, Premio Sor Juana Inés de la Cruz 2021«, in: Noticias NCC, https://noticiasncc.com/cartelera/articulos-o-noticias/12/02/democratizar-letra-fernanda-trias-premio-sor-juana-ines-cruz-2021/ [17.06.2024].

Woodmansee, Martha (1994): The Author, Art, and the Market. Re-reading the History of Asthetics, New York: Columbia University Press.

Yásnaya, Elena A. (2019): »La sangre, la lengua y el apellido. Mujeres indígenas y Estados nacionales«, in: Gabriela Jauregui (ed.), Tsunami, Barcelona: Sexto Piso, pp. 25–39.

Zipes, Jack (2006): Fairy Tales and the Art of Subversion. The Classical Genre for Children and the Process of Civilization, New York: Routledge.

Citation as/and Relation
Chronic Pain, Autotheory, and Horizontal Writing in Jennifer Bélanger and Martine Delvaux's *Les allongées*

Hannah Volland

> How do you throw a brick through the window of a bank if you can't get out of bed?
> (J. Hedva, »Sick Woman Theory«)

1 Sick Women Solidarity

In what has since become a seminal text of disability activism and scholarship, Johanna Hedva, who began to draft »Sick Woman Theory« at the time of the Black Lives Matter protests in Los Angeles in 2014, writes from their personal experience of chronic illness to reflect on modes of protest and collective action afforded to sick people. Their autotheoretical manifesto recognizes the ways in which sick and crip bodies engage in modes of resistance against regimes of capitalism, white supremacy, and cis-heterosexism, demonstrating that crip agency – because it is »lived, embodied, suffering« (Hedva 2020: 9) – often remains invisible to a larger public. As Hedva argues for the transformative potential of care as an interdependent sociality grounded in acts of nursing and nurturing, of caring and sharing, they urge us to consider the relational politics connecting illness with action. In the collaborative essay from Québec that I will turn to in this chapter, *Les allongées* (2022),[1] Jennifer Bélanger and Martine

---

1   All subsequent references to this text will be cited in the text with page numbers in parentheses.

Delvaux take up Johanna Hedva's urgent question, cited above my introduction, and thread it into their own narrative on chronic illness. Tending to another sick woman figure, the »allongées« (literally translating to the elongated or supine women), Bélanger and Delvaux create a similarly capacious onomastic signifier – one that equally holds space for those who are sick and sickened by structures of domination and oppression. Their use of the *féminin générique* further echoes Hedva's (2020: 9) choice of ›woman‹ as a strategic placeholder for »the un-cared-for, the secondary, the oppressed«. In *Les allongées*, Delvaux and Bélanger thus not only attend to the bed-ridden women, as the nominal adjective of their book's title would have it, but they make visible the larger community of those who have been and continue to be marginalized, excluded and left behind.[2]

The initial comparison of *Les allongées* and »Sick Woman Theory« helps to establish two points that will guide my analysis: their intertextual relation attests to a political and ethical kinship based on shared tendencies and commitments, and since this is an intimate connection, it also brings to light how citation can transform into a practice of relating. Put differently, the intertextual links between the two texts point to citing and referencing as discursive strategies that move beyond a purely textual phenomenon and involve closeness, mutuality and camaraderie between writers and their ideas. In my reading of *Les allongées*, I argue that Delvaux and Bélanger make use of a feminist citation practice by leaving behind the conventional logics of citation[3] and emphasizing instead a personal and deeply emotional engagement with intertexts

---

2 »[N]ous écrivons sans arrêt vers ce qui agonise, ces femmes accidentées malades mortes disparues ou vivantes, qui font entendre à nos tympans leurs chants de sirène [...]« (129).

3 In its conventional use, citation is a means of providing proof, of recognizing an authority and making a lineage visible. In academic contexts, citations are embedded in institutionalized structures and disciplines; they determine the ways in which bodies of texts and ideas relate to each other. Such discursive power is inevitably bound up in sociopolitical forms of power: Sarah Ahmed and Donna Haraway (2010: 53) thus aptly speak of institutionalized citations as »reproductive technologies«, ones that, as Ahmed (2013) puts it in one of her killjoy blog posts, are successfully »reproducing the world around certain bodies«. Exposing the heterosexist and racist logics that often undergird academic uses of citation, both theorists present a compelling critique of the socio-discursive implications of citation and make evident the urgent need to rethink and renew our literary and academic practices critically.

as sources of support and inspiration. My reading itself is inspired by the multiple interventions of queer and feminist artists, writers, and theorists who have argued for critically conscious approaches to citation.

While feminist inquiry into citation practices dates back to Katie King's influential article on »Bibliography and a Feminist Apparatus of Production« (1991), more recent debates have been sparked by the independent curator Maiko Tanaka in an article published in *C Mag* in 2015. In »Feminist Approaches to Citation«, Tanaka analyses queer feminist artist's projects that build on citation as a tool for communal thought, reflection, and action. She notes that, in these projects, citation »is not only an acknowledgment of sources of inspiration, but also realizes the community it references, performatively bringing it into being« (2015). Feminist citational strategies often coincide with collaborative modes of working, where citation acts as a shared source of wisdom and reflection and forms part of an embodied experience, of »something felt, lived and particular« (ibid.). Commenting on the same artistic projects as Maiko Tanaka, Lauren Fournier (2021: 191) asserts that, in a more general sense, »citation forms an integral part of a queer feminist practice of world-making«. Fournier implicitly alludes to an argument that has been pivotal in the thought and work of Sara Ahmed. In *Living A Feminist Life* (2017), the theorist makes a convincing case for feminism as »a building project« (Ahmed 2017: 14), comparing citations to »feminist bricks« (ibid.: 16) that need to become the building materials of our writing: »if our texts are worlds, they need to be made out of feminist materials« (ibid.: 14).

I take heed of Ahmed's call for – intertextual – action and turn to *Les allongées* as an example of a relational writing practice that is sustained and supported through acts of citation. My reading implicitly attempts to respond to Johanna Hedva's initial question by way of another interrogation: if one cannot get out of bed and throw a brick through the window of a bank, can one turn to writing and citing as a form of collective action and an expression of solidarity? Can citations be textual resources for relationships and community-building? In my attempt to respond to these questions, I will begin by discussing autotheory, a contemporary literary-artistic practice that has most fruitfully harnessed a feminist citation practice. I then continue with an analysis of citation as/and relation[4] in *Les allongées*, moving from paratextual considerations

---

4   My title indirectly cites and rewrites a chapter title from Lauren Fournier's monograph (2021: 133).

on shared authorship to close readings on lateral citation, intertextual companionship, and figuration. As I follow these discursive paths, my hope is to show that citation can indeed enact and act upon relationality – be it by staging active conversations, making visible personal and political connections, or rewriting the cultural narratives of wellness and well-being through multiple viewpoints.

2 Autotheory's Citational Relations

Like »Sick Woman Theory«, *Les allongées* features autobiographical elements alongside a large body of intertextual references. Cited in the margins of the texts, numerous writers, journalists, cinematographers, and theorists enter the collaborative writing space of Bélanger and Delvaux, coming to form a close-knit community, held together by a shared involvement in intersectional feminist approaches to dis/ability, care, and social justice. This performative use of citation – one that enacts the community it wishes for – is characteristic of autotheoretical modes of writing and artmaking.

Autotheory is a genre-bending, intermedial queer feminist practice that can be situated in-between and across different modes of writing, performance, visual arts, philosophical reflection, and social criticism, and has been attributed to different genealogies.[5] In my use of the term, I refer to Lauren Fournier's seminal work on *Autotheory as Feminist Practice in Art, Writing, and Criticism* (2021) and her consideration of autotheory as a post-1960s practice rooted in feminist epistemologies and »tied to a politics of radical self- reflection, embodied knowledge, and sustained, literary nonfictional writing through the self that has been, and continues to be, suppressed and repressed by certain patriarchal and colonial contexts« (Fournier 2021: 38). It should be noted that Fournier's understanding of autotheory emerges from a large corpus of works that have been developed and disseminated in North America and can thus be considered specific to a geographical and cultural context

---

5   The *Arizona Quarterly* issue of 2020, edited by Robyn Wiegman, links the origins of autotheory to the cross-pollination of poststructuralist theory and autobiography. Wiegman's emphasis on autotheory as a fusion of autobiography and theory stands in contrast to Lauren Fournier's approach of autotheory as a transmedial feminist practice that questions the »master discourse« of T/theory. (cf. Brostoff and Fournier 2021: 491).

marked by ongoing histories of settler colonialism, capitalism, as well as a Euro-American-centric art, literature and theory scene (cf. Fournier 2021: 102).

This context also has to be taken into consideration for the study of autotheoretical works from Québec where cultural productions have been equally affected by longstanding histories of racism and colonialism (cf. Huberman/Kirouac-Massicotte 2021). The authors of *Les allongées*, Jennifer Bélanger and Martine Delvaux, seem well aware of the intersecting histories and locations that can be mapped throughout their text and its intertextual network. In their self-reflective fragments, they not only uncover and criticize the androcentric perspective of medical discourse and its hyper-capitalist injunctions, but also address the longstanding systematic exploitation and neglect experienced by racialized and indigenous communities in Québec. In what follows, I take on Fournier's historically and geographically astute definition to situate autotheory in politically consequential terms and recognize the ethical-political stakes of its formal features. A brief overview of the main ramifications spawned by autotheory's performative use of citation will form the basis of my study.

Citation in autotheory most importantly departs from previous models of intertextuality: where New Criticism and poststructuralism consider intertextuality as either a loss of authority or an integral component of literature's open-endedness (cf. Brostoff 2021: 97), autotheorists employ citation to foster a sense of belonging and community. Maggie Nelson illustrates this point most eloquently when she turns to Barthes' notion of »coexistence« (2002) to exemplify the reciprocity between human and textual bodies who both need to be nurtured and sustained by others. Reflecting on the critical role played by the thinking and writing of others in her creative practice, Nelson (2012) remarks:

> I've often found myself very interested in dramatizing this coexistence – showcasing the situation we find ourselves in, in which dependence on others—or at least relation to them—is the condition of possibility for self-reliance. This is what I mean by »writing with, from, or for others« – the problem of performing relationality in a text.

For Nelson (as is the case for other autotheorists), citation represents one of the key elements of a relational writing practice which redefines the creative act as one that is collective without necessarily being collaborative. As autotheorists angle the discussion of intertextuality into the direction of a deeply personal, emotional engagement with citation, they mark a shift away from an individualist conception of the author/creator, leaning towards relational modes of writing and artmaking where citation is a means of engaging in active and ongoing conversations as well as of »making visible [...] lineages and legacies of inspiration and support« (Tanaka 2015).

In autotheory, intertextual relations illustrate an intimate, personal connection to the artists cited, often grounded in a similarity of lived experiences. As autotheorists reference works that resonate with their own embodied life, they practice what Lauren Fournier (2021: 147) refers to as »comparative life-reading«, meaning a tendency to critically reflect on the past by comparing it to the »life-texts« (ibid.: 149) of others. These discursive gestures not only link texts and intertexts but also point to the intrinsic relationship between subjectivity and sociality and reveal a self bound up in the relations that sustain it. What is at stake in autotheory, then, is a transfiguration of the »I« – the *autos* – into a plural and interconnected subject (cf. Brostoff 2021: 92; Laubender 2020: 39). As Carolyn Laubender (2020: 55) notes, the move to a plural self is spurred by an aspiration to counteract narratives of essentialized selfhood and to achieve relational justice through narrative collaboration and cumulation. While the sociopolitical potential of polyvocal acts of narration is potentially hindered by the risk of (involuntarily) appropriating and usurping the voices of others (ibid.: 59), autotheory's gesture toward a pluralistic subject represents one of the most significant interventions in existing paradigms of authorship, selfhood, and self-writing.

Throughout *Les allongées*, Bélanger and Delvaux indirectly quote autotheory's experimental formal conventions: they divide their text into short, non-chronological paragraphs, use italicized text – instead of quotation marks – and place citations in the margins. Their performative use of citation supports and enacts a relational writing practice that allows different speakers to commingle and their voices to converge. In their commitment to a truly collaborative and collective text, Delvaux and Bélanger cite and rewrite autotheory's approach to citation as/and relation, setting the stage for new modes of cooperation and community through writing.

3 Connecting through Chronic Pain: on Collaboration and Lateral Citation

Les allongées is written from the authors' lived experiences and a mutual commitment to intersectional feminisms and their politics of mental health, dis/ability, and pain, a commitment informed by their respective research on illness narratives.[6] Their project on chronic pain and fatigue began as a spontaneous dialogue, a conversation that had to be conducted in written form due to the context of the global COVID-19 pandemic and a new lockdown in Montréal. In their solitary confinements, exchanging short fragments became a way of connecting and staying close; »c'était une manière de sortir de l'isolement, à distance, mais ensemble« explains Martine Delvaux in an interview with Félix Morin (2023: 6:46) for the podcast *Les longues entrevues*.

This private exchange – a coping mechanism or, as Jennifer Bélanger laughingly adds in the interview, a sort of »medical prescription« (Morin 2023: 7:37) that helped to get through months of social isolation – transforms into a literary text bearing few traces of the initial dialogic form since we can never be sure who wrote which passages, nor if their order and sequencing have been modified in the course of publication. In the paperback edition of *Les allongées*, the back-and-forth between the two writers is only tacitly present in the short and loosely connected fragments that form the non-linear and discontinuous text but invisible on a formal or typographical level. The lack of authorial markers inside the book presents a novelty in autotheory's relational writing practices: where other writers employ citation to *stage* relational gestures, Bélanger and Delvaux actively incorporate the voice of each other, hence creating a plurivocal first-person subject that takes autotheory's idea of a ›plural self‹ a step further. As their writing gets interwoven in the fabric of a text made from no singular thread, the lines between self and other are constantly blurred and become unrecognizable. Thus, their collaboration allows for a generous collective practice in which the shared act of writing partially[7] renounces authorship/ownership

---

[6]   Jennifer Bélanger and Martine Delvaux are pursuing research projects related to illness narratives, and they have collaborated on academic projects. Both are non-/fiction writers: Bélanger is the author of an autofictional novel, *Menthol* (2020), and Delvaux has published numerous essays and novels, three of which deploy a form and style that resemble *Les allongées* (*Thelma, Louise et moi* [2018], *Je n'en ai jamais parlé à personne* [2019], and *Pompières et pyromanes* [2021] come to mind here).

[7]   The author-function is reaffirmed, however, through paratextual naming and the media promotion of the book.

of the written text and honors instead »more equal playing fields or footings« (Fournier 2021: 178).

Delvaux and Bélanger not only share authorship in *Les allongées*, but they also welcome the presence of others in their text. While some are cited with their names placed in the margins, others remain anonymous. These latter, lateral, citations are of close friends, family members, colleagues, and health practitioners. They are characteristic of autotheory's commitment to a relational politics, which, according to Lauren Fournier, aims at »destabilizing hierarchies of influence« (ibid.: 154) by granting discursive space and legitimacy to non-established thinkers, such as friends and lovers. Citing alongside rather than »upward« – the spatial metaphor points to the epistemic and institutional hierarchies involved – gives way to a communal knowledge-production in which one's peers contribute as much knowledge and expertise as so-called ›authority figures‹.

Concretely, though, as we can see in *Les allongées*, lateral modes of citation do not always reveal a harmonious relationship since, in this text, they also disclose the disparities and power imbalances that can exist between individuals and become most evident in medical and professional relationships where the unwell person has to assert themselves against mechanisms of silencing, gaslighting and erasure. Where lateral citations stem from more equal grounds, they do, however, portray the intimacy and closeness of friendship and shared narratives of illness:

> une amie me confie que son épuisement est un ruisseau qui n'afflue nulle part, et devant ses mains qui miment l'avancée infinie de l'eau, je me dis que malgré la sensation de flotter, malgré l'état d'inertie dans lequel il nous arrive de plonger, nous demeurons brûlantes minérales volatiles liquides, éminemment terrestres (107).

In this conversation between friends, the fluidity of liquid metaphors describing the sick body, their movement from one speaking subject to the other, creates a connection and allows for the articulation of shared knowledge: where the friend's metaphoric gesture of a stream flooding out into nowhere describes a sensation of inertia and floating, the continuous movement of her arms testifies to the sick body's liveliness. Recounting (or citing) her friend's gesture and her response to it is then a way of acknowledging their collaboration in the process of critical reflection; it is the friend's gesture which makes the narrator realize that, despite their feeling of a passive drifting, their bodies are well alive and constantly changing – and it is her metaphor that inspires the narrator's own recourse to natural imagery as she depicts unwell bodies as »burning minerals volatile liquids, eminently earthly« (107). Like the collaboration between the two authors, lateral citation is thus a form of cooperation and reciprocity; in both cases, writing is not a singular act, but arises out of conversations and intimate attachments to others.

On a stylistic level, the motifs of mutuality, reciprocity, and dialogue translate into a recurring use of enumerations and accumulations, both rhetorical devices that allow the narrators to create impressions of simultaneity and multiplicity. Accumulation, in particular, serves as a means to stretch out and diversify nominal categories, such as in the above-cited description of sick bodies as »brûlantes minérales volatiles liquides, éminemment terrestres« (107) or another fragment referring to the sick and unwell as »personnes contaminées incandescentes irradiées« (30). The absence of commas (a typographical choice that remains constant throughout the text) underscores a desire to create non-hierarchical syntactical structures while the juxtaposition of adjectives lends itself to a semantic exuberance and as such attests to the multifaceted ways sickness and wellness can be experienced and communicated.

4 (Inter)Textual Companionship

The intimacy and closeness afforded by way of citing others also manifests itself in the citations placed in the margins. Quoting from a heteroclite corpus of writers, artists, and activists, Bélanger and Delvaux create an intertextual network that is also an archive of the sick, the crip, the un-cared-for, the *allongées*. In this archive, not all texts have the same vocation: some canonized works – like the philosophical treatises of Aristotle and Nietzsche – are critically re-cited, and their misogyny and ableism exposed, while others are solicited to provide inspiration, support, and comfort. Those who continually reappear across the fragments, entering the thoughts and reflections elaborated, eventually become »companion texts« to borrow the expression from Sara Ahmed (2017: 16). Just like friends and lovers, such texts can provide direction and encouragement, as Ahmed (ibid.) explains: »companion texts can prompt you to hesitate or to question the direction in which you are going, or they might give you a sense that in going the way you are going, you are not alone.« In *Les allongées*, the texts that accompany the authors along the way are written by those who could be associated with a feminist dis/ability counter-canon and whose working methods, similar to those of Bélanger and Delvaux, can be linked to an autotheoretical impetus (Chantal Akerman, Catherine Blackburn, Anne Boyer, Hélène Cixous, bell hooks, and Michele Lent Hirsch come to mind here).

For Delvaux and Bélanger, incorporating the works of these authors into their writing is a way of paying tribute, as well as a means of staging active and open-ended conversations. Quoting from Audre Lorde's *Cancer Journals*, the authors use citation to enact a dialogic movement, their sentence closely echoing the italicized text:

> *je suis peut-être trop maigre mais ça ne m'empêche pas de danser*, et nous, nous sommes peut-être trop endolories pour nous déhancher, mais avec chaque esquisse de mouvement, nous voulons enfreindre les interdits, nous soulever sans feinte ni ruse dans le désir [...] (115–116).

The dialogic movement unfolds in two ways; first through direct quotation and then through semantic and lexical reiteration, a way of both taking up the citation and creating a variation. Lorde's writing here not only inspires the thoughts and reflections of the writing subject but also provides a structure on which their writing relies in turn. In the pronominal transition from »I« to »we«, one senses that the words cited resonate more widely and are capable of creating a shared feeling or longing, maybe akin to what bell hooks (2006: 256) has referred to as a »*commonality of feeling*« and »a potential place of community building«. When intertextual relations provide community and companionship, they often invoke a mode of »intimacy and identification« (Fournier 2021: 147) in which the narrator identifies with those s/he cites. Such identifications not only manifest in dialogic movements like the one I described above but also appear at sites of enunciative entanglements. In those instances, the speakers are no longer distinguishable, and speech is – conscientiously – appropriated. Citing *Care Work. Dreaming Disability Justice* (2019) by queer, non-binary poet and disability justice activist Leah Lashmi Piepzna-Samarasinha, Bélanger and Delvaux create such a site of identification through citation and ›shared‹ enunciation:

> *je rêve ici j'écris ici* dans mon lit, entourée de livres de bougies d'ailes invisibles pour me déplacer dans le sens contraire des aiguilles d'une montre et avancer sur ce chemin d'encre qui noircit les pages, prolonge la vie en dépit de ce qui la fragilise (35).

Not only do the narrator and Piepzna-Samarasinha refer to similar lived experiences (the quote is taken from a letter addressed to Gloria Anzaldúa in which the author reflects on the relationship between creativity and time spent in bed), but they also, quite literally, speak with one voice. The ›I‹ is attached to multiple speakers and becomes a locus of intimacy and identification, creating a confusion of speakers which, again, occasions a staging of the plural self – a self whose words are ›tangled‹, interwoven with those of others. In these fragments, citations then lay bare affectionate attachments; they show how texts can become intimate companions who provide meaningful resources for (self-)knowledge, inspiration, and support.

5 Citation and Feminist Figuration

Ultimately, citation also relates to a process of figuration that transforms the figure of the *allongées* into the capacious onomastic signifier I described in my introduction. In feminist theory, figuration refers to a critical practice involved in wor(l)d-making; it is a speculative, semiotic tool crucial to imagining different worlds and new relationships within them. Drawing on the work of Rosi Braidotti and Donna Haraway, Katrin Thiele (2021: 232–233) explains figuration as follows:

> Figuration, in the sense presented here, is about the creation of different relations between words and things – between wording and worlding. Figures [...] can be read as tools to produce thought; they constitute rather than they reflect. Figures intervene into the world; they are, and they do their work, by participating in the stories told instead of speaking from outside or beyond.

More than mere metaphors, figures and figurations are agentive textual creatures: they *produce* thought and *intervene* in (hi)stories. As conceptual tools, they always act in relation to a world that is both discursive and material, aiming to shift perspectives and thus to allow for new ways of seeing and being. Framing the citational creation of the *allongées* as figuration is a way of attending to its sociopolitical and critical potential, of bringing to light the interventions it stages into several material-semiotic territories, such as medical discourses, narratives of chronic illness, as well as feminist history and epistemology.

The critical work of figuration is most thought-provoking in the engagement with second-wave feminist figures that have contributed significantly to new understandings of subjectivity and agency. By coming back to these figures, Bélanger and Delvaux intervene in their stories and rewrite them from a sick and crip perspective. For instance, Hélène Cixous' laughing medusa is no longer characterized by a daunting exuberance and vivid self-determination. Instead, she takes on the *allongées*' frailness as she finds herself stranded on the beach, wrecked and weary: »nous sommes des méduses qui ne rient plus, fatiguées exténuées échouées sur le sable d'avoir pris un cocktail d'antidépresseurs, de somnifères et d'alcool«(34). The first-person plural creates an impression of community and inclusiveness – in the textual world of the *allongées*, the sick medusas are no longer laughing, but they are salvaged and revived through the act of citing and rewriting. Here, the syntactical accumulation (»fatiguées exténuées échouées«) not only stylistically reproduces the exuberance of Cixous' figure (and her writing), but also brings out an aspect that has not been given enough attention in this analysis: the poetic language and, more specifically, the recourse to assonances, consonances, alliterations, and anaphoras. Throughout the text, these sound devices generate iterations that hold together words and phrases, prompting a feeling of unity and togetherness despite semantic differences.

As it participates in the semiotic-discursive process of figuration, the figure of the *allongées* stands against an all too optimistic image of embodied agency; she enters the storyworld of the medusa in order to change its plot and characters and to invent a new heroine that no longer corresponds to an idealized image of vigour and autonomy but discloses the reality of illness and its effects on the body. We can further see this in a reference to Monique Wittig's *Les Guérillères*. In this experimental novel, the *guérillères*, inspired by the mythical Amazons, form an army of queer feminist warriors who wage a guerilla warfare against heteropatriarchy. As Bélanger and Delvaux cite from the novel, they merge Wittig's charismatic figure and the *allongées*, endowing the latter with a similar combativeness and joyful solidarity and lending their story an equally utopian ambition. Their fusion even becomes apparent on a grammatical level, since both figures are conjugated in the feminine plural:

> les allongées *se meuvent lancées les unes contre les autres*, épaule à épaule, bras noués, elles se suivent et se tiennent compagnie, à tour de rôle elles se rattrapent dans cette existence oblique qui les force à apprivoiser le déséquilibre, à anticiper le bris de cadence, mais toujours, elles reprennent cette valse qui n'abandonne personne (77–78).

One could object that the comparison of the figure of the *guérillères* to that of the *allongées* seems somewhat paradoxical: while Wittig's epic protagonists are vigorously engaged in battle, the sick and sickened women referred to by Bélanger and Delvaux are bed-ridden, constrained, and immobilized by physical and/or emotional pain. However, as with Cixous' medusas, there is a subtle rewriting at play that goes in both directions (the text and the intertext) and brings the two figures closer. More so, their kinship is not only the result of direct citation but also of an allusion to another essay by Wittig. Where the fragment refers to the life of the *allongées* as »cette existence oblique«, we can indeed discern a hint at »The Point of View: Universal or Particular?«, an essay in which Wittig reflects on the productive contradictions that occur when marginalized writers occupying non-hegemonic subject-positions enter literary discourse and are confronted with literature's claim to universality. Arguing that »[a]ll minority writers (who are conscious of being so) enter into literature obliquely« (Wittig 1983: 65), Wittig uses obliqueness as a metaphor to capture the perspective framed by a minoritized point of view. Bélanger and Delvaux take up the notion of the ›oblique‹ in a way that speaks to both its figurative and literal meaning: as a critical perspective and as bodily posture. This rewriting of the ›oblique‹ then opens Wittig's writing to new meanings and affords the *allongées* a certain conceptual intelligibility, a visibility in language and thought.

Finally, the intertextual references participate in figuration as the process that not only intervenes in feminist thought – citing and rewriting it from a crip perspective – but that, in turn, also revisits the story of the *allongées* and their narrative of chronic illness. Incorporating the wor(ld)s of figures who symbolize bodily strength and agency, *Les allongées* creates an open-ended and ever-evolving story of chronic illness – one in which multiple plots unfold through a continual rewriting.

6 From Citation as/and Relation to Horizontal Writing

Throughout my reading of *Les allongées*, I have been interested in how citational acts perform relational gestures. As can be noted for all autotheoretical texts and artworks, the correlation of citation as/and relation marks a shift from traditional models of intertextuality – focused on questions of authority and influence – to ones attuned to modes of intimacy and connection that bring closer human and textual bodies alike. In *Les allongées*, such closeness is afforded through collaboration, lateral citation, identification, and figuration, all of which inscribe citational modes of belonging and community into the fabric of the text. Delvaux and Bélanger's relational writing foregrounds dialogic and plurivocal scenes of enunciation where the lines between self and other are constantly blurred and rearranged. Their use of citation as/and relation thus eventually forms part of what I propose to call ›horizontal writing‹, meaning a scriptural practice that reaches outward, shares its (textual) space and resources, and invites us to reconsider writing, thinking, and reading as intrinsically relational processes and practices.

Within literary theory and creation, the notion of horizontality emphasizes a particular *modus operandi* of writers who seek to redefine established ideas of influence, hierarchy, and coherence. Maggie Nelson (2012) speaks for instance of a »horizontal plane of action« when she refers to the ways in which her writing performs relationality:

> [...] this relationality, this »leaning against« and its performance, is quite different from performing »influence«, or an »inherited tradition«, or some such. [...] The leaning against I'm talking about takes place on a horizontal plane of action, not a vertical one. It brings one into the land of wild associations, rather than that of grim congenital lineage. It is a place, as Gertrude Stein would have it, in which »the difference is spreading«.

A similar way of working can be ascribed to the fragments composing *Les allongées*, which – as I mentioned above – are only loosely connected, often following diffuse leads and »wild associations«. However, it should be noted that, for Nelson, horizontal writing is always associated with a »*staged* interaction with other texts« (Nelson 2012, emphasis added), that is to say, a consciously arranged performance of dialogue. In contrast, in Bélanger and Delvaux's text, horizontality is firmly rooted in collaboration and a continual exploration of literary possibilities for reciprocity. Less drawn to an individualist posture, their writing finds solace and comfort in the presence and thought of others. One could – figuratively – compare the relational aesthetics of their text to a community of care, held together by the embrace of quotations and reiterations.

On a formal level, horizontal writing in *Les allongées* materializes not only through the relational modes of citation and collaboration analyzed in this chapter but in all textual elements that signal a foundational openness and hence evoke a feeling of hospitality – one can think here of the fragments as a way of breaking out of linear narrativity, of leaving blank spaces as entry points for readers, or even the absence of capitalized letters and punctuation marks as a means of refusing grammatical hierarchization and composing open-ended thoughts. Horizontality is itself a conceptual figure/ation that ties together different meanings of the *allongées*, from bodily posture to relational writing and a critical positionality. It appears at the juncture of both the aesthetics and the ethics of *Les allongées*, referring to modes of relational writing where citation enacts conversation and collaboration, as well as to criticality, emerging from the intertextual engagement with feminist and crip perspectives. As it moves between form, style and content, the notion of horizontality allows me to conclude this chapter with a brief look to the larger sociopolitical implications of literary and artistic projects working towards crip and sick counternarratives, such as the performances and installations of choreographer and theatremaker Raquel Meseguer Zafe.

In »The Potential and Poetics of Rest«, Zafe (2023: 204) refers to horizontality as a »counterpoint to normative culture«. The artist lives with chronic pain and develops performances and installations that invite participants to lay down together and linger for a moment. Her works are committed to an inquiry into the »evolving and collective knowledge on the aesthetics of rest« (2023: 209) – an aesthetics that is fluid and cannot be pinned down but becomes most apparent in the feelings of openness and vulnerability her pieces provoke in visitors, facilitating more intimate conversations on the experience of living with invisible disabilities (ibid.: 209). Zafe's almost playful interrogation of normative ›vertical culture‹ closely resonates with *Les allongées* and its poetic resistance to capitalist and neoliberal imperatives of productivity. Bélanger and Delvaux employ the neologistic portmanteau »lits-terreaux« (40) to refer to the places where the *allongées*, fielded in their own temporal cycle, need to be left fallow, to rest, in order to thrive again: »l'utopie des allongées, c'est d'être laissées en jachère, ne plus tendre vers l'activité pour se prouver qu'elles peuvent exister autrement, et enfin fleurir à l'endroit fertile de leurs révoltes« (137). Bélanger and Delvaux's *allongées* then ultimately join Hedva's ›Sick Woman‹ and Zafe's horizontal spectatorship to engage in a critical interrogation of the gendered social and cultural narratives we associate with wellness and illness, relegating one to the realm of action and significance, and the other to that of idleness and triviality. Deconstructing the normative (and oppressive) logics of these narratives while also reimagining the supposedly private, hidden spaces of rest and recovery as active sites of critique and community-building, their texts and performances bridge the gaps between feminist and crip perspectives and create bonds among a multitude of lived experiences, embedded in relations of care and of mutual understanding.

Bibliography

Ahmed, Sara (2017): Living A Feminist Life, Durham: Duke University Press.

Ahmed, Sara (2013): »Making Feminist Points«, in: feministkilljoys, https://feministkilljoys.com/2013/09/11/making-feminist-points/ [29.04.2024].

Barthes, Roland (2002): »Sade, Fourier, Loyola«, in: Œuvres complètes (vol. 3), Paris: Seuil, pp. 699–870.

Bélanger, Jennifer (2020): Menthol, Montréal: Héliotrope.

Bélanger, Jennifer/Delvaux, Martine (2022): Les allongées, Montréal: Héliotrope.

Brostoff, Alex. (2021): »An Autotheory of Intertextual Kinship. Ambivalent Bodies in the Work of Maggie Nelson and Paul B. Preciado«, in: Synthesis. An Anglophone Journal of Comparative Literary Studies 14, pp. 91–115.

Brostoff, Alex/Fournier, Lauren (2021): »Introduction. Autotheory ASAP! Academia, Decoloniality, and ›I‹«, in: ASAP/Journal 6.3, pp. 489–502.

Delvaux, Martine (2018): Thelma, Louise et moi, Montréal: Héliotrope.

Delvaux, Martine (2020): Je n'en ai jamais parlé à personne, Montréal: Héliotrope.

Delvaux, Martine (2021): Pompières et pyromanes, Montréal: Héliotrope.

Fournier, Lauren (2021): Autotheory as Feminist Practice in Art, Writing, and Criticism, Cambridge, Massachusetts: MIT Press.

Hedva, Johanna (2020 [2016]): »Sick Woman Theory«, https://johannahedva.com/SickWomanTheory_Hedva_2020.pdf [15.03.2024].

hooks, bell (2006 [1994]): Outlaw Culture. Resisting representations, New York/London: Routledge Classics.

Haraway, Donna (2010): »When Species Meet: staying with the trouble«, in: Environment and Planning D: Society and Space 28(1), pp. 53–55.

Huberman, Isabella/Kirouac-Massicotte, Isabelle (2021): »Introduction. Colonialisme et race dans les productions littéraires et culturelles québécoises«, in: Arborescences. Revue d'études littéraires, linguistiques et pédagogiques de langue française 11, pp. 1–7.

King, Katie (1991): »Bibliography and a Feminist Apparatus of Production«, in: TEXT 5. Transactions of the Society for Textual Scholarship, pp. 91–103.

Laubender, Carolyn (2020): »Speak for Your Self. Psychoanalysis, Autotheory, and The Plural Self«, in: Arizona Quarterly. A Journal of American Literature, Culture, and Theory 76.1, pp. 39–64.

Morin, Félix (2023): »Entretien avec Martine Delvaux et Jennifer Bélanger«, in: Les longues entrevues, https://www.cfak.ca/balados/les-longues-entrevues [09.04.2024].

Nelson, Maggie (2012) »Writing With, From, and For Others«, in: Tin House, https://tinhouse.com/writing-with-from-and-for-others/ [09.04.2024].

Tanaka, Maiko (2015): »Feminist Approaches to Citation«, in: C Magazine 126, https://cmagazine.com/articles/feminist-approaches-to-citation [09.03.2024].

Thiele, Kathrin (2021): »Figuration and/as Critique in Relational Matters«, in: Haas/Haas/Magauer/Pohl (eds.), *How to Relate*. Wissen, Künste, Praktiken, Bielefeld: transcript, pp. 229–243.

Wiegman, Robyn (2020): »Introduction. Autotheory Theory«, in: Arizona Quarterly. A Journal of American Literature, Culture, and Theory 76(1), pp. 1–14.

Wittig, Monique (1983): »The Point of View. Universal or Particular?«, in: Feminist Issues 3.2, pp. 63–69.

Zafe, Raquel Meseguer (2023): »The Potential and Poetics of Rest«, in: Backhausen/Wihstutz/Winter (eds.), Out of Time? Temporality in Disability Performance, London: Routledge, pp. 203–212.

Exploring the *Intersectional I* in Transgender Autobiography
A Study of Camila Sosa's Early Works

Juan Zapata

1 Introduction

The hypothesis I will begin with is that the earliest autobiographical trans narratives did not initially take a written form but were originally created for performance. As trans performer Nicolas Shannon Savard demonstrated in his 2021 dissertation *Queer Legacies. Tracing the Roots of Contemporary Transgender Performance*, the origins of trans life narratives can be traced back to communities practicing queer solo performances at the margins of the mainstream stages, primarily in bars and nightclubs. Tracing the history of trans-queer narratives outside of the traditional domain of writing offers a dual advantage. First, it enables us to challenge literature-centrism by taking into account the poetic and political claims of those members of the queer community who did not have access to writing and/or publication. In doing so, we counteract an elitist *posture* that only considers autobiographical trans narratives of those who had access to writing due to their privileged social position.[1]

---

[1] Regarding the first trans autobiographies to be published, see As Rajani B. and Sonima K. (2021: 29): »until the early 1990's, the only mode of discourse through which trans people externalised their thoughts and feelings was autobiographies. The earliest attempts at such modes of self-expression were made by Europeans. The first known book length account in the narrative of Lile Elbe, a male-born Danish painter who began to identify and live as a woman in the 1920s. The major transsexual women autobiographies of the 1970s were written by Jan Morris (*Conundrum*, 1974), Renée Richard (*Second Serve*, 1983) and Nancy Hunt (*Mirror Image*, 1978) and Mario Martino (*Emergence. A Transsexual Autobiography*, 1977) which raided greater awareness of transsexual experience«.

The second advantage of understanding autobiographical trans narratives as originally performative practice – which will be the focal point of my study – lies in highlighting the pivotal role played by the body in both the production and reception of queer autobiographical stories. In fact, this performative dimension distinguishes autobiographical trans narratives from cis-autobiographical narratives, such as class transfuge narratives, all of which give a voice to those who have been excluded from public spaces and discourses.[2] And this is due to a fundamental reason. Being transgender or transvestite not only involves acknowledging the performative construction of sex, gender, and sexuality, revealing that »corporeal styles are nothing other than those punitively regulated cultural fictions that are alternately embodied and disguised under duress« (Butler 1988: 522), but also challenges the dichotomy between appearance and reality that structure the cultural conventions of both theatre and identity. As Judith Butler has pointed out in »Performance Acts and Gender Constitution«:

> The transvestite can do more than simply express the distinction between sex and gender, but challenges, at least implicitly, the distinction between appearance and reality that structures a good deal of popular thinking about gender identity. If the ›reality‹ of gender is constituted by the performance itself, then there is no recourse to an essential and unrealized ›sex‹ or ›gender‹ which gender performances ostensibly express. Indeed, the transvestite's gender is as fully real as anyone whose performance complies with social expectations (1988: 527).

It is this performative dimension in autobiographical trans narratives that I would like to analyze in this article, focusing on the early works of Camila Sosa, an Argentinian trans writer who began to perform her autobiography before writing it. How does this performative dimension manifest itself in her autobiographical narrative? What role does the body play in both the production

---

2 I am thinking about the testimonial narratives that have proliferated in recent decades in Europe, particularly in the narratives of Annie Ernaux, Didier Eribon, or Édouard Louis. While the concept of »hexis corporelle« (Bourdieu, *Le Sens pratique*, 1980) plays a significant role in these narratives, illustrating how socio-economic determinations are embodied by individuals in their manner of standing, speaking, and behaving, their discourse on the body still reproduces the binary oppositions of gendered discourse.

and reception of her autobiography? And, perhaps most importantly, what are its aesthetic and political implications?

To answer these questions, I will begin by situating Camila Sosa's work within a second tradition to which she can also be associated: the narrative of the class transfuge. This traditionally cis-hetero-centered narrative is both expanded and challenged by the Argentinian writer. I will use the term class transfuge to refer to anyone who transgresses social classes and, in doing so, experiences what it is like to occupy borders and intersections. In the same way, I will use the term transgender to refer to anyone who transgresses the boundaries imposed by binary heteronormative social constructs and, in doing so, experiences what it is like to occupy the borders and intersections of traditional gender categories. Camila Sosa's early works embody both aspects, as they exist at the crossroads of gender and class intersections. This is why her dual perspective, as a class transfuge and transgender woman, converges in a self-reflexive narrative capable of comparing the embodied psychosocial effects of classism, sexism, and cis-heteronormativity.

2 Towards an Intersectional I

One of the most pertinent concepts to describe the discursive strategies in class transfuge narratives is the concept of the ›Transpersonal I‹. This term, coined by Annie Ernaux in 1993, characterizes a form of writing that transcends individual subjectivity to express a collective experience:

> Le Je que j'utilise me semble une forme impersonnelle, à peine sexuée, quelquefois même plus une parole de ›l'autre‹ qu'une parole de ›moi‹: une forme transpersonnelle, en somme. Il ne constitue pas un moyen de me construire une identité à travers un texte, de m'autofictionner, mais de saisir, dans mon expérience, les signes d'une réalité familiale, sociale ou passionnelle (1993: 222).

This ›Transpersonal I‹, through which Annie Ernaux shows how we embody the collective experience of domination, could also be described as an *Intersectional I*. This label seems appropriate as it emphasizes the perspective of a writer who has become aware of the convergence of various forms of discrimination. This is precisely what Annie Ernaux highlighted in 2022 upon receiving the Nobel

Prize for Literature, illustrating how her writing emerges from the intersection of classism and patriarchy:

> C'est ainsi que j'ai conçu mon engagement dans l'écriture, lequel ne consiste pas à écrire ›pour‹ une catégorie de lecteurs, mais ›depuis‹ mon expérience de femme et d'immigrée de l'intérieur, depuis ma mémoire désormais de plus en plus longue des années traversées, depuis le présent, sans cesse pourvoyeur d'images et de paroles des autres. [...] Dans la mise au jour de l'indicible social, cette intériorisation des rapports de domination de classe et/ou de race, de sexe également, qui est ressentie seulement par ceux qui en sont l'objet, il y a la possibilité d'une émancipation individuelle mais également collective (2022: s.p.).

However, this *Intersectional I* would remain incomplete without acknowledging the experiences of transgender subjectivity. As Emmanuel Beaubatie (2021: 15) has noted in his study *Transfuges de sexe: passer les frontières du genre*, transgressing binary boundaries also entails transgressing social class boundaries: »les FtMs [female-to-male or trans men] vivent une promotion et les MtFs [male-to-female or trans women] sont déclassées«. In this regard, by highlighting the intersection of both social class mobility and gender/sexual mobility, autobiographical trans narratives not only expose the cis-hetero-centric nature of class transfuge narratives but also shed light on the experience of being marginalized by exposing the psychosocial effects of gender binarism and classism. It is precisely these effects that Camila Sosa portrays in *El viaje Inútil* (2018), her first published autobiographical narrative, in which she deals with the feeling of illegitimacy she experienced when challenging the imperatives of both class and gender constructs:

> Escribo para que una historia se sepa. La historia de mi travestismo, de mi familia, de mi tristeza en la niñez, de toda esa tristeza prematura que fue mi familia, el alcoholismo de mi papá, las carencias de mi mamá [...] También para decir la lucha de mi familia en contra de la pobreza, una pelea que nos devastó y nos enfermó de rencores y desamor e indiferencia, contra todos (2018: 26).

But what I am interested in emphasizing here is that trans autobiographical narratives articulate the *Intersectional I* through bodily consciousness, whose initial expression usually emerges on the stage. As Rebecca Schneider (1997: 7) pointed out in *The Explicit Body in Performance*, feminist and queer solo performers in late capitalism often »use their bodies as stages across which they re-enact social dramas and traumas that have arbitrated cultural differentiations«. And this is not merely because »gender performances in non-theatrical contexts are governed by more clearly punitive and regulatory social conventions« (Butler 1988: 527), a censorship that has led transgender communities to privilege the stage to express themselves, but also because the body's plasticity and versatility empower performers to re-enact subjectivities that resonate with their own experiences.

That is also true for Camila Sosa. It was through performance – and not through writing! – that the Argentinian trans writer initially embodied the otherness of those who share the experience of domination. In her first solo performance *Carnes tolendas. Retrato escénico de una travesti* (2009), Sosa embodies the dramas of other subjectivities with the aim of shedding light on her own experience. In one of the most significant moments of the performance, the Argentinean performer re-enacts Yerma, a cisgender woman that Federico García Lorca portrays to depict the feeling of shame and illegitimacy that women can experience when they are faced with the impossibility of motherhood.[3]

Fig. 1: Teatro la Cochera, Córdoba, Argentina

Camila Sosa identifies with the feelings of shame and illegitimacy experienced by Yerma. Furthermore, Yerma's shame enables Camila Sosa to understand her own sense of illegitimacy as a trans woman. But, why does

---

3   Link to the extract: https://youtu.be/fcpA8JnSf84.

the performer choose to use her body to re-enact Yerma's feelings of shame in front of her audience? Is it only to show that trans women have also embodied the binary and heteronormative stereotypes associating women with motherhood? Certainly, the *Intersectional I* from which Camila Sosa enunciates herself is fully aware of the heteropatriarchal matrix that oppresses both trans and cis women. Consequently, can we not consider that, by comparing trans and cis women's experiences, there is also a call to transcend gender and cultural boundaries, to break through cis-heteronormative assignments that confine individuals to a reified identity?

The question seems crucial to me in a context where reactionary thought seeks to delegitimize the political claims of feminist, queer, and decolonial movements by accusing them of promoting a sort of communitarianism and self-isolation within an identity, a self-isolation that undermines democratic values and fractures society.[4] If Camila Sosa advocates for an *Intersectional I*, it is not to be isolated within a chosen identity. This would perpetuate the particularisms responsible for deuniversalizing subjectivities that do not fit into the hegemonic binary system. On the contrary, by recognizing a convergence between trans and cis women, Camila Sosa enables her audience to gain a deeper understanding of the experience of being marginalized. This is why the universal dimension of shame cannot be fully comprehended without taking into account the shame produced by cis-heteronormative gendering. In a way, the social and historical experiences of transgender individuals open a new chapter, without which the human experience would remain incomplete, mutilated, even amputated. Denying their historical reality equates to denying human experience as a whole.

Throughout her performance, Camila Sosa embodies even more universal feelings, such as love and loneliness, which serve to universalize transgender subjectivity and free it from any retreat into communitarianism. However, is this a form of abstract, disembodied, ahistorical universalism? In other words, could the search for a universal deny the political value of a work that speaks from a community that has traditionally experienced exclusion, invisibility,

---

4   A notable example of this form of delegitimizing the political claims of feminist, queer, and decolonial movements is L'Observatoire des idéologies identitaires, where French academics and editorialists converge to criticize what they label as WOKE ideology, invoking France's democratic values of universalism, scientific rationality, freedom of expression, and laïcité. At this regard, see: https://decolonialisme.fr.

and marginalization? To think this would be to overlook the fact that Camila Sosa's insight into domination is enunciated from the historical body of someone who has painfully transgressed gender and class boundaries. A painful transgression, indeed, as it compels her to exist at the intersections without any possibility of assimilation, but also a joyful transgression, as it empowers her to understand the mechanisms governing the shifts between borders. This is why the Argentinian performer chose to re-enact social experiences such a shame, love or loneliness. She refuses to be relegated to any form of communitarianism that would reduce her narrative to a mere testimonial value. Instead, in her performances, Camila Sosa claims the universality of her transgender experience.

Furthermore, Camila Sosa uses her dual perspective as a class transfuge and transgender woman to deconstruct the stereotypes imposed by a classist, patriarchal, and cis-heteronormative society. This is what happens in *Carnes Tolendas* when she caricatures the feeling of superiority that overwhelms those who claim to embody the social norm and, in doing so, reinforce the boundaries between ›normal‹ and ›other‹. The performer embodies not only the racialized, cis-gendered, and classist discourse that has characterized the most reactionary thought in Latin America but also the supposedly »open-minded« discourse, though no less stigmatizing, of her own audience:[5]

Fig. 2: Teatro la Cochera, Córdoba, Argentina

---

5   Link to the extract: https://youtu.be/Aju2wOrsJWs.

The position from which Camila Sosa speaks is fundamental to understand the impacts and motivations of her embodied caricature. When caricatures are produced from hegemonic and dominant positions, laughter is used to discredit and denigrate bodies that deviate from societal norms. In other words, caricatures emerging from the center serve to reinforce boundaries by perpetuating stigmatizing stereotypes that relegate certain individuals to the margins of society. On the contrary, caricatures produced from the borders and intersections reverse the relationships between the center and periphery to disrupt the established order. Therefore, by laughing at those who claim to embody the social norm, caricatures emerging from the borders not only expose the stigmatizing stereotypes produced from hegemonic positions but also challenge the center by questioning its universality.

This is precisely what Camila Sosa does in *Carnes Tolendas* when she invites the audience to laugh at the classist, patriarchal, and cis-heteronormative stereotypes that she caricatures. If the audience agrees to laugh with her, the centre shifts to the borders, and those who claim to embody the norm are discredited. Conversely, those who refuse to laugh with the performer are automatically exposed as accomplices of a classist and heteropatriarchal society. The power of the caricature produced from the borders lies in its ability to encourage us to explore intersections and meeting points while also inviting us to build a community based on the pleasure of sharing the same awakening.

3 How to Embody the Body in Writing?

Ten years after the first performance of *Carnes Tolendas*, Camila Sosa published *El Viaje inútil* (2018), which revisits her experience as a class transfuge and transgender woman. Many of the episodes depicted on stage find their textual form in this autobiographical work. However, this shift from performance to writing is not without its challenges. When publishing her autobiography, the performer is deprived of direct contact with the audience. Her narrative is no longer an embodied narrative but rather a text delivered to an anonymous public that extends far beyond the boundaries of the stage. In other words, the logic of the printed world not only separates the performer from the act of communication but also deprives the reader of the performer's corporeality. And, as we demonstrated in the first part, this corporeality was fundamental for her scenic self-portrait. From the moment Camila Sosa oriented her narrative towards an autobiographical interpretation, her body became the guarantor of the value and authenticity of her monologue. This is why the theatre audience sought to correlate the self-image constructed by the performer with her physical presence. Any disparity between her self-portrait and her body, any suspicion of insincerity or dissimulation, would have been punished by an audience avid for honesty and authenticity. This is precisely the reaction that the audience often has after her performances, or at least, that is how Camila Sosa parodically portrays their reaction in *Carnes Tolendas*:

> Mira Camila, yo como presidenta de la liga de madres de familia madrileña quisiera hacerte una par de preguntas puesto que es la primera vez que tengo sentado frente a mí un travesti en carne y hueso, y te veo a ti como muy responsable, muy atenta y muy dispuesta a responder todas estas dudas que me están comiendo el seso: [...] ¿Te has puesto las tetas? ¿Te has puesto el culo? ¿Te prostituyes? Pues, digo, ¿los hombres cuando están contigo te pagan... ¿te gritan cosas espantosas por la calle? [...] Bueno, pero no lo tomes a mal, si no quieres responder no me respondas. Lo único que quisiera saber, y esto sí te lo agradecería que me lo respondieras con toda sinceridad, porque me está carcomiendo el seso: ¿en dónde mierdas te escondes la polla?[6]

How can this absence of the body be compensated in writing? How can Camila Sosa embody the body in text? To continue authenticating her autobiographical narrative, to give it a body serving as a guarantor to her work, Camila Sosa needed to find a way to inscribe her presence in the text. And the only way to achieve this was by adopting the testimonial ethos that characterizes all autobiographical writing.[7] This is what she explains in *El viaje inútil*, detailing the mechanisms and motivations of her writing:

> Para escribir, voy detrás de esos recuerdos, incluso de sueños y expectativas que no son otra cosa más que recuerdos. Escribo a partir de mí y para mí. Eventualmente me comparto, comparto lo que escribo, pero eso no quiere decir que yo me abra al mundo, sino que traigo a los visitantes a mi intimidad. Prefiero que el lector entre en mí a ir a buscar al lector [...]. Podría decir que hay dos clases de escritores, los que escriben fantasías y los que escriben recuerdos. Yo me encuentro entre estos últimos (2018: 43–44).

---

6 Minute 02:00 from the extract: https://youtu.be/Aju2wOrsJWs.
7 Regarding the testimonial ethos that characterizes autobiographical writing, see Meizoz 2010.

Certainly, the testimonial ethos enables Camila Sosa to establish an implicit agreement with the reader, in which she commits to telling the truth, staying faithful to reality, and being sincere.[8] This promise of transparency legitimizes her narrative and enhances its political value. As a result, readers seek all kinds of extratextual information to corroborate the authenticity of her testimony. This is precisely what the critics and journalists did after the publication of *El viaje inútil*: they not only labeled the book as an ›autobiographical essay‹ but also endeavored to authenticate its testimonial value by delving into the author's life:

> *El viaje inútil: trans/writing* by Camila Sosa Villada is an autobiographical essay where the writer, playwright, and actress from Córdoba attempts to find an explanation of why she became a writer, or rather, when or under what conditions the urge to write emerged (León 2018).
>
> Camila Sosa Villada has just published *El viaje inútil*, a captivating work that intertwines autobiography with an essay on the mystery of writing, revealing her experience of becoming a writer (López 2018).
>
> Camila Sosa Villada has just published *Un viaje inútil*, a dive into her childhood, her experience as a transvestite, her family relationships, psychoanalysis, and her recognition as an actress and playwright (Mónica López 2018).

But beyond this ›autobiographical pact‹ (cf. Lejeune 1975) that forces readers to seek the author's body and private life, what interests me here is the *Intersectional I* that Camila Sosa used to exhibit in her performances. What happened to this *Intersectional I* that allowed her to embody alterity and, at the same time, keep saying ›I‹? Why did Camila Sosa choose to write a testimonial narrative instead of a work of fiction? Wouldn't fiction, more than autobiography, allow her to embody other subjectivities, other voices, other bodies, as she did in her performance? In other words, wouldn't the polyphony that characterizes fiction have enabled her to continue embodying the *Intersectional I* of the performance?

Once again, the question seems crucial to me in the current context, where testimonial narratives appear to be the only legitimate mode of expression

---

8   Regarding the notion of ›pacte autobiographique‹ advocated here, see Lejeune 1975.

for subjectivities that have traditionally been marginalized. It is as if autobiographical narratives were the only authorized path for trans minorities to access the literary field. This is what the Argentinian writer Juan Forn had in mind when he decided to endorse Camila Sosa by writing a prologue for *Las Malas* (2019), her first novel. Anticipating the potential editorial and media success of a text written by a transgender woman, Forn chose to guide the reader towards an autobiographical interpretation, as Camila Sosa pointed out in an interview:

> Juan Forn también es el culpable de que piensen que *Las Malas* es una novela autobiográfica cuando es el invento más grande del que fui capaz [...] La afirmación de que es un libro autobiográfico se da por sentado sin preguntármelo a mí. Pienso que es responsabilidad del prólogo de Juan. Eso me causó enojo para con él. Por suerte, como siempre he sido lenguaraza, se lo dije apenas me pasó el prólogo y él respondió que era para entrar directamente en el ojo del lector. Tenía razón claro, ahora que las ventas me pagan el bonito departamento en el que vivo y que me codeo con la creme de artistas argentinos y de otros países. Pero mi queja fue que la gente pensaría que no soy una escritora sino una cronista de mi propia vida (Yanke 2022).

Camila Sosa consistently emphasizes that her writing is »an act of cross-dressing« (2018: 35), a way to mask herself, »to lie, to exaggerate, to hide« (ibid.: 24), much as she used to do during her childhood when she created alternative lives for herself in »dirty novels where the protagonists had sex in the mud with their lovers and heroines were always adored by their fathers« (ibid.: 45). However, this act of cross-dressing and masquerade is not viable within testimonial narratives, such as *El viaje inútil*, where any deviation from the ›autobiographical pact‹ is harshly penalized by readers seeking truth and authenticity. We had to wait for the publication of *Las Malas* to see Camila Sosa embodying once again, thanks to the polyphony of fiction, the *Intersectional I* of *Carnes Tolendas*. This is what she implies in her speech upon receiving the Sor Juana Inés de la Cruz award when she presents herself as the «queen of deceit« and a »priestess of hideouts«:

> Me dieron el lenguaje y salí a vivir. Estuve a la intemperie. Maestra en el arte de los trucos, maestra para ensombrecer los ojos, reina del engaño, sacerdotisa de los escondites y las salidas por cualquier rajadura. La que iluminó por las rendijas el paso lento de una escritora que vino a contar su propio cuerpo, no a ser fiel a la memoria (2021: s.p.).

But it was through performance – not through writing! – that this »priestess of hideouts« and »queen of deceit« learned the art of embodiment. It was there that her bodily consciousness first emerged, enabling her to comprehend gender boundaries and inhabit intersections. The *Intersectional I* of performance, the ›I‹ we saw in *Carnes Tolendas*, is an ›I‹ that not only became aware of existing at intersections but also learned how to leverage those intersections to embody other subjectivities, other bodies, other alterities. In short, it brings to life a more universal ›I‹.

Bibliography

Beaubatie, Emmanuel (2021): Transfuges de sexe. Passer les frontières du genre, Paris: La Découverte.

Butler, Judith (1988): »Performative Acts and Gender Constitution. An Essay in Phenomenology and Feminist Theory«, in: Theatre Journal 40.4, pp. 519–531.

Ernaux, Annie (1993): »Vers un je transpersonnel«, in: Serge Doubrovsky/ Jacques Lecarme/ Philippe Lejeune (eds.), Autofictions et Cie, Nanterre: Université de Paris X, pp. 219–222.

Ernaux, Annie (2022): »Conference Nobel«, https://www.nobelprize.org/prizes/literature/2022/ernaux/201000-nobel-lecture-french/ [27.03.2024].

Lejeune, Philippe (1975): Le pacte autobiographique, Paris: Seuil.

León, Gonzalo (2018): »Camila Sosa Villada. Tomé conciencia de que era una escritora trans con este libro«, https://eternacadencia.com.ar/nota/camila-sosa-villada-ldquo-tome-conciencia-de-que-era-una-escritora-trans-con-este-libro-rdquo-/323 [26.03.2024].

López, María Pia (2018): »Transformarse en escritura«, https://www.pagina12.com.ar/140210-transformarse-en-escritora [26.03.2024].

López, Mónica (2018): »Reivindico la inutilidad de la escritura«, https://ediciones documenta.com.ar/2018/07/reivindico-la-inutilidad-de-la-literatura/ [26.03.2024].

Meizoz, Jérôme (2010): »Éthique du récit testimonial, Annie Ernaux«, in: Nouvelle revue d'esthétique 2.6, pp. 113–117.

Rajani, B. and Sonima, K (2021): »Fictionalizing the Gendered Self. A Critique of the Politics of Gendered in Transgender Autofictions«, in: Literary Endeavour 12.2, pp. 28–33.

Savard, Nicolas Shannon (2021): Queer Legacies. Tracing the Roots of Contemporary Transgender Performance, Ohio: doctoral dissertation, 2024, http://rave.ohiolink.edu/etdc/view?acc_num=osu1626384633865101 [26.03.2024].
Schneider, Rebecca (1997): The Explicit Body in Performance, London/New York: Routledge.
Sosa, Camila (2021): »Discurso de aceptación del XXVIII Premio Sor Juana Inés de la Cruz«, https://www.caratula.net/discurso-de-aceptacion-del-xxviii-premio-sor-juana-ines-de-la-cruz/ [26.03.2024].
Sosa, Camila (2019): Las Malas, Buenos Aires: Tusquets.
Sosa, Camila (2018): El viaje inútil, Córdoba: DocumentA/Escénicas.
Sosa, Camila (2009): Carnes Tolendas. Retrato escénico de una travesti, performance directed by María Palacios, Theatre »La Cochera«.
Yanke, Rebeca (2022): »Camila Sosa: ›con mis cuentos intento demostrar de qué clase de veneno está hecha mi escritura‹«, https://www.elmundo.es/cultura/literatura/2022/03/14/622df86521efa0671c8b4578.html [26.03.2024].

Fighting to Exist in a World Where You Don't Belong
Forms of Relationships and Struggles in Lauren Delphe's *Faite de cyprine et de punaises* (2022)

Alex Lachkar

1 Introduction

> Ce soir, tu as si froid que tu ne sens plus tes doigts, et la joue contre la vitrine de la laverie, tu te jures de ne plus jamais prendre une décision que tu pourrais regretter. Tu te jures d'être forte.
> *(Delphe 2022: 175)*

The narrator of *Faite de cyprine et de punaises* tells her story in the second person singular. Over the pages, she looks back on her childhood, adolescence and adulthood, characterized on the one hand by precariousness, discrimination and trauma, and on the other by the joys of a feminist and lesbian life and culture. First novel by French author Lauren Delphe, published in 2022 by the small independent feminist publishing house iXe, *Faite de cyprine et de punaises* can be read as an apprenticeship novel: the narrator tries to make a place for herself in a world that is not made for her and does not want her. Fundamentally feminist and lesbian, but also a victim of ableism, lesbophobia and sexual violence, this »you« whose name stays unknow navigates between environments, relationships, questioning, discrimination and the pleasures of every-day life.

Nothing is ever really fixed in the novel: temporalities overlap, traumatic memories follow great moments of joy, lovers come and go, and the tone alternates between entusiasm, anger, fierce irony and melancholy. Hopes and disappointments multiply and intermingle, even within the lesbian community the narrator belongs to in Montreal, which is not exempt from discrimination. In the midst of all these emotions, events, encounters and hostile world, she wonders about her place and role in a world that was not designed for her, a disabled and precarious lesbian whose memories are mostly linked to trauma.

In this article, we will be looking at the extent to which the narrator tries, through and in spite of these different types of relationship, to make her way in a world and a life of omnipresent violence. By relationships, are not only meant relationships with other people, but also with objects and attitudes, such as the one the narrator has with alcohol or with lesbian culture. First, we will look at why the world in which the narrator lives is unbearable for her, before exploring possible modes of escape, which are nonetheless temporary in each case. Finally, we will see that lesbian joys – the happiness found in living a lesbian life – are perhaps the best and most lasting way of helping the narrator to evolve in the world.

2 Living in an Unlivable World

Faite de cyprine et de punaises opens with a list of »sujets potentiellement traumatisants qui se doivent d'être mentionnés« (10), including sexual violence, ableism, lesbophobia and alcohol. This not only sets the tone for the novel's violent narratives, but also for the author's desire to reduce the risk of awakening traumatic memories in her readership.[1] Throughout the novel, the narrator describes her life in a world that is unbearable for her, due to the discrimination she suffers, both from individuals and from society in general (institutions, infrastructures etc.). She is a young lesbian, in a precarious situation, with a visible disability: all parts of her identity liable to be attacked, either directly or more indirectly. As a result, her relationship with the world in general, and with certain individuals in particular, is necessarily built from a marginalized position. As the novel unfolds, a vicious circle of discrimination and violence emerges, with one kind of violence leading to another: the narrator loses her self-confidence as the discrimination she suffers increases. The novel has several overlapping dimensions: life under capitalism and neo-liberalism; con-

---

[1] Trigger warnings at the beginning of books are not yet widespread in France – unlike in the USA or the UK, for example – but are increasingly common in feminist and/or queer and/or independent publishing houses.

stant rejection by the family; everyday ableism; sexual violence, which are analysed in more detail below.

2.1 Living Under Capitalism and Neo-Liberalism

The narrator is a full-time salesperson in a Montreal boutique, a job that does not bring her any satisfaction, but does pay her rent. Aware of the uselessness and absurdity of her job, she makes a mockery of the capitalist system while being obliged to comply with its productivity demands, but above all she must navigate between her own contradictions. On the one hand, her anti-capitalist convictions are nourished by her reading of Angela Davis and her conversations with other queer people, while on the other, she is obliged to visit »ces quelques mètres carrés climatisés meters« (75) several times a week, to abide by the store's rules and to put up with the sexism of certain customers (cf. 85). From then on, she tries, through actions that may seem superficial or insufficient, to restore a certain balance: »Tu likes un tweet sur une grève et te remets au travail en te déhanchant sur du Queen« (75). The narrator also recalls the career plans she had as a teenager (»Christiane Taubira en gouine, afin de pouvoir retourner les insultes déplacées à l'envoyeur«, 40[2]) and, with bitterness, compares her dreams with her current situation: »A quel âge as-tu troqué tes ambitions présidentielles contre l'espoir de gagner des points auprès d'un employé à temps plein d'une Coop qui ne ferme pas le dimanche?« (76) The money she earns from this job is good enough for her, but the novel is peppered with anecdotes and reflections revealing the narrator's disgust with her job, and with the system more generally.

2.2 Constant Rejection by the Family

If the narrator's relationship with the world of work and capitalism is complicated, her relationship with her parents is broken. As the story unfolds, she gives us snippets of memories, sometimes delivered as they are, sometimes revisited through her own feminist, lesbian and anti-ableist prism:

---

2 French Justice Minister from 2012 to 2016, she championed the bill authorizing marriage for all. She also ran – unsuccessfully – in the 2002 and 2022 presidential elections. Here, reference is made to Christiane Taubira's talent as an orator, who, when it came to passing the law, as at other times in her life as a politician and minister, always met political and personal attacks with a sense of repartee and verve that are still remembered today.

> Tu ne devrais pas oublier que son amour [de ta mère] est conditionnel, relatif à la couleur de tes cheveux, à la longueur de tes ongles, aux chiffres de ta balance, aux dessins sur ta peau, aux bijoux sur ton visage. Ton anneau, elle ne l'aurait accepté qu'à l'annulaire, et selon des critères bien précis (39).

The author hijacks the expression that a parent's love for a child is unconditional, and uses the ring motif to crystallize the two antagonistic positions: on the one hand, there is the ring she wears on the septum, a piercing site favored by lesbians (Octavia, one of her lovers, also wears one, cf. 29); on the other, the wedding ring hoped for by her mother. The antagonization of the two positions is reinforced by other lesbian features of the narrator's outfit, such as dyed hair and tattoos.[3] The lesbian critique of marriage as an institution to be abolished is presented as follows by Monique Wittig, in La Pensée straight, a work which, as we shall see, serves as a survival manual for the narrator:

> [L]e lesbianisme est historiquement la culture grâce à laquelle nous pouvons questionner politiquement la société hétérosexuelle et ses catégories sexuelles, sur la signification de ses institutions de domination en général et en particulier sur la signification de cette instruction de dépendance personnelle qu'est le mariage imposé aux femmes (94).

While the emphasis in this extract from the novel is on lesbophobia,[4] ableism also plays a role in the break-up between the narrator and her parents. In fact, it was her parents who kicked her out of the house, although we do not know how old she was at the time (see 129). The majority discourse on disability is not held by disabled people, but by abled people – notably the parents of disabled children[5] – who formulate opinions and demands that rarely correspond to those

---

3   More generally, lesbian fashion occupies an important place in the novel, as for example certain brands of shoes popular with lesbians are often evoked to describe the characters (DocMartens, Vans). About lesbian fashion, see Medhurst 2024.
4   On parents' lesbophobia, or more broadly on their deeply sexist and heterocentric upbringing, see also 97–98 and 189–191.
5   In French literature, see S'adapter, a novel by Clara Dupont-Monod published in 2021, which tells the story of a disabled child through the eyes of his abled siblings. Strongly criticized by activists for its ableist discourse, it has received critical acclaim and several literary prizes.

of disabled people.[6] None of this is the case in the novel, which unabashedly exposes the ableism at work in her family:

> [L]a mère de ton père t'en coupait vite fait des quartiers [de pamplemousse] chaque matin, en t'expliquant, placide, que de son temps les filles comme toi leur place était à l'hôpital. Tu y voyais une subtile allusion d'hétéro à ton lesbianisme, que tu prenais pourtant soin de cacher, mais les reproches de ta grand-mère visaient aussi, tu le savais, d'autres aspects de ton identité plus difficiles à camoufler – en particulier ton corps handicapé si ouvertement différent, si ouvertement énervé (72).

Although the antiphrase »subtile allusion« is ironic, the seriousness of the subject is underlined, as the narrator's grandmother's words refer to the fact that, in Western societies, many disabled children are placed in institutions and thus ostracized from an early age, where everything is done to ensure that they cannot leave (Marabet 2016). For the narrator, the break with her family is complete, depriving her of one of the most accepted forms of relationship in society.

2.3 Everyday Ableism

Since the disabled narrator's daily life evolves in a world conceived and designed by and for the abled, her daily life is constantly punctuated by difficulties and obstacles. Her relationship with the world is necessarily conditioned by the way the world is conceived, and there is not a place, whether in public space or in the places where she lives, in which she is not confronted with ableism. As it is omnipresent in her daily life, it is also present in the narrative: when it comes to taking stairs (11, 102), opening doors (17, 90, 154), reaching for objects at height (18), changing sheets (112–113), tie or untie shoelaces (54, 151, 183), cook (153–154), carry certain objects (90, 154), play cards (162), pass through subway gates (167), or put laundry in a washing machine (173).[7]

As is often the case when she is exposed to discrimination, the narrator reacts with humor and irony, as in this scene in the supermarket:

---

6 On this subject, and on the links between homophobia and ableism, particularly within families, see Kafer 2013: 77–89.

7 The novel also includes several scenes in which the narrator displays internalized ableism: I do not have space to develop this here, but see in particular 153–154 and 168.

Le caissier enfourne tes provisions dans un sac en papier sans poignées que tu attrapes poliment, sans oser mentionner ton bras droit ballant, trop occupée déjà à calculer avec quel membre tu vas bien pouvoir pousser la porte et sortir de la boutique. Il faudra jouer du pied et des épaules, puisque ta main gauche est prise. Tu es toujours à court de mains gauches, ça en devient agaçant (154).

Here, she shows us the chain of her thoughts, focused on finding an exit strategy, and plays with the expression »avoir deux mains gauches«,[8] which she ironically reverses. This example underlines the difficulties of her relationship with the abled world around her, but it also shows the extent to which the world is ableist, insofar as architecture, in particular, has been designed by and for the abled, forcing disabled people to struggle constantly to carry out everyday gestures that the abled see as simple, requiring no particular effort.[9]

2.4 The Underlying Theme of Sexual Violence

Another omnipresent element in the story is the subject of sexual violence, and more specifically sexual violence between lesbians. Throughout the novel, the character of Marcela recurs: the narrator's former partner raped her during their relationship, and continues to do so regularly once they have separated. At the end of the novel, the narrator is also raped by Zineb's wife, who was her first partner when she arrived in Montreal. Evoking sexual violence, in life as in literature, is never insignificant, but it is all the more so when the violence is perpetrated by people who are themselves marginalized. Violence within queer couples and within the queer community is little discussed, both in culture[10] and in the activist world,[11] with most activists believing that these are issues to be dealt with within the community, as their public exposure is likely to fuel the LGBTI-phobias already omnipresent in society.

---

8   Which in French means »to be clumsy«.
9   On the lack of accessibility to public spaces, see in particular Kafer/Jarmann 2014. This extract also refers to the notion of crip time, see Alison Kafer 2013.
10 This partly explains the success of American author Carmen Maria Machado's *The Dream House. A Memoir* (2019), in which the author explores the motives, implications and consequences of psychological and sexual violence within a lesbian couple.
11 In France, things seem to be gradually changing, notably with the launch in 2023 of the association Violences en milieu queer.

When the narrator moves into a new shared apartment at the start of the novel, she has just come out of an abusive relationship with Marcela, who is introduced to us in the second chapter as follows: »Parfois ton exe, Marcela, arrive à l'improviste en fin d'après-midi et tu ne sais pas comment lui dire non« (20). This is followed by a description of a rape, during which the narrator dissociates. In all, there are thirteen passages devoted to the subject of sexual violence, eleven of which concern Marcela, who, as the story progresses, we learn was already raping the narrator when they were together, and continues to do so after their separation. The style of these passages is particularly spare, the narrative is factual, and emotions are generally absent. In an almost clinical way, the narrator tells us about the violence she suffers. While the passages devoted to joyful, enthusiastic lesbian sexuality are sometimes almost lyrical in style, those recounting the repeated rapes are the opposite.

The narrator is lucid: as early as page 35, she uses the terms »viol«, then »violeuse« (45), »couple abusif« (68) and »relation abusive« (136). But, as is often the case when sexual violence takes place in the context of a romantic relationship, she is unable to hate Marcela or truly detach herself from her, even after the break-up. Several passages illustrate this ambiguity:

> Marcela avait le gout des mochas chocolat noir et curcuma qu'elle rapportait de son travail de barmaid au café libanais de la rue Ontario. [...] Tu choisis, tu le sais, d'oublier qu'elle avait aussi le gout de la sueur et de la contrainte (64).

The synaesthesia employed here underlines the physical impact of Marcela's rapes on the narrator, as well as the significance of the trauma, since it also suggests – a reality for many victims – that any smell similar to Marcela's is likely to awaken her trauma.[12]

The narrator's relationship with the world is therefore complex and painful: all too often synonymous with suffering and discrimination, it offers few prospects for a happy future. To avoid this, the narrator puts in place temporary solutions: escape, which takes many forms and which she practices assiduously in order to escape reality.

---

[12] Beyond the question of trauma, the links between the senses and memories occupy a certain place in the novel, notably through Proustian intertextuality, see for example 73 and 87.

3 Possible and Temporary Escapes

3.1 Anesthetizing Reality

Is it possible to escape reality when it is unbearable? *Faite de cyprine et de punaises* is also an account of various possible escapes: escaping from harmful relationships, by developing others, not only with individuals. These escapes are all characterized by their temporary aspect, and some are also unhealthy for the narrator, and in this regard have little to envy the relationships discussed in the first part of this article.

Whatever form the escape takes, it is always a question of forgetting suffering and forgetting oneself, leaving certain thoughts aside, a process that is more or less conscious depending on the case. Four types of escapist relationship can be identified in the novel: lesbian sexuality; dissociation; alcohol consumption; TV series consumption. Whether it's dissociation, sexuality or alcohol consumption, the aim is always the same: to anaesthetize reality, to make it less palpable for a given period of time. Insofar as the theme of lesbian sexuality also has a lot to do with the potential prospect of a saving relationship, this point will be developed in the last part of this article.

Several passages in the novel are devoted to relatively precise descriptions of the phenomenon of dissociation as experienced by the narrator, which consists, to put it briefly, of a temporary psychological absence: the body is there, but no longer the mind. Dissociation is a common (and usually unconscious and uncontrolled) reaction of the brain to avoid the full force of trauma, and is particularly common in cases of sexual violence. The first instance of the phenomenon occurs in the second chapter, when Marcela visits the narrator in her new apartment to rape her. While the description of the rape is fairly brief, the account of the dissociation spans several pages, with no clear indication of when the narrator returns to herself.

> Parfois ton exe, Marcela, arrive à l'improviste en fin d'après-midi et tu ne sais pas comment lui dire non. Tu ne sais pas lui expliquer que tu n'aimes pas ses mains qui pressent ton crâne vers son entrejambe et comme convenu, car on t'a bien éduquée, tu restes polie et tu te plies sagement à ses demandes, appuyée sur tes coudes rugueux, la tête entre ses cuisses. Son clit aux lèvres, tu te demandes qui est ce »on«, et quand est ce qu'il est apparu dans ta vie. (20)

Here, we are treated to a series of reflections by the narrator, who begins with a question about a pronoun (»on«) and goes on to discuss, in turn, her desire to be discreet so that her roommate, Octavia, does not find out, the first time they spoke, the decoration of their bathroom, the Twitter account of an actress, her first lesbian kiss, and so on. All subjects that seem to have nothing to do with each other, and certainly nothing to do with the action taking place in parallel. The absence of any clear indication of when the narrator returns to herself also suggests that this episode of dissociation is particularly long.

By dissociating, the narrator anesthetizes herself, so that she feels less strongly the violence directed at her. However, this escape is only temporary, since she is well aware of having been raped, a scenario that recurs several times in the novel. To anesthetize herself, she also resorts to alcohol consumption, which seems far removed from simple festive drinking, reserved for certain clearly identified occasions. Alcohol is mentioned many times, and is almost systematically associated with a desire to escape the present moment and/or the emotions felt by the narrator. This exaggerated consumption takes such a place in her life that, towards the end of the novel, she »descen[d] machinalement« a bottle of cider found at the home of Zineb, her first girlfriend who is temporarily taking her in (169).

At times, the narrator is conscious of drinking for the sole purpose of forgetting the world around her: »[h]ier, tu essayais de t'oublier en éclusant les bières d'une quasi-inconnue« (160). Her relationship with alcohol (which may be akin to alcoholism) deteriorates over the course of the novel: at first, she drinks in order to dare tell Octavia that she would like to kiss her (29, 35) – thus combining two escapes in one, alcohol and sex – while wondering »Comment font les gens pour survivre à la sobriété?« (35), by the end her consumption has increased and seems to serve no other purpose than to anesthetize herself as quickly and effectively as possible: »Tu achètes quatre canettes de cidre au dépanneur et les vides l'une après l'autre sur le banc du métro Beaudry avant de trainer des pieds jusqu'à l'appart« (141). Alcohol allows her to detach herself, for a time, from the traumas that are still with her, offering a life-saving breath, but solving no problems.

3.2 Escape into Fiction

Another escape is the consumption of TV series. Here, the aim is not so much to anesthetize her as to plunge her into another world, with other characters, other relationships, other problems – all things that do not concern her. Fictional characters play an important role in her daily life, like those in the sitcom *2 Broke Girls* (CBS, 2011–2017), which features the daily lives of two best friends working in a restaurant. It is what she watches before falling asleep (17), and she falls asleep in front of it, only to be awakened by the recorded laughter (19). But the escape does not stop there: »Tu laisses l'épisode en mode lecture sur ton cellphone pendant que tu files aux toilettes, car tu ne penses pas pouvoir survivre seule avec tes pensées« (19). Interrupting the series for even a few dozen seconds seems unthinkable and unbearable, which reveals her profound need to escape. In this way, the characters of *2 Broke Girls* are at her side on a daily basis, with fiction taking precedence over reality.

Turning to series can also be a way of reassuring herself about the possibility of a less bleak future. After her breakup with Octavia, she reacts as follows:

> [T]u grimpes sur ton matelas et tu te construis avec tes oreillers une petite amie que tu serres très fort en regardant Tina et Bette s'embrasser dans ta playlist de baisers lesbiens. Ainsi tu t'inventes un semblant d'amour [...]. Tu pourrais tenter de juguler ton anxiété autrement, murir et jeter un regard franc sur ta réalité à l'aide de ta playlist méditation qui t'attend toujours, si jamais. Mais tu travailles tôt demain (138).

The reference here is clear for the majority of lesbian readers: in *The L World* (Showtime, 2004–2009), the first mainstream series to focus on the lives of a group of lesbians, Tina (Laurel Holloman) and Bette (Jennifer Beals) embody solid, eternal love (although their relationship experiences many difficulties), and may represent a welcome identification for a lesbian audience hitherto mainly accustomed to lesbian characters portrayed as toxic and without hope of a happy ending (Cameron 2018). So it is no coincidence that the narrator, after her break-up, seeks comfort in this couple, who have a special status among lesbians who have seen the series.[13] There is also a brief moment in this excerpt when she questions the wisdom of this umpteenth escape and this umpteenth search for comfort in a relationship with fictional characters, but the sentence falls immediately, cutting short the debate she's having with herself: »Mais tu travailles tôt demain«.

---

13   In the reboot of the series, *The L Word. Generation Q* (Showtime, 2019–2023), Tina and Bette are initially separated, but marry a second time in the final episode of the last season, offering, for the second time, the depiction of a fairy-tale happy ending.

More generally, the possibility of representation, and identification, in cultural works is an important issue for minoritized people. In her own context, this is all the more vital for the narrator, who thus has access to a representation of what her future might, perhaps, look like one day. Even if, as we shall see, a future that meets society's standards (a long relationship celebrated by marriage) may not be what she really wants.

The various escapes evoked here are all temporary, because they are the only ones the narrator has within her reach. To borrow from Foucault, these escapes are »points of resistance« to power, and thus an integral part of it (Foucault 1976: 126. In this sense, they can only be punctual, and cannot really change the order of things, at least not from an individual point of view (ibid.: 127). The alternative would be to overthrow the entire power structure, which the narrator is unable to do alone and isolated.

Fleeing the relationships mentioned in the first part of this article leads the narrator to take refuge in other relationships which, while not all necessarily unhealthy, are only occasional helps, and seem to weigh very little against what she has to face on a daily basis. Perhaps it is in what a lesbian life has to offer that it is possible to find another form of relationship with the world and those around her.

4 The Joys of Lesbian Life

4.1 Lesbian Culture at the Center

The narrator's most constant and strongest relationship is with lesbianism: her life is organized around and according to lesbianism, in every aspect of her daily life. She leads a lesbian life, in the sense that her entire life is organized around what is for her much more than a sexual orientation, but a lifestyle in its own right. The politicisation of her identity gives her a prism through which she views not only her life, but also the world: her sexual relationships, both romantic and friendly, are all lesbian; she consumes a culture that is almost exclusively lesbian, or at least queer and/or feminist; she frequents lesbian places and goes to lesbian events. This activist posture leads her to reject much of the established order, such as the cisgender men who approach her on the street (141). Referring to Alice Coffin's *Le Génie lesbien*, she asserts that »sans les lesbiennes les combats féministes perdraient en flamboyance« (124).

Her life is thus organized around the triptych of lesbian culture, theory, encounters/sexuality. Lesbian culture is shown in the novel in all its facets, be it music (the duo Teagan and Sara), series (*The L Word*, *Orange Is The New Black*, *Work in Progress*), films (*Jennifer's Body*, *The Watermelon Woman*), or of course books. In the latter case, a whole string of names of English- and French-speaking authors are listed, including Monique Wittig, Audre Lorde, Emily Dickinson, Jeanette Winterson, Eileen Myles, Toni Morrison, Mary Oliver and Joan Nestle, to name but a few. Lesbian thinkers are also mentioned, including Adrienne Rich, who conceptualized compulsive heterosexuality. Through all these names and references, she celebrates a culture as prolific as it is invisibilized, of which only insiders know the most famous names as well as those more confidential to the general public, but well known to the lesbian (or more widely queer) community. This omnipresence of lesbian culture can be interpreted as the narrator's need to surround herself with works through which she finally feels represented, and which she often mobilizes in order, perhaps here too, to feel less alone. Nevertheless, this escape is less temporary or doomed to failure than the aforementioned escapes: books, music, films and those who create this culture remain, enabling her to surround herself permanently with people, real or fictional, living or dead, but very much present in her imagination and bookshelves. While these relationships do not, at first glance, solve the problems, the narrator encounters on a daily basis, they certainly seem healthier than the temporary ones. They also complement the romantic and/or sexual relationships that take place throughout the novel. In this sense, they do not replace the relationships that are possible in life, but nevertheless fill a gap.[14]

4.2 Embracing Sexuality

Dating and sexuality also play an important role. Alongside the three important relationships in the narrator's life (chronologically Zineb, Marcela, Octavia), she also has flings, and is on dating apps. Her writing about sexuality is all at once raw, precise and enthusiastic, lyrical at times. Far from the preconceived notions of lesbian sexuality – perceived as non-sexuality – the passages in question portray an uninhibited, pleasurable sexuality. It must be said, however, that the shadow of sexual trauma often hangs over these scenes, but when

---

14 Nonetheless, the novel's absence of friendship is glaring, even though friendly lesbian relationships could provide the narrator with a certain stability and comfort.

the narrator manages to rid herself of it, her sexuality becomes joyful and powerful:

> Elle ouvre sa chambre et tu la suis, affamée, écartes les jambes sobrement, coules dans ses draps en attendant un doigt qui finalement se glisse en toi, puis deux, puis trois, un poignet, un bras, son corps tout entier plongeant entre tes grands courants, un point sur la mer immense. Tu n'es qu'océan pour son bassin qui ruisselle à tes lèvres, elle s'écoule dans ta bouche et tu bois la tasse pendant que contre tes cuisses sa housse s'engorge d'un torrent sans fin. La source tarie, elle allume une cigarette qu'elle fume adossée à son oreiller, les sourcils froncés. Le flux de ta cyprine pourrait la noyer (37).

The gradation, the aquatic and marine metaphors, the use of the term »cyprine« – mostly used by lesbians[15] – and the allusion to squirting, all these elements, combined with the fact that this is the first time she sleeps with Octavia, her roommate in her new apartment, are representative both of other scenes of sexuality in the novel and of some of what can be found in other contemporary lesbian novels, which address and write about lesbian sexuality head-on.[16] The author also explicitly adheres to a certain literary tradition, referring to Monique Wittig: »Tu voudrais citer Wittig, glorifier avec des mots d'amour ses cheveux étalés ses joues pâles, mais tu as peur que ta langue se laisse emporter, fourche et dise *je t'aime* au lieu de *je te désire*. Ta cyprine parle pour toi« (183).

For the narrator, lesbian sexuality is at once a relationship, a place, a time and a practice where she feels, momentarily, at home. She knows and appreciates the codes specific to this sexuality, and makes numerous references, for example, to sex toys, which she describes as a »queue de sirène en silicone« (177), which she puts on or sucks, depending on the partner and the moment. She knows what she is doing, what she wants, what she likes: she is in the right place, in a joyful, egalitarian interaction, whether it lasts just one night or much longer.

---

15 Not least thanks to and since Monique Wittig, who uses it on numerous occasions in *Le Corps lesbien* (1973) and *Brouillon pour un dictionnaire des amantes*, written with her partner Sande Zeig (1976).
16 See, for example, novels by Al Baylac, Albane Linÿer or Wendy Delorme.

4.3 Lesbianism as a Path to Emancipation

Thanks to her lesbian life and her »uniforme de gouine« (140), the narrator manages to detach herself, at least in part, from the gaze the outside world may cast on her, and in particular from male gaze, a term she uses several times (79, 85, 89) and a concept she condemns and seeks to escape. But we can look at things more generally: the lesbian identity is that of a fighter (the »uniforme de gouine« is also presented as »une tenue de combat ou deuxième peau« 140) who seeks to dismantle the entire system of discrimination. This goes hand in hand with her critique of ableism, insofar as the two are sometimes analyzed and mobilized jointly, notably within the framework of crip theory.[17] The narrator's struggle, then, is likely to bring about significant changes in the relationships she needs to have with others, and more specifically with the world around her.

Moreover, Monique Wittig's influence is particularly perceptible in the novel, in more or less explicit ways, particularly with regard to writing about lesbian bodies and sexuality. But there is one use of her thought that is particularly original:

> Dans l'appli Notes de ton cell, faute d'argent pour te payer des séances de thérapie tu peux trouver en quelques clics trente-six citations de Wittig; et quand ton père te balance ce genre de pique, tu te répètes comme un mantra, »Et vivre en société c'est vivre en hétérosexualité«[18] jusqu'à sentir la boule au creux de ta nuque se dégonfler. À juste titre, cela te parait très sain d'utiliser un recueil d'articles féministes et lesbiens en lieu et place d'un livre de développement personnel. Salutaire, même (81).

A key figure in lesbian theory and activism, Monique Wittig here takes the place of therapy and personal development, her thinking thus becoming, by association, a method for better living and surviving in society, a method that is obviously very political, particularly insofar as, unlike therapy or personal development, it's not so much a question of reflection and change by and for oneself, but rather of reflecting on what, in society as a whole, needs to be changed.

---

17 See, for example, the work of Alison Kafer, quoted in the novel, and in particular *Feminist, Queer, Crip*.
18 This quote is taken from Monique Wittig's *La Pensée straight*, 73.

5 Conclusion: »Muse of Yourself«

All these lesbian elements – culture, sexuality and encounters, theory – thus seem to be what constitutes a truly effective survival manual for the narrator. As with the temporary escapes mentioned in the second part of this article, the establishment of this lesbian life and the environment that accompanies it enables her to break out of her isolation and loneliness and form a community, by entering into relationships with people, fictional or real, who resemble her. But the relationships established in the context of this lesbian life are more enduring and healthy than the others, and although they do not – at least for the time being – launch a revolution, they do offer the narrator a little happiness and respite.

The link must also be made with anti-ableist struggles, insofar as crip theory is influenced as much by disability studies as by feminist and queer theory. The final chapter, entitled »Muse de toi-même«, focuses on the breaks with unhealthy relationships she has managed to make, and dwells on the changes she wants to put in place in her everyday life: refusing the ableism fetishization that some lesbians impose on her, putting off opening a bottle of wine, taking the time to fully appreciate the lesbian culture she loves so much. She also mentions a possible return to writing, consisting of »[f]aire de l'Art et tout bruler sur [son] passage« (193), and concludes thus: »Tu y arriveras, un non à la fois, maintenant que pour la première fois tu as irrationnellement envie d'essayer d'être vivante« (194).

Without denying the life she has lived up to now, she decides to take a different approach to the »arène ennemie« of society, described and criticized by Monique Wittig, in which she lives (Wittig 2024). She wants to live by and for herself, to be nobody's muse but her own. Belonging to one or more discriminated social groups implies having a different relationship to the world from the outset, evolving in a world that, at best, does not take her needs and particularities into account, at worst doing everything to make life within it unbearable. Since it is impossible to extract oneself completely from the world, the challenge is to find breathing space through a variety of relationships. This is what the narrator tries to do, and what the author offers us as we read her novel.

Bibliography

Coffin, Alice (2020): Le Génie lesbien, Paris: Grasset.

Delphe, Lauren (2022): Faite de cyprine et de punaises, Donnemarie-Dontilly: iXe.

Foucault, Michel (1976): Histoire de la sexualité (vol. 1). La volonté de savoir, Paris: Gallimard.

Jarman, Michelle/Kafer, Alison (2014); »Growing Disability Studies: Politics of Access, Politics of Collaboration«, in: Disability Studies Quarterly, 34.2.

Kafer, Alison (2003): »Compulsory Bodies. Reflections on Heterosexuality and Able-bodiedness« in: Journal of Women's History 15.3, pp. 77–89.

Kelsey, Cameron (2018): »Toxic Regulation. From TV's Code of Practices to ›#Bury Your Gays‹«, in: Participations. Journal of Audience & Reception Studies 15.1, pp. 1–14.

Machado, Carmen Maria (2019): In the Dream House. A Memoir, Minneapolis: Graywolf Press.

Marabet, Bénédicte (2016): »Les IME. Qui sont-ils? Où vont-ils?«, in: Empan 4.104, pp. 53–61.

Medhurst, Eleanor (2024): Unsuitable. A History of Lesbian Fashion, London: Hurst Publishers.

Rich, Adrienne (1980): »Compulsory Heterosexuality and Lesbian Existence«, in: Signs. Journal of Women in Culture and Society 5.4, pp. 631–660.

Wittig, Monique (1973): Le Corps lesbien, Paris: Minuit.

Wittig, Monique (1976): Brouillon pour un dictionnaire des amantes, Paris: Grasset.

Wittig, Monique (2007): La Pensée straight, Paris: Amsterdam.

Wittig, Monique (2024): Dans l'arène ennemie, Paris: Minuit.

»D'autres femmes continueront, elles réussiront«
Reception of Violette Leduc's Work in *Colza* d'Al Baylac, *Fiévreuse plébéienne* d'Élodie Petit et *Au temps du sublime* de Louise-Amada D.[1]

Alexandre Antolin, Luciano Verzeletti

1 Introduction

Violette Leduc was a French author, born in 1907 and died in 1972, she comes from a destitute background: the son of the bourgeois family she worked for impregnated her mother. She remained financially unstable for much of her life, even when living with her partner Denise Hertgès, and later with her husband Jacques Mercier. She had a series of odd jobs, and during the Second World War she entered literature by publishing short stories and news reports in a women's newspaper after being recommended by the homosexual writer Maurice Sachs. During this period, Sachs, fed up with Leduc's constant complaining, told her to get under a literal apple tree and write. This act marked the beginning of Leduc's career in writing novels. In 1945, Violette Leduc brought her manuscript to Simone de Beauvoir: the philosopher thought she would be receiving the dull confessions of a *bourgeoise* but after a full night of reading, she was convinced of her mistake.[2] A literary mentoring relationship began which would only end with Leduc's death. Simone de Beauvoir reread all her protégée's manuscripts, corrected them, defended them to Gallimard and allowed for the publication of Leduc's work.[3] Almost all of which was autobio-

---

1 This text has been translated from French to English by Luciano Verzeletti.
2 »Quand, au début de 1945, je commençai à lire le manuscrit de Violette Leduc – ›Ma mère ne m'a jamais donné la main‹ – je fus tout de suite saisie: un tempérament, un style« (de Beauvoir 1996: 10).
3 »[Catherine Viollet:] Toutes les œuvres de Violette Leduc ont été lues par Simone de Beauvoir au fur et à mesure de l'écriture. C'est à dire que Simone de Beauvoir

graphical. *L'Asphyxie* (1946) is a childhood memoir, *L'Affamée* (1948) the diary of Leduc's incandescent passion for Beauvoir (who wrote back to her: »malgré ma colossale indifférence, j'ai été très émue par votre lettre et votre journal«, Viollet 2012: 130) and *Ravages* (1955), an autobiographical novel in which she recounts her three great loves: Isabelle, her lover at boarding school; Cécile, her partner, outside of marriage; and Marc, the love of married life. At no point does she rank them in order of importance, on the contrary, together they form a continuum of sex and emotional life of her alias Thérèse. However, this literary project never came to fruition, due to Gallimard's editorial censorship. At that time, french law forces publishers to be their own censors, to avoid costly lawsuits.[4] Despite Beauvoir's negotiations, the novel is disfigured, putting heterosexuality at the front, and the beginning of the novel, devoted to the three nights of love in the boarding school between Thérèse and Isabelle, is simply deleted. Leduc narrated the discovery of sexuality between two teenage girls from a point of view situated in poetic realism, outside of any male gaze. The episode was not published until 1966, under the title *Thérèse et Isabelle*, after Leduc became famous with *La Bâtarde* (1964), the first volume of her autobiography.

In the second part of his autobiography, *La Folie en tête* (1970), Leduc looks back at the writing of *Ravages*, explaining:

> Mon texte est plein d'images. C'est dommage. Mes roses, mes nuages, ma pieuvre, mes feuilles de lilas, ma mouture, mon paradis du pourrissement, je ne les renie pas. Je visais à plus de précisions, j'espérais des mots suggestifs et non des comparaisons approximatives. Il y avait autre chose à dire, je n'ai pas su. J'ai échoué, je ne doute pas de mon échec. Je ne regrette pas mon

---

a lu toutes les versions, des différentes séries de cahiers... des milliers, des milliers de pages« (Hoffenberg 2013).

[4] »L'autocensure existe notamment chez les éditeurs. Et les éditeurs peuvent se charger, avant même que la censure, au sens juridique, intervienne, de faire savoir à un auteur, et notamment lorsque son manuscrit existe, parfois même avant qu'il existe, qu'il doit tenir compte d'un certain nombre de contraintes. Parce qu'il y a, et pour mieux comprendre il faudrait rentrer dans le détail, des mesures qui existent au XXème siècle qui pèsent sur l'édition, qui pèsent encore aujourd'hui sur l'édition. Y a toute une série de contraintes économiques qui vont peser sur l'éditeur, au cas où l'un de ses volumes subissent, l'une ou l'autre forme de ces censures. Donc l'éditeur d'emblée se place dans cette position lui-même de censeur, avant le censeur en titre, et transforme l'écrivain en autocenseur lui-même« (Brun 2005: s.p.).

labeur. C'était une tentative. D'autres femmes continueront, elles réussiront (Leduc 1994: 498).

After the author's death on 28th May 1972, her friends started to fan her legacy, beginning with Simone de Beauvoir in her *Mémoires*. Also, the press, whether *Gai pied* or *Masques* – two famous gay and lesbian French magazines from the 1980s and beginning of the 1990s –, continued to publish about her. The turn of the century proved to be a rich period in terms of Leducian news. The first two volumes of her autobiography appeared in the collection »L'Imaginaire«, in 1994 and 1996, a biography came out in 1999 and a reissue of *Thérèse et Isabelle*, presented as »uncensored« was published in 2000, to which we can add a volume of correspondence in 2007 for the centenary of her birth. In 2006 a book brought Violette Leduc back into the spotlight: *King Kong Théorie* by Virginie Despentes. At the end of her feminist manifesto, she discusses the censorship of *Ravages*, putting herself in a direct filiation with Leduc, as an unapologetic author who refuse the socio-economic establishment and to be part a of it:

> Moi, je suis de ce sexe-là, celui qui doit se taire, qu'on fait taire. Et qui doit le prendre avec courtoisie, encore montrer patte blanche. Sinon, c'est l'effacement. Les hommes savent pour nous. Et les femmes si elles veulent suivre doivent apprendre à comprendre l'ordre. Qu'on ne vienne pas me raconter que les choses ont tant évolué qu'on est passé à autre chose. Pas à moi. Ce que je supporte en tant qu'écrivain femme, c'est deux fois ce qu'un homme supporte (Despentes 2007: 137–138).

From this stems an image of Leduc as one who suffered censorship, because she told the experiences of a minority group, both by having lesbian and heterosexual love affairs, whilst being from the working class and being poor throughout most of her life. She also renewed the way of writing about sexuality and, more broadly, invented her own style to describe her perception of the world. Authors from outside her generation, such as Nina Bouraoui and Wendy Delorme, claim her as an influence. Leduc appears in several novels with this aura, whether in Annie Ernaux's *Mémoire de fille* (2016), Wendy Delorme & Fanny Chiarello's *L'Évaporée* (2022) or, again, Virginie Despentes' *Cher Connard* (2022). Nevertheless, Leduc's influence mostly appears in their later works, when they are sufficiently part of the literary world.

For this article, I will focus on a new generation of authors who, from the moment they published what is now designated as their first novel, claim a

Leducian aesthetic or even use Leduc, namely: *Colza* by Al Baylac, *Fiévreuse plébéienne* by Élodie Petit and *Au temps du sublime* by Louise-Amada D.[5] My selection is not comprehensive – we could also mention Mathilde Forget, Pauline Gonthier or Albane Linÿer – but I prefer to limit myself to the three first novels published in 2022, the year commemorating the 50th anniversary of Leduc's death. My observations will be divided into two parts. First, the appropriation of Leduc's figure in the books studied, in terms of style, authorial position and the image of Leduc that emerges. Then, I will look at the editorial strategies put in place by the authors and their publishing houses, in relation to Leduc's case.

2 The L author, Violette Leduc's Reception

First of all, let us explore how the authors present their relationship with Leduc. While they all claim to know her by name, their knowledge of the work varies. Baylac, in his autobiographical novel, for example, boasts to Manon, a lover, before changing her mind:

> je dis que moi aussi j'adore Violette Leduc mais en réalité, à part *L'Affamée*, je n'ai jamais ouvert un seul autre de ses livres. elle m'a offert *Thérèse et Isabelle* et je ne l'ai pas lu. maintenant c'est une relique. et peut-être qu'il me faudra dix ans pour la profaner (Baylac 2022: 68).

Louise-Amada D., on the other hand pointed out that she has read *L'Asphyxie*, *L'Affamée*, *Thérèse et Isabelle* and *La Bâtarde*, at the very least. For her part, Élodie Petit does not explicitly mention the books she has read, but her references allow us to assume that she is at least aware of *Thérèse et Isabelle* and *La Bâtarde*, traces of which can be found in her manifesto of a »bastardized« language, to which I will return later. The three works include Leduc's two best-known books: *Thérèse et Isabelle* and *La Bâtarde*, and it is from these books that they weave a filiation with Leduc: through the affirmation of writing from a minority point of view and a revival of lesbian erotic writing.

In the incipit to *La Bâtarde*, Leduc explains the position in which she writes:

---

5   Each of the authors has published previously (Al Baylac 2018; Petit/Le Louvier 2021; D. 2021). However, the Éditions Blast and Éditions la Peuplade indicate that this is Élodie Petit's first novel, and her first book published under her own name.

> Mon cas n'est pas unique: j'ai peur de mourir et je suis navrée d'être au monde. Je n'ai pas travaillé, je n'ai pas étudié. J'ai pleuré, j'ai crié. Les larmes et les cris m'ont pris beaucoup de temps. [...] Le passé ne nourrit pas. Je m'en irai comme je suis arrivée. Intacte, chargée de mes défauts qui m'ont torturée. J'aurais voulu naître statue, je suis une limace sous mon fumier (Leduc 1996: 23).

She does not portray herself as a conqueror, like Beauvoir;[6] she asserts herself as a »zéro magnifique« (Leduc 1960: 63). Throughout her autobiography, she presents a minority point of view, as a bastard, a poor woman, a smuggler and a woman who has had lesbian and heterosexual love affairs, among others. Each of the authors we studied also drew this portrait. In the prologue to *Colza*, Al Baylac sketches who he was as a child until he writes:

> j'ai aimé la ville; vraiment. la ville ça voulait dire être cette femme, lesbienne, étudiante, employée précaire, flexitarienne, amoureuse, tatouée, impatiente et sagittaire. OK. la ville ça voulait dire devenir cette gouine, butch, misandre, manifestante, écrivaine, ascendant lion, drag et agnostique (Baylac 2022: 13).

In *Fiévreuse plébéienne*, Elodie Petit situates her fictional alter ego, Johnny Castle, also at the end of the first chapter:

> AA [Antonin Artaud] Je suis Johnny Castle et j'habite aux Genêts depuis 1968 – ma tour est en béton et je suis vivante – [...] à l'entrée des immeubles on trouve les vendeurs de drogue, et les vieux qui restent – un tag 92 – ma sexe ne me sert à rien à part à commander des cocktails moins chers et passer devant les autres à la caisse – [...] je ne suis pas vieille et je ne suis pas folle – toute le monde court et pratique la peur des machines qui ont sorti mon grand-père de l'usine – je pense que le peuple qui respire souffre et que les ouvrier·es ont peur de réussir et frustrent une vie entière – je ne suis pas vulgaire même quand j'ai l'impression de l'être – ma chance est ma langue (Petit 2022: 12–13).

---

6   »Je suis terriblement avide, aussi, je veux tout de la vie, être une femme et aussi un homme, avoir beaucoup d'amis, et aussi la solitude, travailler énormément, écrire de bons livres, et aussi voyager, m'amuser, être égoïste et aussi généreuse... Vous voyez, ce n'est pas facile d'avoir *tout* ce que je veux. Or quand je n'y parviens pas, ça me rend folle de colère« (de Beauvoir 1999: 60).

As for Louise-Amada D., in the incipit of *Au temps sublime*, she describes the racist humiliation she suffered at the airport security and the fact she was denied entry on French soil, even though she was due to enroll for a doctorate. By repeating the same sounds and phrasing, the last sentence is a direct echo of Leduc: »J'arriverais au Québec comme on arrive au monde: choquée et nue, dans la lumière éblouissante« (D. 2022: 13).

Nevertheless, through the construction of the first pages of their books, each of them regains their agency and they are the ones telling about themselves, and how to present who they are. They subscribe to Beauvoir's words in the foreword to *La Bâtarde*, »qu'une vie, c'est la reprise d'un destin par une liberté« (Beauvoir 1996: 10), and this freedom is conquered through writing. Louise-Amada D. makes this clear in her incipit and reiterates it regularly, declaring: »Si je lisais, si j'écrivais, si j'étais publiée, je m'en sortirais« (2022: 22). For his part, Baylac, after her lawyer uses her butch appearance as an argument to convict her pedocriminal piano teacher, comforts herself by saying, »heureusement, il existe une autre justice qui est de s'écrire soi-même« (2022: 89). Like Leduc, who took back her destiny through her notebooks and her writing, the authors we are discussing can take back the moments they were discriminated against, because of their gender identity, race, sexual orientation, class, and no longer suffer these humiliations, by transforming them into literature that addresses their peers. Élodie Petit shows this in a different way by writing two manifestos in *Fiévreuse plébéienne*. In the first, that of living poets, she reminds us that »8. La poésie est l'affaire de toustes« and invites everyone to write: »12. Sens-toi libre d'écrire ce que tu veux, ce qui te fait plaisir, ce qui t'exprime et t'excite« (2022: 29). Then the manifesto of a »bastardized« language, which she defines as follows:

> La langue bâtarde est le fruit névrosé de l'accouplement d'une langue littéraire ténue avec un langage de rue, un argot rural, une langue de trottoir, un dialogue vide de repas de famille./Elle est vulgaire dans le sens où elle ne se soucie pas de sa réception, elle est./Elle parle trop fort, elle ne s'arrime pas là où il faut, elle se contrefout des règles. Elle s'invente au fur et à mesure qu'elle raconte (Petit 2022: 66).

Petit's encouragement of unrepentant writing recalls Leduc's intrepid sincerity. All these authors are unapologetic in their use of bastard language, echoing what Leduc said of *Ravages*: »C'est dur, c'est précis, c'est raréfié, c'est complexe. Il n'y a pas une courbette. Voilà ce que j'ose dire de mon livre« (1973: 89).

This approach applies to the telling of their stories, and particularly in the writing of lesbian eroticism influenced by the Leducian style. Petit specifies in her manifesto: the bastardized language »n'a pas peur d'être dramatique, dramaqueen, lyrique dans ses larmes, élégiaque à l'amoure, saphique, mielleuse, ouvertement érotique, pornographique et gênante« (2022: 66–67). Their rewrites are not pastiches; they use Leducian elements to put their feelings into words. Louise-Amada D, who keeps a diary of her orgasms, gives an example: »Troisième. Je comprends la fragile épiphanie thérèse-et-isabelléenne des *genoux pourris de délices*. Cette affolante lumière, qui irradie dans les jambes et ravit les pieds jusqu'aux orteils, me traverse fugitivement« (2022: 134). These borrowings bring lesboerotic writing and intertextuality linked with the scene of the first kiss between Thérèse and Isabelle:

> Isabelle me tira en arrière, elle me coucha en travers de l'édredon, elle me souleva, elle me garda dans ses bras: elle me sortait d'un monde où je n'avais pas vécu pour me lancer dans un monde où je ne vivais pas encore; les lèvres entr'ouvrirent les miennes, mouillèrent mes dents que je serrais. [...] Mes yeux étaient gros d'étonnement sous mes paupières, la rumeur des coquillages trop vaste (Leduc 2000: 23–24).

Al Baylac takes up two key elements of the scene, both the shift from one world to another, from heterosexual society, in Monique Wittig's words,[7] to a third space outside heterosexual society, thanks to the nocturnal kiss, and the eyes that discover this newness. He succeeds in reinterpreting the most quoted extract of the opus:

> on raconte qu'un soir – ça n'arriva qu'une fois – MiuMiu de Lalave embrassa Colza. On dit que la terre trembla si fort qu'une brèche s'ouvrit dans le sol et avala le monde, un quart de seconde, avant de le recracher dans un sens différent. que Colza, quand elle rouvrit ses yeux, vit que le monde était enfin à l'endroit (Baylac 2022: 30).

---

[7] »En fait, les conventions sociales et le langage font apparaître avec une ligne en pointillé le corps du contrat social désignant ainsi l'hétérosexualité. Pour moi les deux termes de contrat social et d'hétérosexualité sont superposables, ce sont deux notions qui coïncident. Et vivre en société c'est vivre en hétérosexualité« (Wittig 2007: 56).

The act of seeing is twofold. At first, through the eyes of the main character, who regains a capacity for agentivity by observing the world around her. Secondarily, this particular apprehension of the world is reflected in the authors' writing, as each works on his or her text, sometimes giving it an experimental form. Leduc's work on literary is echoed in the manifesto of bastard language:

> Elle n'a pas de trame narrative directe – évidente – elle raconte brutalement ce qu'elle traverse. Elle colle aux réels, elle a les mains moites. Elle dérange par sa franchise et son manque de politesse./Elle n'est pas là pour être gentille (Petit 2022: 67).

This lack of concessions on the part of Baylac, Petit and D. makes them unsuitable for publication by commercial publishing houses, where more accessible texts are favored and solid social capital is required. This led them to develop other editorial strategies, which can be compared with Leduc's case.

3 'Cause We are Living in an Hetereopatriarchal Publishing World and We are Queer Authors

Violette Leduc began writing her novels in 1942, when she was living off the black market with Maurice Sachs in Normandy. Exasperated by her complaints, he told her: »Vos malheurs d'enfance commencent de m'emmerder. Cet après-midi vous prendrez votre cabas, un porte-plume, un cahier, vous vous assoirez sous un pommier, vous écrirez ce que vous me racontez« (1996: 422). Sachs then abandoned her, as he was no longer able to stand her and her constant complaining, but Leduc carried on writing. In 1943, she discovered Simone de Beauvoir's novel *L'Invitée*. Literary admiration and a kind of groupie relation began to form, with Leduc observing Beauvoir in the cafés of Paris's Saint-Germain-des-Prés, almost in a stalking-like manner. Through a friend, she handed over the manuscript of *L'Asphyxie*. The quality of the writing marked the beginning of a literary mentoring relationship, as defined by Marine Rouch:

> Une mentore littéraire a un rôle actif dans l'élaboration d'un texte littéraire. Elle se charge non seulement de relire les manuscrits, mais aussi de faire des suggestions de réécritures, d'ajouts ou de suppressions. Les échanges, qui peuvent avoir lieu par correspondance ou en personne, ont autant pour

but de discuter du texte littéraire que d'encourager et d'apporter un soutien psychologique souvent nécessaire. Une aide matérielle ou financière peut accompagner le processus, le cas de Leduc est à ce titre édifiant. Une mentore littéraire ne le devient que parce qu'elle a déjà publié elle-même des textes littéraires et qu'à ce titre elle fait partie de ce champ (Rouch 2017: 6).

As an author, through her friendship with Camus and as Sartre's companion, Beauvoir managed to have *L'Asphyxie* published in Camus's »Espoir« collection at Gallimard. Then, with *Le Deuxième sexe* (1949) and the Prix Goncourt for *Les Mandarins* (1954), Beauvoir gained great recognition in the literary field. From there, she was able to pay a pension to her protégée and defend her books to Gallimard publishing house. Beauvoir's editorial choices may be debatable, but without her, no Leducian work could have existed, whether *L'Asphyxie*, the post-*Ravages* works (Leduc wanted to give up literature after the censorship episode) or *La Chasse à l'amour*, the posthumous edition of the last autobiographical volume.

From Beauvoir to the present day, other cases of literary sponsorship, more or less famous, exist: Marguerite Duras and her article on Monique Wittig's *L'Opoponax*, Françoise Mallet-Joris writing songs for her partner Marie-Paule Belle or, closer to us, Virginie Despentes helping to publish Fatima Daas's first novel, *La Petite dernière*. A common denominator for these »godmothers« is the possession of substantial Bourdieusian capital, notably symbolic and cultural, which enables them to act in the literary field. In the case of the three authors in my corpus, we observe the implementation of different literary strategies to enter the field or, rather, to exist outside it. They create third spaces, defined by Maël Maréchal as follows:

[Les tiers espaces] ne constituent pas une contre-attaque ni une défense. Dans le tiers espace, les enjeux se jouent sur un autre niveau. Sa présence ne requiert pas de validation de la part des dominants. Le tiers espace court-circuite leur échiquier. Il ne les empêche pas de se déplacer sur cet échiquier, il n'annule pas la partie en cours, mais il crée un nouveau jeu, en parallèle, où le but ultime n'est pas de posséder du pouvoir au détriment d'un-e autre. […] Ce que le tiers espace permet, pour les marginalisé-e-s, est la formation d'une vision qui échappe aux dominants et par laquelle repenser leur identité individuelle et collective. Il leur procure du pouvoir en cela qu'il légitime l'existence des marginalisé-e-s par et pour eux et elles-mêmes et non plus en regard d'un système où toute la réalité est organisée autour de la reproduction d'un seul modèle identitaire (Maréchal 2018: 19).

It is through the creation of these third editorial spaces that authors are able to create a new queer literature outside of hegemonic editorial systems. The aim is not to please a majority, by respecting heterosexual society, as theorized by Wittig, but to put forward a minority voice, unchallenged by the dominant. This approach echoes an article by Virginie Despentes, reacting to Adèle Haenel's departure from the 2020 Césars, after Roman Polanski won the Oscar for Best Film. The formula »on se lève et on se casse«, depoliticized and repeated ad nauseam today, has a radical dimension: create a third space immediately and now, and let the dominant ransack their spaces alone on their own. Despentes writes:

> Vous n'aurez pas notre respect. On se casse. Faites vos conneries entre vous. Célébrez-vous, humiliez-vous les uns les autres tuez, violez, exploitez, défoncez tout ce qui vous passe sous la main. On se lève et on se casse. [...] La différence ne se situe pas entre les hommes et les femmes, mais entre dominés et dominants, entre ceux qui entendent confisquer la narration et imposer leurs décisions et ceux qui vont se lever et se casser en gueulant. C'est la seule réponse possible à vos politiques (Despentes 2020, s.p.).

Beyond the authors studied, it is important to focus on the editorial structures that publish them. All are independent and have chosen a corporate social responsibility status: blast is a non-profit association under the French law of 1901, the Éditions du Commun is also a non-profit association, before becoming a SCOP, and the Éditions de la Peuplade does not indicate its status, only that the management is assured by the couple, with tasks divided equally. The choice of economic structure coherent with the editorial line of these publishing houses, each of which affirms its support for experimental, political and non-commercialized literature: »La Peuplade a toujours un pied posé dans son époque et l'autre dans l'avant-garde« (Association nationale des éditeurs de livres 2023, s.p.), states the Quebec-based association of book publishers. While Éditions du Commun, in their podcast, asserts that their aim is to ›éclairer de différentes manières les enjeux sociaux et politiques du monde dans lequel nous vivons‹ with their catalog (Daval 2023). And the blast publishing house indicates their radicalism from the very first sentence: they »défendent une littérature d'essai et de création politique, une littérature qui pense l'articulation des oppressions et des luttes et qui ouvre des perspectives depuis le champ des résistances antiracistes, féministes, queers, anarchistes« (Ouaghenim/Sol 2023). Finally, a new political reflection takes place with the geographical decentralization in relation to the major economic and cultural centers of publishing most notably in Paris. La Peuplade is based in Chicoutimi, Québec, the Editions du Commun are based in Rennes, Brittany, and les Éditions blast in Toulouse, in the south of France.

These independent structures are based on the triptych: CSR, radical editorial line, geographic decentralization, which allows them to form another editorial space out of the mainstream. Each materializes this desire for community, in different forms. As co-founder Simon Philippe Turcot reminds us, »L'idée de La Peuplade, c'était la tribu, la bande«, and adds, »ça demeure toujours une préoccupation pour nous d'essayer de faire travailler d'autres artistes provenant d'autres formes d'art« (Dumais 2016). Éditions Blast, for its part, recalls a detail often overlooked in the publishing world: »ça demeure toujours une préoccupation pour nous d'essayer de faire travailler d'autres artistes provenant d'autres formes d'art« (Ouaghenim/Sol 2023). As for the Éditions du Commun, in their press release announcing their change of status to SCOP on 7th March 2022, they point out that »nous nous envisageons avant tout comme un collectif: notre ligne éditoriale, nos choix, notre fonctionnement sont le fruit d'une élaboration collective continue« (2022).

From there, thanks to social networks and newspaper articles, we can trace a constellation – to use the term from the »Constellations créatrices« a conference organized by Les Jaseuses (cf. Turbiau et al. 2022) – about queer solidarity. I will take the case of Élodie Petit as an example. She is a member of the RER Q collective, as is Wendy Delorme. On 26th June 2022, on Instagram, Delorme made a »déclaration publique [...] bouleversée« (2022) about a book her publisher, Cambourakis, had sent her: *La Vie têtue* by Juliette Rousseau. She adds: »Je pressentais, de par les mots qu'elle avait eus pour en parler voici un an, qu'il allait toucher à la fibre de l'émotion« (ibid.). There is an established relationship between the two authors, and we return to Élodie Petit by pointing out that Juliette Rousseau is a member of the editorial board of Éditions du Commun. In particular, she was responsible for launching the company's poetry collection (cf. Éditions du Commun 2022). This example is not intended to question Petit's literary talents, by justifying her publication by a game of cronyism. Rather, I want to highlight the new networks of lesbiarity or queerity, to use Camille Desombre's term pédérité/sissyrity (cf. Desombre 2023: 49–87), which third editorial spaces enable and even encourage to sustain themselves. They finally offer us places where we can express ourselves, build our society outside heterosexual society, where Leduc and Beauvoir had to keep playing with it. We are even finding that, without having a dominant position in the literary field, we can be actors in our queer literary fields.

My new example again involves Wendy Delorme. As part of his doctorate, before he was awarded a contract, Delorme spoke with Alex Lachkar. This led to a friendship that went beyond the strict confines of research, with a strong emphasis on lesbian literature. In the course of their exchanges, Lachkar joked that he cannot remain friends with Delorme unless she reads Al Baylac's *Colza*. The author finds herself overwhelmed by the text. This private queer-feminist friendly interaction, mixing literary and academic fields, is already interesting. However, it goes beyond the private sphere and materializes in the editorial third space when Wendy Delorme asks Al Baylac to write the afterword for the paperback reprint of *La Mère, la Sainte et la Putain*. This preface allows her to express her appreciation of Baylac's work, but also to use her reputation to highlight an newly-published author. In this way, we can see that the adelphic relationships of minority figures really influence the editorial third space, whereas Leduc and Beauvoir could only have an influential force after having obtained a dominant position in the field.

4 Conclusion

Since Virginie Despentes' *King Kong Theory*, the image of Violette Leduc has changed. She is no longer seen simply as a martyr to censorship. The new generation of lesbian authors is seizing on the Leducian figure as a mean of gaining auctorial legitimacy. They can write from a minority position (poor, working-class, lesbian and other minority positions where Leduc is not concerned, such as the POC position Louise-Amada D. speaks from), just as Leduc did in her own time. Violette Leduc thus becomes a model in not asking the dominant for permission to speak out, as Élodie Petit expresses in her manifesto: »[The bastardized language] n'est pas là pour plaire aux hommes, à la bonne société, aux bien éduqués, aux lettres françaises, à la rentrée littéraire« (2022: 66).

The authors studied have no interest in the current heteropatriarchal, white, bourgeois literary field. Each in their own way seek to create a language that allows them to tell the story of their experiences, both social and erotic, which play a large part in the three books studied. They all take up Leduc's phrase: »D'autres femmes continueront, elles réussiront« (1994 [1970]: 498), using new images, linguistic or typographical innovations, etc., in their own way, even going beyond gender issues.

However, this field of literary possibilities can only exist if there is a space in which to express oneself. Unlike the authors studied here, Leduc found herself limited by editorial censorship and the heteropatriarchal society of the 1950s. The creation of independent, politicized and activist publishing houses in the 21st century, such as blast, du Commun and la Peuplade, offers new lesbian literary spaces for writing experimentation that hegemonic publishing houses do not, or no longer, grant them. These structures thus become editorial third spaces where the stakes of the dominant literary field do not arise. However, it must be remembered that they are fragile, both economically and in human terms, as they rely heavily on voluntary work. Queer and feminist solidarity networks help support these structures, but do not guarantee their continuity. Yet it is essential to preserve them, so that we can also develop our literatures outside white, bourgeois heteropatriarchal society. Freed from these shackles, authors will be able to go further, inventing new ways of talking about our lesbian and queer loves and continuing to recount them.

Bibliography

Baylac, Al (2022): Colza, Toulouse: Éditions Blast.
Beauvoir, Simone de (1996 [1964]): »Préface«, in: Violette Leduc, La Bâtarde, Paris: Gallimard, pp. 9–21.
Beauvoir, Simone de: (1999 [1997]): Lettres à Nelson Algren. Un amour transatlantique (1947–1964), Paris: Gallimard, 1999.
Brun, Catherine (2005): La Littérature face à la censure. Tire ta langue, France Culture, INA.
D., Louise-Amada (2022): Au temps sublime, Saguenay: Éditions La Peuplade.
Daval, Corentin (2024): »Éditer, La Mécanique du livre, saison 1, épisode 1«, in: Podcast Éditions du Commun, https://www.editionsducommun.org/blogs/podcasts/podcast-1-alias-soluta-enim-illo-necessitatibus [29.09.2023].
Delorme, Wendy (2022): »J'ai beaucoup de chance...«, in: Instagram, https://www.instagram.com/p/CfRb4B3jEhA/ [01.10.2023].
Despentes, Virginie (2007 [2006]): King Kong théorie, Paris: Grasset.
Despentes, Virginie (2020): »Césars. Désormais, on se lève et on se barre«, in: Libération 01.03.2020, p. 24.
Desombre, Camille (2023): »Pédé·s dans la peau«, in: Florent Manelli (ed.), Pédés, Paris: Points, pp. 49–87.

Dumais, Manon (2016): »Entre québécitude et nordicité«, in: Le Devoir, https://www.ledevoir.com/lire/469870/edition-entre-quebecitude-et-nordicite? [29.09.2023].
Leduc, Violette (1960): Trésors à prendre, Paris: Gallimard.
Leduc, Violette (1996 [1964]): La Bâtarde, Paris: Gallimard.
Leduc, Violette (1994 [1970]): La Folie en tête, Paris: Gallimard.
Leduc, Violette (1973): La Chasse à l'amour, Paris: Gallimard.
Leduc, Violette (2000): Thérèse et Isabelle, Paris: Gallimard.
Maréchal, Maël (2018): Conjurer l'absence. Pratiques du tiers espace dans les littératures lesbiennes francophones, Ottawa: Unpublished Doctoral thesis.
Moraga, Cherrie and Anzaldúa, Gloria (2021): This Bridge Called my Back. Writings by Radical Women of Color, NY: State University of New York Press.
Ouaghenim, Karima/Sol (2023): »À propos«, in: Éditions Blast, https://www.editionsblast.fr/a-propos [29.09.2023].
Petit, Élodie (2022): Fiévreuse plébéienne, Rennes: Éditions du commun.
Turbiau, Aurore et al. (2022): »Constellations créatrices, dépasser les redécouvertes de créateur-trices effacé-es«, in: Glad! 12, https://doi.org/10.4000/glad.3723 [14.10.2023].
Viollet, Catherine (2012), »Lettre à Violette Leduc« in: Cahier de l'Herne 100, p. 130.
Wittig, Monique (2007 [2001]): La Pensée Straight, Paris: Éditions Amsterdam.

https://www.anel.qc.ca/membre/editions-la-peuplade/ [29.09.2023].
https://www.editionsducommun.org/blogs/actualites-evenements/les-editions-du-commun-se-transforment-en-scop [01.10.2023].
https://www.editionsducommun.org/blogs/actualites-evenements/fievreuse-plebeienne-est-disponible [01.10.2023].

Literary Performance Festivals as a Space for Feminist and Queer Sociability

Anna Levy

1 Performing Literature in Festivals

For several years now, literary festivals have been multiplying, offering a space for the deployment of literary performance. Literary performance has acquired some form of institutional legitimacy: the proliferation of literary festivals has provided an opportunity for this practice to flourish. This oral literature is part of what Magali Nachtergael calls »neoliterature« (2017) or what Lionel Ruffel and Olivia Rosenthal refer to as »literature outside the book« (2010). More precisely, literary performance constitutes a »contextual« literature (D. Ruffel, 2010) that cannot be analysed outside its context of enunciation. The studies on »neoliterature« or literature outside the book look at what happens to literature when it leaves the pages of the book and are interested in all the forms it can take outside those pages. The literary performance is part of this »neoliterature«, and encompasses all instances where the text is declaimed, recited, or performed by its author. The text may have a printed existence, be published in a book, or it may not be published at all. It may be performed in theatres, in bookshops or/and at literary festivals. There are many types of literary performances: some could be confused with theatre, others with public readings, while others are closer to slam poetry or spoken word.

Contrary to the tradition of French performance poetry, which follows in the footsteps of the avant-gardes of the early 20th century and of sound poetry in the 1960s, in the Anglo-Saxon tradition, spoken word is superimposed on literary performance. These days, a certain branch of performance literature claims to be spoken word, or at least to place itself fairly explicitly in that tradition. Although definitions may vary, the term »spoken word« generally signals a contemporary trend towards the oralisation of texts. It is performed at festivals, can be the subject of spoken word competitions and marks a revival of poetry whose publishing market was beginning to run out of steam (Craig and Dubois, 2010). At the same time, the development of slam poetry in the USA since the 1980s (and since the 1990s in Europe), an art form which initially involved verbal jousts and invitations to the audience to judge the candidates – thereby giving the public greater involvement – has, according to Julia Novak (2011), led to the development of poetry performance. For the researcher, the distinction between slam, poetry performance, spoken word and readings is not so obvious, and she places the practice of poetry performance within the same poetic counterculture. Literary performance festivals are part of all these traditions, offering a space for expression on the margins of published and canonical literature. These spaces aim at building relationships and are also part of the turning point in what has been called relational literature (Viart, 2019).

> Relational practices do not consist in taking over art venues, but rather the social field. It's not so much a question of expanding the territory of literature than to question its nature, to experiment with the links it forges with society, readers and networks, and to rethink the status of the creator and the nature of the literary work through the relationships established during its production and reception (Ruffel 2010, my translation).

Literary performance festivals are particularly well-suited to forging relationships between the various bodies that make up the festival (author, spectator, programmer etc.). In recent years, these festivals have multiplied and diversified: they are no longer mere book fairs organised around selling books, but artistic events based around literature.

This paper will focus on three festivals: the *Littérature etc.* festival in Lille, created in 2013 by Aurélie Olivier, the *Sturmfrei festival* created in 2021 in the Paris region by Arnaud Idelon and Samuel Belfond, and *Mots à Défendre* at the National Theater of Brussels (one instance is of particular interest to me: in March 2023, slam poetry artist Joëlle Sambi was invited to create a weekend-long programme). Based on the study of these three festivals, I will show how they create new literary spaces, not only creative spaces for authors but also listening spaces for the public. I also aim to examine how literary performance festivals take on a political dimension because they require authors and readers to be present together. In addition, the festival format, which takes place over a long period of time, allows people to meet. On the one hand, it is not uncommon for festival-goers (myself included) to go as a group to these festivals, which are seen as queer and feminist gatherings. Indeed, the people in attendance are often disproportionately gender and sexual minorities. The festivals are also an opportunity for authors to meet, and the overlap in the programming of the different festivals helps create constellations of artists. The atmosphere at these festivals is also conducive to encounters (among spectators, between spectators and authors). These links are professional, artistic, friendly, and/or political. But, first and foremost, the festival format is a festive format (as its etymology indicates) that puts links and relationships at the centre of the festival-goers' experience. This relationship is not necessarily a lasting one, but we are witnessing the creation of a temporary community for the duration of the festival, and it is the collective dimension of this experience that makes it a political one. In the case of the three festivals studied, the double-event dimension of literary performances (they are an event: the performance within an event: the festival) takes on a very clear political meaning, not only in the subjects tackled (feminist and anti-racist struggles, etc.) but also in the fact that these festivals bring together a large number of authors who belong to these minorities. By proposing to transform the solitary experience of reading into a collective moment the literary performance festival politicises the literary experience. By making literature a living art form and narrowing the distance between author and reader, the literary performance festival is a particularly apt space for alternative forms of social interaction. This has two main effects. On the one hand, practising literature in a community helps to create social links, and these relationships have several variants. Secondly, the festival format redefines the position of the author and the reader.

2 The Expansion of Queer and Feminist Literary Festivals

While the oral practice of literature is nothing new, but on the contrary harks back to practices that are both ancient and non-Western, it has recently been developed and institutionalised. Literary festivals are a response to this paradigm shift in literature. Readers increasingly crave the mediation of the author.[1] Literature is thus becoming a social moment: because it is experi-

---

1 As Vincent Kaufman explains in his essay *Dernières nouvelles du spectacle vivant, ce que les médias font à la littérature*, Paris, Seuil, 2017, far from being dead, authors are subjected to a certain spectacularisation. In his book, *A voix haute: poésie et lecture*

enced in society, in a community, and because it encourages social interaction. Literature festivals respond to readers' need for a presence and a relationship.

According to the words of its creator Aurélie Olivier, *the Littérature etc.*'s mission is to disseminate »as widely as possible literature that concerns everyone and/or spares no one«.[2] Each year, a new theme is selected: »Risks« in 2022, »Ritual« in 2021, »Conflict« in 2020 or »Reproduction« in 2019. The festival brings together a wide range of proposals: readings by authors, performance readings, writing workshops, collective readings. The guest authors do not all share the same status or the same recognition. The festival's stated aim is to showcase literature that has developed outside the canon. In a private interview, its director and founder explains:

> The texts I find interesting are those that are not expected. The idea of a canon, of a text that follows rules, is very limiting: it becomes conventional and loses its interest in terms of creativity. There's also a political issue at stake in giving visibility to a literature that is less visible, or that will always be considered marginal and never put centre stage. Paradoxically, that's where the most creative work is to be found (Aurelie Olivier, personal interview, February 2023, my translation).

The promotion of these literatures is political then, since they are produced by authors who are not very well represented on the literary scene, and because they convey little-heard discourses at the intersection of gender, race, and class. By proposing innovative and intermedial formats that present themselves as work in progress, *Littérature etc.* festival places itself in opposition to canonical published literature, whose forms are classified in relatively fixed categories (novel/theatre/poetry etc.). The programs are always made according to this dual aesthetical and political standard: to offer something new and contemporary, and to work towards greater representativeness in the literary field.

The Sturmfrei Festival, subtitled »festival of writing in presence: performance, celebration and poetry«, has been held twice (2021 and 2022). The aim of the festival is to combine literature and techno parties. The venues, chosen in the eastern Parisian suburbs, reflect the desire to move literature

---

publiques/performées, Les Impressions nouvelles, Bruxelles, 2016, Jan Baetens reminds us that writers no longer have a choice, and must read their texts in public if they do not want to condemn themselves to non-existence.

2   In the words of its creator, http://litterature-etc.com/le-projet/.

to alternative structures, outside the institution, so as to welcome/foster an emerging artistic scene. The programme features a variety of performances ranging from hybrid, highly musical forms to readings in which the text plays a central role. The eclectic mix of dance, music, declamation, performance, slam poetry, video, DJsets, etc. generates artistic effervescence, rejecting the fixity of form in favour of movement and transformation.

The *Mots à défendre* festival is slightly different from the other two because it was organized around one artist, Joëlle Sambi, who was invited to organise a three-day festival. Another difference is that it took place at a major institution: the Brussels National Theatre. Joëlle Sambi created a programme and brought together different figures to »queer« the theatre, in her own words. The programme included readings, literary performances, slam poetry, literary massages, a rap night, literary wrestling, a round-table discussion, and so on. In a video of presentation for the festival,[3] Joëlle Sambi establishes a connection between political engagement and poetry and explains that the artists were brought together around issues of desire, queerness, class and race. For her, this meeting and gathering of artists must take place »around words«.

3 Shaping New Constellations of Artists

Sociability operates at the level of artistic proposals – authors quote one another and refer to each other's work – but also at the level of programming – a network of feminist and queer authors and artists is being set up, leading to the development of a queer and feminist constellation of artists creating alternative spaces for literature: the same process is bringing literature out of the book and out of the closet. The concept of constellation has found an echo in feminist studies (Turbiau et al. 2022, Bonilla et al. 2021). Breaking away from the linear model of inheritance or genealogy, the concept of constellation is closer to that of rhizome and shows the complex and horizontal entanglement of the different parts.

---

3   https://www.theatrenational.be/fr/articles/3109-des-paroles-que-l-on-n-entend-pas-souvent-dites-de-maniere-inattendue-joelle-sambi.

3.1 The Programs

The overlaps in the programs of these festivals are a sign that these festivals create constellations of artists. In the case of festivals, I noticed various intertwining configurations:

a) The same performance can be presented at several festivals: as is the case of the performance *Brûler danser* by Lisette Lombé and Chloé du Trèfle or *Caillasses* by Joëlle Sambi and Sarah Machine, presented at *MAD* festival in 2023 and then at *Littérature etc.* the same year.
b) The same authors/artists move from one festival to the next: the artist Law organised a writing workshop at *Littérature etc.* in 2020 and was behind the *Liquid lyric erotic* rap show at *MAD* in 2023; Aurélie Olivier organises the *Littérature etc.* festival but performed *Mon Corps de ferme* at *MAD*; some of the members of the RER Q collective were present at *MAD* in 2023, at *Littérature etc.* in 2021, and at the *Sturmfrei festival* in 2021 and 2022.
c) Some artists return to the same festival several times: Joëlle Sambi, Lisette Lombé and Milady Renoir have been invited to *Littérature etc.* several times for example.

Analysis of the programs reveals that both friendly and artistic relationships are being forged between the various members on the art scene. These networks of social interaction take place on the fringes of a canonical and hegemonic literature, since they bring together authors and performers who are either not published or are published by independent publishing houses. The festival thus becomes the space-time that makes this encounter possible between artists who are doubly minoritised: on the one hand because they produce a literature on the fringes and on the other because they belong to minorities (women, queer people, people of color etc.).

3.2 Showing the Relationships Between Authors

Littérature etc. organises exchanges between artists and between artists and publishers and booksellers. At *MAD*, moments of discussions took place between different authors. *MAD*'s literary wrestling staged a confrontation between six authors/slam artists. The processes by which literature is mediated at festivals, not only through performance but also through meetings, discussions, and this type of creation, also have an influence on the creative process, and the links that can be forged between authors are more prolific and are even encouraged. Sharing the same time and space at the festival creates moment of conviviality. The slam artist Lisette Lombé wrote the foreword to the book *Caillasses* (a collection of texts that were first performed on stage by the artist):

> For me, Joëlle Sambi is not just a voice that counts among contemporary French-language authors. Joëlle Sambi is a sister, in the sense that Audre Lorde speaks of a sister. We were born together on stage, spat out of the belly of a burn-out [...] Yes, everything in Joëlle Sambi's writing is political, and she stands by it as such! Her poetry is social, militant and intersectional. It is also lyrical and unifying (Lombé/Sambi 2021: s.p.).

Lisette Lombé's words underline not only the political purpose of Joëlle Sambi's poetry, but also the unifying dimension of oral performance in front of an audience. This union is strengthened by the fact that the performance brings together an audience around a shared struggle.

3.3 Gathering Around a Shared Commitment

Contrary to *Littérature etc.*, *MAD* and *Sturmfrei* do not set a specific theme for each year. However, all three festivals follow under the same queer and feminist line by offering performances that tackle these subjects. Lesbian love and relationships are evoked (in Al Baylac's reading of *Colza* at *Littérature etc.* or in Law's concert at *MAD*), as are the oppressions experienced by trans people (through the performances of Rose Canine Griffe Chromée at *Littérature etc.* or in Hashem Hashem's performance *Ni tout à fait le même, ni tout à fait un autre* at *MAD*. Anti-racist struggles also feature prominently in the programme (with a reading of *Aux vies anecdotiques* by Karima Ouaghenim, the show *À nos humanités révoltés* by Marie-Julie Chalu and Marina Monmirel, the performance *Deux secondes d'air qui brûle* by Diaty Diallo and DJ Oret Pape at *Littérature etc.*; Joëlle Sambi's show *Koko Slam Gang* at *MAD* brought together eight Congolese women, ›tantines‹, who were invited to speak on stage about their arrival in Belgium). The modes of enunciation involve the audience, particularly through the different enunciative addresses made to them. The idea that literature can and must act on reality,[4] that it has »words to defend« as the title of the festival suggests, is very firmly rooted in this type of festival, as shown by the names of some activities, such as »literary wrestling« at the MAD festival, and its opening performance, a slam titled »why are we fighting?« The performativity of literature is echoed in the performativity of language as theorised by Austin: to put literature *into performance* is also to give it the capacity to act directly on reality, which explains why literary performances appear to be a medium of choice for the expression of minority voices.

4 Building Reader/Spectator Communities

Producing a performed literature enables aesthetic canons to be reconfigured: authors are pushed to go beyond the simple framework of the page and onto the stage. Sharing the *here* and *now*, the *hic et nunc* constitutive of performance art (De Duve 1980; Phelan 2003) and which can also be found in literary performance adopts a political dimension.

4.1 A New Community of Spectator Readers

The presence of literature outside the book and at queer and feminist festivals is also renewing the audiences for literary festivals. The question of representativeness also arises in the composition of the audience: while the report by the French National Book Foundation estimates that the average age of attendees of literary events is fifty,[5] *Littérature etc.* draws a thirty-five-year-old average audience, according to its organiser Aurélie Olivier. This can partly be explained by the choice of the formats presented at this festival. Literary performances, which are over-represented at the festival, allow literature to be mediated more easily outside the book itself. This does not mean, however, that books are excluded from the literary experience: the festival offers a number of meetings to discuss published books, readings where books are physically present, as well

---

4   This is also one way of understanding the term ›literary performance‹, which is also in line with Austin's work on language and its performative dimension (Austin 1975).
5   CNL report drawn up in 2018 on literary events supported by the CNIL in France in 2017: https://centrenationaldulivre.fr/donnees-cles/poids-et-impact-des-manifestations-litteraires-soutenues-par-le-cnl-dans-les [08.03.2024].

as a bookshop. What is at stake is the question of access to books and solitary reading:

> Who, sociologically speaking, are the people who walk into an elitist bookshop? Who, geographically, has access to an elitist bookshop? Who spends twenty euros on a book with no picture on the cover that they have never heard of? Who has the capacity to read ten books at the risk of finding just one of them nourishing? Who enjoys being taken aback by a text? Literature needs to be presented outside the book so that the answers to all these questions are less depressing (Olivier, 2010: 108).

Taking these material conditions into account helps create a friendly atmosphere and space, better suited to welcoming audiences with less literary capital, a particular form of Bourdieu's cultural capital according to literature sociologist Gisèle Sapiro (Sapiro/Picaud/Parcouret 2015). Aurélie Olivier explains that she wants to differentiate herself from other literary festivals that reproduce a strict separation between stage and audience, between authors and readers:

> In 2013, I felt that the authors whose work interested me were not being invited to Lille. More generally in France at the time, when I attended literary fairs and festivals, I often felt a sense of unease between the coldness of the staging and the texts that I found galvanising to read. I wanted to show that this distancing, which is sometimes hushed, is no guarantee of quality or objectivity and that, on the contrary, the commitment to warmth and encourages the circulation of texts (Olivier 2010: 100).

The festival's political commitment can be seen not only in its choice of programming, but also in its approach to welcome and integrate audiences into a community where stage and audience merge, where authors and spectators share a space-time. The venues for the three festivals were quite different: while *Littérature etc.* and *MAD* took place in theatres or concert halls, the *Sturmfrei festival* took place in a hall where the stage and the hall were not spatially demarcated. Lisette Lombé and Chloé du Trèfle presented the same *Brûler Danser* performance at *Littérature etc.* and at *Sturmfrei*: while at *Littérature etc.*, the audience was seated, they danced during the performance at *Sturmfrei*. At the end of the performance at *Littérature etc*, Lisette Lombé invited the audience to come and dance on stage and began performing the text again.

Far from being dead, the author is present on stage, easily accessible, and it is not uncommon to bump into the authors and chat with them in informal moments during the festival. This ethos of a benevolent host can also be found at the other two festivals. The reception facility creates a community of readers turned spectators already gathered around common struggles, »a crowd of optimistic idealist feminists« in the words of Lisette Lombé in the forewords to Joëlle Sambi's book *Caillasses*:

> So when the spotlights go down, when the violence of the cops, systemic exclusion and racism have barely subsided; when the spotlights go down and the lights go out, you look out over the vast plain and say to yourself, what a beautiful thing a collective is. The elbows that stick together, the energies and souls that boost each other. It's beautiful, this crowd of optimistic idealists and feminists (Lombé/Sambi 2021: 6).

In his essay *Cruising Utopia* José Esteban Muñoz looks at performance from several angles. In his view, performance art, which is largely practised by minority artists, has a strong political power in that it makes us see a future in the present. While performance art is first and foremost an art of the present, it opens up the possibility of making this present utopian. It also enables the creation of new minority groups:

> I use the term minoritarian to index citizen-subjects who, due to antagonisms within the social such as race, class, and sex, are debased within the majoritarian public sphere. […] Minoritarian performance – performances both theatrical and quotidian – transports us across symbolic space, inserting us in a coterminous time when we witness new formations within the present and the future. The coterminous temporality of such performance exists within the future and the present, surpassing relegation to one temporality (the present) and insisting on the minoritarian subject's status as world-historical entity. The stage and the street, like the shop floor, are venues for performances that allow the spectator access to minoritarian lifeworlds that exist, importantly and dialectically, within the future and the present (Muñoz 2009: 56).

This analysis can be extended to literary performance festivals, which through its »unifying dimension« contribute to the »creation of new groups« in which a utopian future becomes possible.

4.2 Creating Spaces for Care

The possibility of building relationships between spectators or with authors also comes from the fact that festivals create spaces for encounters between spectators and authors and amongst spectators, and for the well-being of both parties. The *Littérature etc.* 2023 festival and *MAD* are offering »literary massages«, where professional masseurs give a massage while an author reads a text. The 2022 edition of *Littérature etc.* featured an installation: *Overshare* by Avril Avilas. In this installation, comfortable beds were laid out along with books to allow the public to settle in comfortably for a nap. These different offerings reflect the festival organisers' desire to move away from a consumerist logic. Audiences are no longer consumers who have come to consume a show (in fact, admission to the *Littérature etc. f* estival is free), but they are invited to take over the festival space, to stay between shows, which of course encourages the possibility of encounters. This rejection of commodification is part of a broader approach to performance art, as analysed by Peggy Phelan. If performance art can have a political impact, it is because it acts on the real, the present, by refusing reproduction and thus commodification:

> Performance's only life is in the present. Performance cannot be saved, recorded, documented, or otherwise participate in the circulation of representations of representations: once it does so, it becomes something other than performance. To the degree that performance attempts to enter the economy of reproduction it betrays and lessens the promise of its own ontology. Performance's being, like the ontology of subjectivity proposed here, becomes itself through disappearance (Phelan 2003: 14).

Festivals of literary performance play an important role in creating a different temporality, one that is detached (as far as possible) from a productive, capitalist temporality.

4.3 Literature as a Party: Celebrating the Margins

One of the common objectives of the three festivals is to bring literature to life. This is partly achieved by treating literature as a party: The *Littérature etc.* festival closes with dancing and/or singing evenings (karaoke, concerts, etc.). The *MAD* festival offered two dance evenings. The *Sturmfrei festival* is a clear example of the desire to combine literature and techno parties. By doing so, the *Sturmfrei festival* is appealing to new audiences, some of whom are regulars at Parisian techno parties. The venues for the festival's three nights were either third-party venues (Sample in Bagnolet, near Paris) or techno party venues (La Station). These places can be considered examples of Foucauldian »heterotopias« (Foucault2009), spaces that constitute »real« utopias, where usual rules do not apply and which are separate from the rest of the world. Angela Jones develops Michel Foucault's concept by looking at queer heterotopias:

> Unlike utopias, heterotopic spaces can be created in reality…They are sites where actors, whether academics or activists, engage in what we might call a radical politics of subversion, where individuals attempt to dislocate the normative configurations of sex, gender, and sexuality through daily exploration and experimentation with crafting a queer identity (Jones 2009: 1–20).

Of course, apart from the *Sturmfrei festival*, the two other festivals take place in institutional venues and receive public funding. Nevertheless, the concept of heterotopia remains relevant, not to describe what these festivals actually do, but rather to understand the intention of their founders. By moving outside of Paris and into venues that are not designed to host literature, the festival is forcing a reconfiguration of the audience. This audience does not recognise itself in the classic, elitist conception of literature. It is easy to see how literature becomes a space for celebration. Making literature a party, and even more so a queer and feminist party, reveals a change in cultural and social practices: access to this literature is no longer based on a certain cultural capital but on belonging to a community, in these cases a queer and feminist community.

5 Conclusion

Beyond the aesthetic renewal of the forms that literature can take in these places, the literary festivals propose a new vision of what makes literature by rejecting a certain idea of literature that some have described, as Magali Nachtergael does, as the literature of »dead white men« (2015). The three festivals studied take literature out of the book by offering innovative formats that are politically committed, feminist and intersectional. The overlapping programmes and invitations to artists to engage in dialogue with each other and with the public help to create new constellations that stand in opposition to literature that is perceived as canonical, edited and published by major publishing houses. The festival format, which defines a here and now, encourages the creation of relationships and creates a temporary community of readers turned spectators. This ephemeral community encourages the creation of friendly, artistic and/or professional relationships. Performance festivals also show how literature can be an art of relationships-building, by making these relationships the condition for the reception of works.

Bibliography

Austin, John Langshaw (1975): How to do things with words, Harvard: University Press.
Baetens, Jan (2016): A voix haute. Poésie et lecture publiques/performées, Bruxelles, Les Impressions nouvelles.
Bonilla, Marie-Laure Allain/Blanc, Émilie/Renard,Johanna/ Zabunyan, Elvan (2021): Pour une histoire féministe de l'art, Donnemarie-Dontilly: iXe.
Bourriaud, Nicolas (1998): Esthétique relationnelle, Dijon: Les presses du réel.
Craig, Ailsa/Dubois, Sébastien (2010): »Between Art and Money. The Social Space of Public Readings in Contemporary Poetry Economies and Careers«, in: Poetics 38.5, pp. 441–460.
De Duve, Thierry (1980): »La Performance *hic et nunc*«, in: Chantal Pontbriand (ed.), Performance, Text(e)s & Documents, Montréal: Parachute, pp. 18–17.
Deleuze, Gilles (1990): Pourparlers (1972–1990), Paris: Minuit.
Foucault, Michel (2009 [1966]): Le corps utopique, les hétérotopies, Paris: Lignes.
Kaufman, Vincent (2017): Dernières nouvelles du spectacle vivant, ce que les médias font à la littérature, Paris: Seuil.
Jones, Angela (2009): »Queer Heterotopias. Homonormativity and the Future of Queerness«, in: A Journal of Queer Studies 4, pp.1-20.
Muñoz, José Esteban (2009): Cruising Utopia. The Then and There of Queer Futurity, New York: University Press.
Nachtergael, Magali (2017): »Le devenir-image de la littérature. Peut-on parler de ›néolittérature‹?«, in: Pascal Mougin (ed.), La tentation littéraire de l'art contemporain, Dijon: Les presses du réel.
Novak, Julia (2011): Live Poetry. An Integrated Approach to Poetry in Performance, Amsterdam: Rodopi.

Phelan, Peggy (2003): Unmarked. The Politics of Performance, London: Routledge.

Rosenthal, Olivia/Ruffel, Lionel (2010): »La littérature exposée. Les écritures contemporaines hors du livre«, in: Littérature 160, online.

Rosenthal, Olivia (2018): »Publication de la littérature. Entretiens croisés avec Olivier Chaudenson, Jean-Max Colard, Olivier Marbœuf et Aurélie Olivier«, in: Littérature 192, online.

Ruffel, David (2010): »Une littérature contextuelle« in: Littérature 160, pp. 61–73.

Sambi, Joëlle (2011): Caillasses, Bruxelles: L'arbre de Diane.

Sapiro, Gisèle/Picaud, Myrtille/Parcouret, Jérôme (2015): »L'amour de la littérature. Le festival, nouvelle instance de production de la croyance. Le cas des Correspondances de Manosque«, in: Actes de la recherche en sciences sociales 206–207, pp. 108–137.

Turbiau, Aurore/Leïchlé, Mathilde/Islert, Camille/Renné Hertiman Marys/Gauthier Vicky (2022), »Constellations créatrices. Dépasser les redécouvertes de créateur-rices effacé-es«, in: Glad! 12, https://doi.org/10.4000/glad.3723.

Viart, Dominique (2019), »Terrains de la littérature«, in: Elfe 20–21.8, http://journals.openedition.org/elfe/1136.

Contributors

Alexandre Antolin has a PhD in French literature and gender history. After a thesis on Violette Leduc (*Étude d'un cas de censure éditoriale : »Ravages« de Violette Leduc*, PUL 2023), he continues his research on questions of censorship, French women authors and French lesbian literature of the 1950s (Aurore Turbiau et al., *Écrire à l'encre violette. Littératures lesbiennes en France de 1900 à nos jours*, Cavalier Bleu, 2022). He edited the uncensored version of Violette Leduc's *Ravages*, published by Gallimard in 2023.

Audrey da Rocha has been a French lecturer since 2018 at the department of Romance Languages and Literatures of the University of Tübingen, Germany. She holds a bi-national Master's degree in Comparative Literature and a Bachelor's degree in German and American Studies from the Universities of Mainz and Dijon. Her research topics have included the relationship between language and migration and its effect on the female body, female subjectivity in the works of Assia Djebar. An article on the figure of the witch in Wendy Delorme's *Viendra le Temps du Feu* was presented last December at a conference in Mulhouse and is currently being prepared for publication.

Alkisti Efthymiou is a PhD candidate at the Department of Social Anthropology at Panteion University (Athens, Greece). Closely engaging with works of queer feminist film in Chile, Argentina and Brazil, her thesis focuses on the cultural politics of love and the critical state of intimacy under conditions of neoliberal governmentality. Running in parallel with her doctoral research, her film practice is inspired by queer feminist affectivities and translocal forms of resistance. She has presented her filmic projects and given talks and performative lectures in collaboration with various institutions around the world. Her most recent publications have been included in the *Journal of Greek Media* *and Culture*, *The Cambridge Journal of Anthropology*, and *Fabrik Zeitung*. She has been awarded with a Fulbright Visiting Research Scholarship at UC Berkeley for 2023–24.

Teresa Hiergeist is a professor of French and Spanish literature and cultural studies at the Department of Romance Studies at the University of Vienna. Her research focuses on alternative concepts of society and relationships, imaginations of social and communal cohesion, negotiations of the sacred and spiritual, human-animal relations in literature and culture, literary and cinematic imaginations of work. She works on the early modern period, the turn from the 19th to the 20th century and the present.

Gabrielle Jourde is a PhD candidate in feminist theory at Sciences Po Paris's CEVIPOF, co-supervised by Réjane Sénac in political theory and Marie de Gandt from Université Bordeaux-Montaigne in comparative literature. She holds a Master's degree in Gender Studies from the University Paris 8 Vincennes Saint Denis and a second Master's degree in Political Theory from Sciences Po Paris. Her research centers on a feminist theory of freedom post-#MeToo and queer literature. Gabrielle Jourde's doctoral research investigates the reconfiguration of queer-feminist subjectivities since the fourth wave, with a particular focus on autotheoretical practices that blur the boundaries between literature and political theory.

Alex Lachkar is a PhD candidate and university assistant in Literary and Cultural Studies at the Department of Romance Studies at the University of Vienna. In his doctoral project, he is working on contemporary lesbian literature in France and investigating the influence of Virginie Despentes work. He is the co-author of *Écrire à l'encre violette. Littératures lesbiennes en France de 1900 à nos jours*, and does science popularization regarding lesbian and trans literature on social medias. He is also is part of Teresa Hiergeist's podcast-project *Fabulari*.

Anna Langewiesche is a PhD candidate in the Department of French at Columbia University. Their dissertation is on the subject of utopia and uchronia during the French Revolution and the first two thirds of the 19th century, specifically on the intersections between the historical novel and the utopian genre during this period, and the use of counterfactualism in historical writing.

Anna Levy is a contractual doctoral student at the University of Bordeaux Montaigne. Her work focuses on literary performance. She studies how these forms, by breaking out of traditional publishing channels, have opened up a space for women artists and poets to make a feminist claim. She is a member of the feminist research and creation collective *Les Jaseuses*.

Stefanie Mayer is PhD candidate and university assistant in Literary and Cultural Studies at the Department of Romance Studies at the University of Vienna. She is currently working on her doctoral project, in which she investigates conceptions of female authorship in 21st century Mexico. Her research interests lie in contemporary Latin American literature and cinema, with a focus on gender issues. She co-organises the Central American Film Festival in Vienna and, together with Teresa Hiergeist, she initiated the pre-graduate online journal *vistazo*. She also is part of Teresa Hiergeist's podcast-project *Fabulari*.

Pierre Niedergang holds a PhD in philosophy and is an affiliate researcher at IRePh (Institut de Recherches Philosophiques), Paris-Nanterre University. His doctoral thesis is entitled »Sexual desire and power. Normalization, normativity, real«. He is the author of *Vers la normativité queer* (Toward Queer Normativity), published in April 2023 by Blast edition, as well as several academic articles, including »Sexual Violence or ›Initiation‹? Queer Commons, Trauma, and Normativity« written with Tal Piterbraut-Merx and »Cultural Seduction as a Modality of the Desire/Power Immanence: a Proposal for Queer Psychoanalysis«.

Julia Obermayr is a cultural studies and media scholar who worked until recently at Graz University of Technology. In 2019 she received the 14th Scientific Award of the Austrian-Canadian Society for her research on *Female Identities in Lesbian Web Series* (2020, transcript) in Palm Springs, Los Angeles, San Francisco, Toronto, Montreal, Madrid, and Barcelona. She specializes in LGBT+ studies and diversity, minority identities, female representations and social change in audiovisual media – currently in Corona Fictions – mainly in Romance speaking Europe and the Americas.

Michaela Rumpikova is a bilateral PhD student in the Department of French and Comparative Literature at Charles University and Sorbonne Nouvelle. She is currently writing her thesis on Virginie Despentes and the poet(h)ics of (non)violence. Her research interests include contemporary French feminist literature and its interdisciplinary intersections with ethics and politics, countercultural movements, AIDS literature and queer identities in narratology, along with others.

Arthur Ségard is a PhD candidate in the Department of French Literature, Thought and Culture and the Institute of French Studies at New York University. His research focuses on the formation of the notion of the monster in the 19th century, between literature, science and performance (freak show), and on the contemporary uses of this notion, particularly in queer practices and discourses. His most recent article is »Des îles et des lunes: Hétérotopies queer dans la fiction contemporaine« in *Genre, sexualité & société* (2023).

Hannah Volland is a PhD candidate at the French Department of the University of Toronto, Canada. Her dissertation analyzes agency and *engagement* in contemporary life-writing from France. Her research interests include feminist and queer theories, affect and trauma studies as well as politically engaged writing in the twentieth and the twenty-first century. Last fall, she published an article on the depiction of trauma in Annie Ernaux's *La honte* in *Women in French Studies*.

Vera Lucía Wurst has a Bachelor's degree in Hispanic Literature from the Pontificia Universidad Católica del Perú and a Master's in Hispanic Philology from the Universität zu Köln. She has taught Literature classes at universities in Lima, Cologne, Bonn and Berlin. She is currently a research assistant at the Institute for Latin American Studies at the Freie Universität Berlin, where she is also doing her doctorate on contemporary representations of motherhood in Latin American women's literature.

Juan Zapata holds a PhD in French Literature from the University of Rennes 2, France, and from the University of Liège, Belgium. He is a full professor at the University of Lille and a translator in the field of sociology of literature, where he has translated authors such as Jacques Dubois, Nathalie Heinich, Jérôme Meizoz, Pascal Brissette and Alain Vaillant. He edited and translated the collective works *La Invención del autor. Nuevas aproximaciones al estudio sociológico y* *discursivo de la figura autorial* (2015), *Baudelaire: de la bohemia a la modernidad literaria* (2017) and *Autorías encarnadas. Representaciones mediáticas del escritor/a* (2021), with Aina Pérez Fontdevila. In 2021 he published *Baudelaire. El heroísmo del vencido*.